STRATEGIC CHOICE AND
INTERNATIONAL RELATIONS

STRATEGIC CHOICE AND
INTERNATIONAL RELATIONS

Edited by
David A. Lake and Robert Powell

PRINCETON UNIVERSITY PRESS   PRINCETON, NEW JERSEY

Library of Congress Cataloging-in-Publication Data

Strategic choice and international relations /
edited by David A. Lake and Robert Powell.
p.   cm.
Includes bibliographical references and index.
ISBN 0-691-02698-X (cl : alk. paper).
ISBN 0-691-02697-1 (pb : alk. paper)
1. International relations. 2. Strategic planning.
I. Lake, David A., 1956– . II. Powell, Robert, 1956– .
JZ1305.S765   1999
327.1'01—dc21   99-12215 CIP

This book has been composed in Sabon

The paper used in this publication meets the minimum requirements
of ANSI/NISO Z39.48-1992 (R1997) (*Permanence of Paper*)

http://pup.princeton.edu

1   3   5   7   9   10   8   6   4   2
Printed in the United States of America

Contents

Acknowledgments

THIS VOLUME grew out of the multicampus Workshop on International Relations sponsored and funded by the University of California's Institute on Global Conflict and Cooperation. The workshop began in September 1990, with a small retreat of scholars from throughout the University of California system to reflect on the end of the cold war and its meaning for international politics. It then grew into a "floating" seminar, meeting on different University of California campuses from 1991 to 1994. Over the course of these gatherings, we came to appreciate that we shared a common perspective on how to study international relations that was, nonetheless, poorly articulated in the existing literature. *Strategic Choice and International Relations* is an attempt to capture this common perspective for ourselves and others, as well as to probe its strengths, weaknesses, and limitations.

The first "brainstorming" session that led to this volume was held in May 1994. In addition to the authors of the chapters included here, Peter Cowhey, Judith Goldstein, Stephan Haggard, John Odell, and Randolph Siverson helped define our subsequent direction. Drafts of the chapters were discussed at meetings in Laguna Beach in December 1994, Santa Barbara in July 1995, and San Diego in September 1996, as well as at the annual convention of the American Political Science Association (APSA) in September 1995. We are grateful for the comments of Benjamin Cohen, James Fearon, Steph Haggard, Lisa Martin, and Paul Papayoanou, who participated in the Santa Barbara meeting, and James Caporaso, Judith Goldstein, and Beth Simmons, who served as discussants on two panels at the APSA meetings.

Perhaps most important, we appreciate the patience and endurance of our authors, who produced numerous drafts of their chapters with good cheer—if not always great speed. We have learned immensely from their efforts and have enjoyed ourselves enormously in the process.

In addition to supporting the Workshop on International Relations, the Institute on Global Conflict and Cooperation (IGCC) funded the preparation of this volume. We are grateful to then IGCC director Susan Shirk for her support and to the staff at IGCC for their assistance. We are also pleased to recognize Jennifer Pournelle and Caryn Sugar at IGCC, Lynn Edwards at Bookmark Media, and Malcolm Litchfield and Rita Bernhard at Princeton University Press for helping to turn seven chapters into a book.

STRATEGIC CHOICE AND
INTERNATIONAL RELATIONS

CHAPTER ONE

International Relations:
A Strategic-Choice Approach

DAVID A. LAKE AND ROBERT POWELL

THE STUDY of international relations has long been rent by large and often unproductive paradigmatic debates. Over its brief history, the discipline has been split between idealists and realists, realists and liberals, and, most recently, neorealists and neoliberal institutionalists—not to mention the various minor sects and other apostasies that have also fractured the field. In addition, international relations scholars have argued endlessly about the role of theory and method, with important divisions occurring between traditionalists and behaviorists, quantitative and qualitative researchers, and now various positivists, postpositivists, and postmodernists. Within each of these so-called great debates, moreover, scholars have disagreed over the relative importance of unit (domestic) and systemic-level (international) causes of behavior, the applicability of theories of security policy (high politics) to economic policy (low politics), and vice versa, and what separates the study of international politics from the rest of political science.[1] These numerous divisions, and the tendency to mistake debate for explanation, have long stymied progress in understanding international relations.

The purpose of any theoretical framework is to bring intellectual order to a domain, identify accepted and contested knowledge, and guide future research. In this volume, we attempt to pull together many diverse strands of existing theory and research in international relations into what we call a strategic-choice approach. This approach begins with a simple insight. Students of international relations, and of politics in general, are typically interested in explaining the choices or decisions of actors—be these actors states, national leaders, political parties, ethnic groups, military organizations, firms, or individuals. These choices, moreover, are frequently strategic; that is, each actor's ability to further its ends depends on how other actors behave, and therefore each actor must take the actions of others into account. Outcomes ranging from the foreign policies of individual

---

[1] For a recent review of the great debates in international relations, see Katzenstein, Keohane, and Krasner 1998.

states to international phenomena such as war or cooperation cannot be understood apart from the strategic choices actors make and the interaction of those choices.

The strategic-choice approach is comprised of three principal components. The first is to make strategic problems and interactions the unit of analysis. Rather than beginning with predefined actors as the units of analysis, such as states, the strategic-choice approach takes the *interaction* of two or more actors as the object to be analyzed and seeks to explain how this interaction unfolds.[2] We believe—and this book is an effort to show—that making strategic interactions between actors the unit of analysis provides a fruitful and productive way to study international politics.

The second component is a way of organizing research on the strategic interactions that arise in international relations. We distinguish first between actors and their environments. In turn, actors are defined by the preferences and beliefs they hold, and the environment is disaggregated into the set of actions and the information available to the actors. These analytic categories serve as the basis for conceptual experiments that recur at all levels of strategic interaction. It is this analytic scheme that gives theories within the strategic-choice approach their explanatory power.

The third is a methodological approach to analyzing strategic problems or, perhaps more accurate, a set of methodological bets about what will prove to be productive ways to think about strategic interactions. United by an essential pragmatism that emphasizes the construction of theories appropriate to the question under investigation, the strategic-choice approach, as will be elaborated below, is agnostic toward the appropriate level of analysis in international relations, presumes that strategic interactions at one level aggregate into interactions at other levels in an orderly manner, adopts a partial equilibrium perspective, and avoids, when possible, untheorized changes in preferences or beliefs as explanations of changes in observed behaviors.

We do not claim that the strategic-choice approach is new. Elements can be found in nearly all the classic works in the field of international relations. As early as 1959, Kenneth Waltz recognized that the essence of a systems or third-image approach is the strategic interdependence of actors: International outcomes, he argued, are always the product of choices made by more than one actor—in his case, states. Morton Kaplan (1957) made early use of game theory to capture this strategic interaction. Likewise, Thomas Schelling was centrally concerned with strategic interaction in *The Strategy of Conflict* (1960) and *Arms and Influence* (1966),

---

[2] This is roughly equivalent to the shift from neoclassical economics, which takes the firm as the unit of analysis, to transactions cost economics, which takes the transaction as its basic unit. See Williamson 1994, 87–88.

as were many other early theorists of nuclear deterrence. Strategic interaction is also the core of John Herz's (1950) and Robert Jervis's (1978) work on the security dilemma. The strategic-choice approach has a long and distinguished pedigree in international relations. Owing to its diversity, however, the approach has not been identified as a coherent research program. By articulating the principles of the approach, we hope to highlight its contributions, identify relationships between bodies of research and theory heretofore unappreciated, reveal lacunae, and clarify the future research agenda.

The strategic-choice approach, in our view, offers three major benefits. The first is simply a useful way of organizing one's thinking about international politics. The analytic categories suggested by the approach differ from those found in prevailing paradigms.

Second, the strategic-choice approach helps sharpen the logic of our theories. As will be elaborated below, many of the debates in international relations can be traced back to disputes about what is actually being assumed in a theory or about the arguments linking assumptions to the conclusions that purportedly follow from them. Sharper and tighter deductive reasoning is a prerequisite to the difficult empirical work that must be done to test and evaluate any theory. By emphasizing microfoundations and a fuller description of a strategic setting, the strategic-choice approach calls attention to assumptions and logical consistency.

Third, the strategic-choice approach tends to break down traditional distinctions that may have been useful at one time but now seem counterproductive. As will be seen, domestic actors often face strategic problems that are quite similar to the strategic problems confronting states. The levels-of-analysis approach tends to obscure this similarity by emphasizing the level at which causes are located, whereas the strategic-choice approach brings this similarity to the fore. Actors also encounter strategic problems in international economic issues that are similar to the strategic problems they confront in the security arena. By making strategic problems the unit of analysis, the strategic-choice approach highlights these similarities and so begins to unite international political economy and security studies within a single framework.[3] Even more broadly, domestic actors face strategic problems in politics—as well as economics—that have little, if anything, to do with international relations and yet are similar to the strategic problems that other actors face in the international political arena.[4] The strategic-choice perspective underscores these simi-

---

[3] A number of scholars have called for trying to unify the fields of security studies and international political economy within a common theoretical approach. See, for example, Jervis 1988; Keohane 1984; Lipson 1984; Powell 1991; and Stein 1983, 1984.

[4] As but one example, compare the application of relational contracting theory, first developed in economics, to the internal organization of Congress (Weingast and Marshall

larities and, ideally, serves as a way of integrating the study of international relations with other areas of political science.

This chapter proceeds in four main steps. The next section elaborates the principal components of the approach. We then highlight several characteristics of the approach that are implicit in these components. Third, we contrast the strategic-choice approach with its principal rivals, especially cognitive and constructivist approaches to international relations. Finally, we provide an overview of the subsequent chapters. Each of these chapters focuses on a different aspect of the strategic-choice approach, and, taken as a whole, they provide a broad survey of the research program.

THE STRATEGIC-CHOICE APPROACH

The strategic-choice approach is theoretically inclusive. Most current theories of international relations recognize, more or less explicitly, the strategic nature of politics. Even unit-level theories that abstract from strategic interactions between states often incorporate strategic interactions within states. This common core provides a foundation for integrating and synthesizing many otherwise competing theories of international relations.

The strategic-choice approach is, to state the obvious, an approach or orientation, rather than a theory. Theories are defined by particular sets of assumptions about, say, human nature or a focus on certain variables, like technology or institutions. As a result, many theories are consistent with any given approach. Nonetheless, the strategic-choice approach possesses certain features that all theories within it share: It assumes actors are purposive, makes strategic interactions the unit of analysis, provides a common framework for organizing interactions, takes an essentially pragmatic view of theory, and makes a series of methodological bets about what will prove to be fruitful ways of analyzing and thinking about international politics.

Purposive Action

The strategic-choice approach is part of the burgeoning literature on "rational-choice" theory in political science. Like other rational-choice analyses, the strategic-choice approach assumes that actors make purposive

---

1988), trade organizations (Yarbrough and Yarbrough 1992), colonialism (Frieden 1994b), and American foreign policy (Lake 1999).

choices, that they survey their environment and, to the best of their ability, choose the strategy that best meets their subjectively defined goals. The approach does not presume that actors always obtain their most preferred ends—indeed, theories are often most useful when they help explain why actors fail despite their best intentions—but it does assume that actors pursue their goals as best they can.

Despite frequent criticisms to the contrary, the strategic-choice approach does not necessarily assume that actors are "human computers" able to perform complicated calculations or to assess the costs and benefits of all possible consequences of all possible choices.[5] By "rational," most theories mean simply that actors can rank order the possible outcomes of known actions in a consistent manner—or, more formally, that they possess complete and transitive preferences (see Morrow 1994a, 18–9). Nor does the approach require that actors be fully informed, able to costlessly access information on themselves or other actors.[6] Extreme views of individuals as "walking encyclopedias" are obviously false, but very few theories rest on such implausible assumptions. The approach typically requires only a minimalist definition of cognitive ability. In short, theories of strategic choice commonly assume not that actors are omniscient, only that they are purposive.

Strategic Interactions as the Unit of Analysis

At the center of the approach lies a vision of international politics as the strategic interactions of actors. These actors might be individuals protesting against environmental degradation, firms lobbying their governments for protection from "unfair" foreign-trade practices, departments or ministries struggling for control over policy, governments seeking to control the spread of nuclear weapons, the United Nations attempting to mobilize countries for an international peacekeeping operation, or states

[5] In developing his "cybernetic theory of decision making," Steinbruner (1974) criticizes rational choice theory on precisely these grounds. In the strong form of rationality he criticizes, tennis players would be required to understand complicated physics, perform near instantaneous calculations of the trajectory of a ball when hit, and identify and choose among all conceivable positions and swings by which the ball might be returned. Few, if any, tennis players fit this model—and we suspect those who do are not particularly good at the sport. In our view, a "rational" tennis player, who presumably desires to hit the ball, need only assess a few practiced alternatives, decide which has the greatest likelihood of resulting in a successful return, and act accordingly.

[6] Actors may also be able to make highly sophisticated decisions on the basis of relatively little information. By knowing who endorses a particular ballot proposition, for instance, voters can often decide accurately for or against a measure even without reading its specific provisions. See Lupia and McCubbins 1998.

locked in a territorial dispute. A situation is strategic if an actor's ability to further its ends depends on the actions others take.[7] If so, then each actor must try to anticipate what the other actors will do. But what those other actors will do, of course, often depends in part on what they believe the first actor will do. For example, whether a state decides to stand firm or make concessions in a trade dispute or a military crisis may depend on what actions it expects its adversary to take. If it believes the other is about to make major compromises, the first state may wait for its adversary to concede. If it believes that its adversary is unlikely to make any concessions, however, it may give in. In turn, whether the adversary concedes may depend on whether it expects the first state to concede. It is the set of decisions made by the relevant actors that constitutes the strategic *interaction* and produces the observed outcome, whether this be war, a crisis, or some form of cooperation.

Organizing Strategic Problems

Like all rational-choice analyses, the strategic-choice approach breaks strategic interactions into two elements: actors and their environments.[8] It is this assumption that actors and environments can be usefully separated, at least for analytic purposes, that divides the strategic-choice approach from constructivism and other sociological perspectives, a point we develop more fully below in the section on alternative approaches.

Actors and their environments can each be further disaggregated into two attributes. All strategic environments are composed, first, of the *actions* available to the actors. Together, the available actions summarize what could happen as the actors interact; that is, the first attribute of a strategic environment is the set of possible ways that decisions and events can unfold. For example, the four cells of the familiar Prisoner's Dilemma matrix show all the possible ways that the interaction can develop (both actors can cooperate, the first can cooperate while the second defects, and so on).[9] More generally, one can envision a game tree as an abstract summary of all the possible ways that events can unfold. Each path

---

[7] This holds whether there are a small number of actors who possess mutually contingent strategies, such as in an arms race, or a large number of actors, none of which can affect the outcome, as in the classic collective action dilemma or a perfectly competitive market. The former is best modeled through game theory, the latter through either game theory or decision theory. Although we draw heavily on insights from game theory, the modeling technique does not define the approach.

[8] Some limitations of this assumption are discussed below.

[9] Readers unfamiliar with the prisoner's dilemma should refer to Figure 3.1 in chapter 3 and the surrounding discussion.

through the tree describes one possible sequence of decisions and actions, and the tree as a whole illustrates all the different paths or ways that events can develop.[10] It is important to emphasize that despite the widespread use of "two-by-two games" in international relations and the typical specification of the possible actions as "cooperate" and "defect" (see Oye 1986a; Snyder and Diesing 1977), the range of actions both in actuality and theory may be quite broad. There is no inherent limit on the number or types of actions that can be considered part of an environment.

The environment is also composed of an *information* structure that defines what the actors can know for sure and what they have to infer, if possible, from the behavior of others. As James Morrow elaborates in chapter 3, what an actor knows may have a profound effect on what it chooses to do. To illustrate the point with a simple but concrete example, suppose a group of people is playing poker and one player is trying to decide whether another is bluffing. If the cards are not marked, then the former has to base her decision on the latter's past behavior. If the information structure is different in that the cards are marked, however, then the first player knows for sure whether the other is bluffing. Obviously, the information structure—that is, whether the cards are marked—may have a significant effect on what a player does. More substantively, Keohane (1984) argues that one of the ways that institutions facilitate cooperation is by providing more information to states, especially by providing better ways for states to monitor one another's behavior. It follows that states in an international system devoid of institutions may choose differently than those in a system with many international institutions. As Morrow discusses, analysts have recently begun to consider environments with varying information structures and are producing important new insights into international politics.

Actors are also composed of two attributes. First, actors possess *preferences*, defined simply as how they rank the possible outcomes defined by their environment. In terms of a game tree, preferences are the rank ordering of the terminal nodes or outcomes of the strategic interaction. What distinguishes the familiar games of Prisoner's Dilemma and Chicken, in these terms, is not the actions or information available to the players. In both these games, each actor has two alternatives and must decide what to do without knowing what the other has chosen. What differentiates these games is the actors' preferences—their rankings of the possible outcomes (e.g., PD posits DD > CD whereas Chicken posits CD > DD).

International relations theorists often use the term *preferences* in ambiguous and conflicting ways, and this has been a source of considerable confusion. One reason for this confusion may be that the simple formal

---

[10] See Morrow 1994a for a discussion of game trees and an introduction to game theory.

notion of preferences as a ranking over the terminal nodes of a game obscures an important subtlety. Where to end a tree, or a historical case study for that matter, is a judgment a researcher makes about how to bound the problem under study. These bounds are not given a priori. History, after all, goes on regardless of where a scholar decides to end her analysis. Or, a general model of, say, trade policy may abstract from and ignore questions of the form that protection will take (tariffs, voluntary export restraints, etc.), simply folding this question into the analysis under the broad outcome of "trade restrictions." These bounds reflect a researcher's bet that conceptualizing the problem in this way will prove insightful.

Because events typically continue even after a tree ends, a terminal node implicitly represents how events will unfold given that the actors have reached that particular node. For example, if one suspect confesses and the other remains silent in Prisoner's Dilemma, then the game ends: The terminal node "confess-silent" is generally assumed to stand for the outcome in which the first suspect goes free and escapes punishment and the second suspect goes to jail for several years. But suppose we were trying to study a situation in which the mob enforces a code of silence. Then the unmodeled sequence of events abbreviated in the "confess-silent" node would be very different. In this case, the suspect that squealed would be severely punished. Clearly a suspect's rankings of the terminal nodes of the game depends on the *unmodeled* way that events will unfold after he leaves the interrogation room. Similarly, a model of nuclear crisis decision making may include a node of "nuclear war," which includes an unmodeled sequence of actions depicting how the war is actually fought. How states evaluate the node of "war" depends on what they expect to happen once they actually begin fighting.

Stated more generally, that a terminal node of tree is an abbreviation for what happens outside the game means that an actor's preferences over the terminal nodes of a game generally reflect two considerations. The first might be called an actor's basic preferences. These are desires that remain the same across a wide variety of situations. Firms, for example, are usually assumed to prefer larger profits to smaller ones in most circumstances. Similarly, in neorealism, states are typically presumed to prefer more security to less. The second consideration is the specific substantive interaction and the implicit assumption about what happens after the formal game ends. An actor's preferences in a particular game combine these more basic preferences or desires with the implicit assumptions about a future or set of more precise actions that continues to unfold.

Sometimes it is trivially easy to combine these two considerations in order to rank the outcomes of a given game. For example, there are only two actors and three possible outcomes in many brinkmanship models of nuclear crises (Nalebuff 1986; Powell 1987). In these models the challenger may prevail in a crisis in which both states avoid a massive nuclear exchange, the defender may prevail in such a crisis, or both states may be destroyed in a nuclear conflagration. In this simple setting, where these are the only possible outcomes, it would seem bizarre not to assume that the challenger's ranking or preferences over these three possibilities is to prevail, followed by the defender's prevailing, and then by nuclear war. At other times, however, it is extremely difficult to move from an actor's basic preferences to the way it ranks the terminal nodes of a particular problem we want to investigate. Indeed, the failure to appreciate these difficulties and to define the game-specific preferences carefully has led to much confusion, as Jeffry Frieden elaborates in chapter 2.

The second attribute of an actor is its prior *beliefs* about the preferences of others. For example, even though an actor is uncertain whether an opponent possesses preferences characteristic of Prisoner's Dilemma or Chicken, it nonetheless holds a prior belief about the likelihood that the opponent has one or the other. Likewise, the essence of Schelling's (1966) description of a nuclear crisis as a "competition in risk taking" is that each state is unsure of the risk the other state is willing to run, but actors must still make some probabilistic assessment of whether the other is risk averse or risk acceptant. When actors are uncertain, beliefs are critical to the choice of strategy and the outcome of the interaction and must be included in a complete description of a strategic interaction.[11] Typically these beliefs are represented by probability distributions that describe how likely an actor believes the various possibilities are.

Assuming actors and environments to be analytically separable naturally lends itself to two broad kinds of conceptual experiments. Whether the interaction is between a legislature and an executive over the formulation of foreign policy or two countries deciding whether to escalate during a crisis, these experiments recur at all levels of strategic interaction and give the strategic-choice approach much of its analytic power. Implicitly or explicitly, all theories in the strategic-choice approach make this distinction between actors and their environment and engage in one or both of these basic conceptual experiments.

The first experiment varies the properties of the actors, that is, their preferences or beliefs, while holding the environment in which they interact constant. What, for example, would happen to the likelihood of war if a state changed its preferences by becoming much more aggressive, as Germany did in the 1930s under Hitler? Or do the preferences of great powers have an important effect on the international economy? What

---

[11] Describing how these beliefs evolve once the interaction has begun is part of analyzing the interaction.

happens if a hegemonic power prefers to remain isolated and is unwilling to assume the burdens of providing public goods? Kindleberger (1973), for instance, argues that this preference was an important cause of the Great Depression. Finally, how do changes in the beliefs actors hold as they enter an interaction affect their choices and the outcome? If a state is confident that another is not revisionist and is primarily motivated by security concerns, is the danger of a deterrence spiral (Jervis 1978) and the likelihood of war smaller because it takes a more tolerant view of the other's arms buildup (Glaser 1994–95) or is that danger and that likelihood larger as the state delays its response and increases the probability that a revisionist state will secure a military advantage (Powell 1996c)?

The second conceptual experiment varies the environment while holding the attributes of the actors constant. For example, do domestic or international institutions matter? In other words, do changes in the institutional structure affect the information or actions available to the actors when they have to act, and do these changes affect the outcomes of the interaction? As already noted, Keohane (1984) argues that international institutions facilitate cooperation by providing information to states. Likewise, Milner (1997) suggests that domestic institutions affect the prospects for cooperation by specifying who gets to decide what, and when, and by providing information to different actors. Similarly we can ask whether bipolar or multipolar systems are more stable? Neorealists posit that bipolarity is more transparent and, as a result, war is less likely (Waltz 1979; Mearsheimer 1990–91). One way to think about this question is to imagine that the preferences and motivations of states remain constant, as neorealists assume, but that the actions and information available to the actors vary. We can then examine how the strategies of states and, in turn, outcomes are likely to change from one setting to another.

Environments, disaggregated into a set of actions and an informational structure, and actors, decomposed into preferences and beliefs, describe a strategic setting. They also form the primary independent variables through which theories of strategic-choice attempt to explain variations in observed outcomes. In principle, at least, actions, information, preferences, and beliefs can vary independently from one another, and analysis can seek to deduce and identify their effects on behavior. Where the distinction between actors and environments suggests two broad conceptual experiments, the disaggregation of these elements into four attributes implies four separate conceptual experiments. Indeed, research within the strategic-choice approach typically proceeds by explicating how these attributes structure interactions and how this interaction, in turn, affects observed behaviors.

Other variables may be featured in strategic-choice theories, but they take on significance only through their effects on one or more of the primary independent variables. For example, analysts have drawn a link between asset specificity and import competition, on the one hand, and trade policy, on the other (Frieden and Rogowski 1996; Rogowski 1989). A full specification of the causal chain, however, would reveal that these factors matter because they affect either the preferences of firms over different types of policy outcomes or the possibility of reallocating assets into alternative uses. Likewise, democracy may lead to peace between similar states either through norms, reflected in different preferences toward war between democracies; domestic institutions, indicated by different actions available to substate actors that, in turn, aggregate into different state preferences (Russett 1993); or greater transparency (Schultz 1999).

Like the distinction between actors and environments, these four attributes recur at all levels of strategic interaction. Whether the actors are individuals forming a lobby group, firms seeking to influence their governments or even the governments of countries in which they are investing, a president negotiating under legislative authority with some foreign partner, the same four attributes describe the relevant strategic interactions. As discussed immediately below, these recurring features of any strategic interaction allow analysts more readily to build theories that bridge the traditional levels of analysis. While for many purposes it may be appropriate to focus on interstate or intrastate interactions, in the traditional fashion, it is equally appropriate to construct a theory that allows for strategic interaction between branches of a government in one country but that treats the second country as a unitary actor (Milner 1997). What matters here is not the level from which the actors are drawn, but their possible actions, information, preferences, and beliefs.

The Pragmatic Nature of Theory

In principle, international politics is a seamless web that links the wants and desires of ordinary individuals to international outcomes, like the first and second world wars, the Great Depression of the 1930s, the economic integration of Europe, or the remarkably peaceful collapse of the Soviet empire in Eastern Europe. Although the comprehensiveness of this image is appealing, the study of international politics would be hopelessly complicated if every international outcome had to be traced back to the goals and actions of individuals or if every individual action had to be traced through to its international consequences. In order to analyze this seamless web, analysts must simplify international politics.

Theories are not necessarily statements about or accurate descriptions of the "real world." Rather, they are tools analysts use to render a complex reality somewhat more tractable intellectually. All theories attempt to simplify a complex reality, and, as a result, they all reflect judgments made by theorists as to what to put into their analyses and what to leave out. This is what Arthur Stein (chapter 7) refers to as the "art of the science of choice," but it applies equally to all social-scientific approaches. The need to make pragmatic judgments at nearly every stage of constructing a theory suggests that there may be multiple ways of approaching the same problem in international relations. There is no true theory of alliance formation or free trade, for instance, only more or less useful ones.

The strategic-choice approach often presupposes that many important issues in international politics can be studied fruitfully by assuming that substate actors interact, that this interaction effectively aggregates these actors into states, and that these states, in turn, interact with each other. At the most basic level, individuals are the actors. But at a somewhat higher level of abstraction, the actors may also be other substate groups like firms, bureaucracies, interest groups, military organizations, political parties, ethnic groups, and so on. These substate actors undoubtedly have conflicting interests and goals that play themselves out in the domestic arena. The interaction of these substate actors in this arena, however, aggregate into a state's preferences and beliefs. States then interact with other states in the international arena. The effect of this particular simplification is to posit states prior to any international interactions, in the sense that these interactions do not shape the underlying preferences of the state (although the anticipation of these interstate interactions may nonetheless affect the strategies chosen by substate actors). This assumption has led to much good and important work, as we believe the following chapters show. However, this presupposition is sometimes inappropriate. Transnational interactions between substate actors and similar actors abroad or even between substate actors in one state and the government of another may also be important (Keohane and Nye 1972; Risse-Kappen 1995). When such transnational interactions are central to a particular strategic setting, they must be included in the analysis.

Beyond individuals, all actors are social aggregates.[12] Given their aggregate nature, there is no right or wrong set of actors in theories of international relations—although disciplinary conventions focus attention on commonly accepted breakpoints such as groups, classes, governments, and states. Without any fixed or inherent actors in international relations,

---

[12] Some theories disaggregate individuals even further into psychological (e.g., ego, id, or superego) or genetic (selfish gene) components.

where one cuts into this aggregation of social actors is a function of the purposes and limitations of the author. While the choice will affect the explanatory power of the resulting theory, which actors to include in a particular model is a pragmatic judgment all analysts must make. In some cases it may be insightful to analyze international relations as the interaction of unitary states, as in present systemic theories. In other cases, however, it may be preferable to focus on the interactions between a legislature, which aggregates one set of societal preferences; an executive, which aggregates another set; and a foreign state which is, for practical purposes, treated as a unitary actor. It may also be insightful, in still other cases, to focus on the interactions of social groups in one country and the state in another.

That actors are generally aggregates of more basic actors and that the appropriate level of aggregation depends on the question at hand means that the strategic-choice approach often resembles a collection of "boxes within boxes." In any given theory, a particular strategic interaction is isolated and explained, one hopes, by the relevant values of the four attributes defined above. In a single box, the preferences of an aggregated actor, for instance, are taken as exogenous, and their effects on choices and outcomes are examined. In a larger box, however, these preferences may themselves become the object to be explained. What is taken to be exogenous in one "box" or formulation may be endogenized or problematized in another. In some formulations it may be useful and insightful to take states and their preferences to be exogenous, whereas explaining these goals and interests is what is at issue in others.[13]

Like all pragmatic formulations, this way of organizing strategic problems has advantages and disadvantages. A major advantage is that it focuses attention on the question of what affects the outcomes of these interactions. How, for example, does a change in the composition of industry affect the way the strategies of firms aggregate into a state's preferences over trade policy (Hiscox 1997)? And how do these national preferences affect the strategies of states within the international economy (Lake 1988)? How does a shift in the distribution of power affect the actions available to states and, in turn, international politics as a whole (Gilpin 1981)? Do international institutions have an important and independent effect in shaping interstate interaction, as institutionalists argue,

---

[13] Given the flexibility of the approach, and the possibility that transnational interactions may be included in a particular theory, the metaphor of boxes fitting easily inside boxes may be partly misleading; rather, the boxes may be oddly misshaped with parts jutting out into other boxes that may, in other theories, be treated as social aggregates. Nonetheless, the idea is that for whatever set of actors is in the box, their actions, information, preferences, and beliefs are determined exogenously by strategic interactions that are not part of the immediate analysis.

either by framing available actions or providing information (Keohane and Martin 1995)? Or do these institutions merely reflect the distribution of power among the states and have no independent effect on their behavior, as neorealists claim (Mearsheimer 1990–91, 1994–95)? And if institutions do have a constraining effect on substate actors and less of an effect on states, what accounts for the difference? Focusing on the interaction and aggregation of substate actors into states and then on the interaction of states brings these questions to the fore. In turn, the four primary independent variables discussed above provide useful mechanisms for thinking through and explicating the questions of how power, institutions, or other factors influence actors' choices.

A disadvantage of the approach, however, is that it may lead to ever more theoretically sophisticated treatments of ever more particularistic problems and cases. Carried to its logical conclusion, an analyst could produce a "theory" of a unique event. Indeed, it would be a useful organizing device to write an account of any historical episode by focusing on actions, information, preferences, and beliefs—this is likely to produce a more complete and useful history than a less directed inquiry. The danger, however, is that we lose our ability to generalize about and ultimately to explain international relations. Typically the desire for generalizable knowledge constrains this tendency toward more specific and precisely tailored theories, but we recognize the temptation inherent in the approach.

Methodological Bets

Methodological approaches, by their very nature, privilege some forms of explanation over others and are, in effect, bets about what will prove to be fruitful ways to attack certain sets of problems. In addition to those already noted above, especially the separability of actors and environments and the pragmatic nature of theory, four central methodological bets underlie the strategic-choice approach.

First, as noted above, the strategic-choice approach is agnostic toward the appropriate level of analysis in international relations. No single level or set of political actors is likely to be everywhere and always helpful in understanding international phenomenon. We intentionally leave open the question of whether individuals, groups, states, international organizations, or other entities are appropriate actors in theories of international politics.

Moreover, in the traditional levels-of-analysis "problem," there is an implicit methodological bet that our understanding of international politics is best enhanced by grouping and isolating causal forces by the level at which they originate, whether this is at the system, unit, or some more differentiated level (Waltz 1959, 1979; Singer 1961; Rosenau 1976). Thus analysts strive to produce theories that locate causes in separate and autonomous categories—with much debate ensuing as to which level this or that causal force should be assigned, as if merely locating a cause within some analytic scheme tells us something meaningful about international relations. The strategic-choice approach makes a different bet, namely, that it is better to focus on the strategic problem regardless of who the relevant actors are and at which "level" they might be located. It parallels Waltz (1959, 1979) and other systems theorists who recognize that actors' intentions are not always a sufficient explanation for outcomes, but it emphasizes strategic action generally—not just interactions between unitary states.

Second, the strategic-choice approach presumes, as already noted, that strategic interactions recur in a seamless web from individuals to international outcomes. By presuming that one can cut into this web at any point, "box" a strategic interaction for purposes of analysis, and thereby gain some understanding of the larger whole, the approach implicitly assumes that social systems are "orderly," that interactions between one set of actors feed into the choices of others at a higher level of aggregation in a well-defined way. An emerging body of work challenges this assumption, however, and assumes that social systems are "chaotic." While "local"-level interactions may be well-behaved in this view, the system as a whole is so complex that "aggregate" outcomes are indeterminate or essentially unpredictable (Fearon 1996; Gaddis 1992–93). If there is some level of aggregation beyond which locally determinant interactions become indeterminate, then the utility of a strategic-choice approach declines. While we share Einstein's intuition about order in the universe, in truth we have no basis at this time for determining which assumption is more accurate or theoretically useful. The methodological bet in the strategic-choice approach is that interactions do aggregate in an orderly fashion. Even if they do not, however, the strategic-choice approach is still likely to prove useful over some ranges of aggregation and behavior.

Third, this "boxes-within-boxes" approach is based on a partial equilibrium perspective. A general equilibrium approach presupposes that everything is significantly related to everything else and therefore tries to incorporate all forms of interactions and feedback. A partial equilibrium analysis, by contrast, simplifies problems by ignoring some feedback effects and thereby bets that everything is not significantly related to everything else or that the gain from simplification will outweigh the distorting effects of ignoring some feedback.[14] As the following chapters show, the

---

[14] Of course even purported general equilibrium approaches still leave things out. General equilibrium theory in economics, for example, does not include political or cultural elements.

current state of the art is that important insights and propositions can sometimes be derived by setting some types of feedback aside. An important goal of future research, however, is to deepen our understanding by incorporating the significant feedback channels which our analyses may have initially excluded.

Fourth, when characterizing a strategic interaction, specifying the attributes of the actors is just as important as specifying the environment. Analysis simply cannot proceed without a specification of the preferences and beliefs of the actors. But when trying to explain changes in behavior, the strategic-choice approach turns to *untheorized* preference- or belief-based explanations as a last resort. We noted above that in any particular theory, the attributes of actors can be treated as exogenous. However, invoking unexplained changes in preferences or beliefs to account for changes in behavior is, in a way, "too easy." In many cases, preferences and beliefs are unobservable and cannot be directly known or measured by analysts. Therefore, to explain changes in behavior as a result of changes in preferences or beliefs often proves tautological. As Jeffry Frieden explains in chapter 2, when preferences (or beliefs) are deduced from some other theory and rest on some observable traits, it is perfectly appropriate to draw a link between changes in the sources of preferences (or beliefs) and changes in behavior. Short of well-developed deductive theories of preferences or beliefs, however, analysis within the strategic-choice approach typically tries to explain changes in behavior primarily through learning, through changes in the actors' environment, or even by decomposing the actors into more basic actors.

Learning is an important part of many strategic interactions. It is, for example, at the heart of models of crisis bargaining, for it explains why a state changes its behavior by backing down rather than continuing to escalate (Morrow 1994b; Nalebuff 1986; Powell 1987, 1988, 1989; Fearon 1994a). In some theories, for instance, the states are initially unsure of each other's willingness to go to war. During the crisis each state watches the behavior of its opponent and tries to reason back from this behavior in order to update its prior beliefs about the other's willingness to fight. The longer the crisis goes on, the more confident each becomes that the other is willing to run high risks or pay high costs. Eventually one state may become sufficiently confident that the other is willing to bear a higher cost or run a larger risk that it chooses to concede. A state backs down when it concludes that its adversary is more resolute. In this way, learning can explain why behavior changes during a dynamic interaction in which a single set of actors acts and reacts to each other.

Changes in the environment may explain why the behavior of different groups of similar actors change. This type of explanation is based on the second kind of general conceptual experiment discussed above. Consider, for instance, the alliance behavior of the Great Powers before the world wars. Thomas Christensen and Jack Snyder (1990) argue that states tended to act like a chain gang before World War I and to pass the buck before World War II. In other words, states before 1914 tended to bind themselves together tightly through their alliance commitments, which had the unintended consequence of making it more likely that they would be entrapped in a war they did not want to fight, but in the interwar years they tried harder to avoid conflict and thereby passed the cost of fighting on to their allies. One way to try to explain these different behaviors would be to argue that there was an important and fundamental change in the basic motivations and goals of states—a change in their preferences. The strategic-choice approach tries to avoid this type of explanation, unless there are good theoretical reasons for expecting preferences to have changed. Instead, strategic-choice theories typically assume that the states' basic goals remained the same in both situations and try to explain the change in behavior through an alteration in the strategic environment, say, in the nature of military technology. Indeed, this is precisely what Christensen and Snyder do by tracing the different alliance behaviors to changes in the perceived balance between offense and defense.[15]

The desire to avoid untheorized preference-based explanations even extends as far as a willingness to change the actors rather than have the same actors change their preferences for some unexplained reason. This willingness is starkest and easiest to see if we contrast the strategic-choice approach to constructivism (Wendt 1992, 1994; Wendt and Friedheim 1995).[16] Alexander Wendt and others argue, correctly in our view, that states' goals and preferences have changed over time, especially if we consider a long enough interval.[17] To explain these changes, Wendt continues to assume that states are unitary actors but seeks to problematize their preferences. The strategic-choice approach would, instead, disaggregate the state into more basic actors. Assuming states to be unitary actors is, after all, only an assumption and, like all simplifying assumptions, it may be useful sometimes and get in the way at other times. The strategic-choice approach would try to decompose the state into more basic actors— be they firms, national leaders, bureaucracies, interest groups, classes,

---

[15] See Morrow 1993 for a criticism of Christensen and Snyder's analysis and an alternative explanation that is also in keeping with a strategic-choice approach. For an example of an explanation based in part on changes in preferences, see Mueller's (1989) discussion of the absence of major war since 1945.

[16] Other contrasts are discussed below.

[17] Jervis, also recognizing that preferences change, suggests that taking tastes and preferences as exogenous may facilitate analysis, "but at the cost of drawing attention away from areas that may contain much of the explanatory 'action' in which we are interested" (1988, 3324–25).

parties, or organizations—whose basic preferences could be considered to have remained constant across time. Analysis would then turn to questions of how the environment has changed—perhaps the distribution of domestic power among different political parties or classes has evolved, for instance—and how these changes affect the way actors interact and, ultimately, the way that their goals aggregate into state goals.[18]

In sum, the strategic-choice approach, like all research approaches, is really a series of bets about what will prove to be fruitful ways to increase our understanding of international relations. Some aspects of this approach will undoubtedly turn out more helpful than others. Indeed, some are likely to prove counterproductive. Unfortunately it is impossible to be sure ahead of time which of these bets will pay off. Future research will have to probe the boundaries of usefulness.

CHARACTERISTICS AND IMPLICATIONS

The strategic-choice approach must ultimately be judged in terms of its empirical utility. How well does it help us understand international politics? Given the current state of much of international relations theory, however, the strategic-choice approach also holds the promise of an important intermediate payoff: It can help tighten and sharpen the logic of our theories and, in so doing, help us to identify which are worth the substantial investment of time and energy necessary to do the hard empirical work of evaluating competing claims and hypotheses. This intermediate payoff derives from two characteristics of the strategic-choice approach.

The first is its emphasis on what might be called microfoundations, that is, on the connection between what actors want, the environment in which they strive to further their interests, and the outcomes of this interaction. This emphasis is especially important because the microfoundations underlying many theories in international relations are weak or poorly specified. This weakness has been the source of much confusion, heated debate, and wasted effort. Focusing on strategic interactions can lead analysts to be more explicit about the microfoundations they employ.

The second source of advantage is that the strategic-choice approach, as noted, tends to break down traditional distinctions between the levels of analysis, security and international political economy, and, most generally, international relations and other areas of political science. Breaking

---

[18] Within the constructivist approach, Katzenstein (1996b) also disaggregates states into more basic actors but continues to emphasize the importance of socially constructed identities and norms.

down these traditional distinctions makes it possible to focus on the logic of the interaction and not on irrelevant and often misleading distinctions. It may also make it possible to draw on new sources of empirical evidence and theoretical insight.

Microfoundations

Existing theories of international relations generally suffer from a weak or inadequate specification of the actors and the environment in which they interact. Theorists have often not given enough attention to specifying who the relevant actors are, their environment, and especially the causal chain linking the actors and their environment to the outcomes claimed to follow from these variables. In brief, existing theories of international relations generally lack firm and secure microfoundations.[19] Even theories that can be broadly grouped under the umbrella of the strategic-choice approach sometimes fail to explicate fully their microfoundations. Part of our ambition in laying out the fundamentals of the approach is to encourage analysts to take more care in specifying the microfoundations of their theories.

The failure to specify microfoundations adequately makes it difficult to understand how changes in strategic settings affect outcomes. This is a significant failing, for being able to trace these effects is often essential for answering important questions in international relations. Does, for example, a change in military technology that creates greater first-strike incentives make war more likely? Do international institutions shape and influence states' behavior in significant ways? How do foreign economic policies vary with domestic institutional structures? Do increasing returns to scale and changes in the level of efficient production make the formation of trade blocks more likely? Each of these questions is, in effect, a different version of the second type of conceptual experiment: how changes in the environment affect outcomes. Answering these questions depends critically on being able to trace the links between assumptions about actors and their environment to the expected outcomes of this interaction.

Several brief examples illustrate that existing theories have generally not devoted sufficient attention to specifying microfoundations. Much attention has been given to the problem of relative and absolute gains in

---

[19] By "microfoundations" we do not intend to imply that all social interaction can or should be grounded in individual behavior. As noted above, who the relevant actors are is a pragmatic modeling assumption in the strategic-choice approach. Rather, we use that term only to refer to the need to specify the goals of purposive actors and the environments in which they interact.

the last few years.[20] Realists and many others believe that if a state must provide for its own security and if an absolute gain but relative loss can be translated into a future threat to that state, then states must be concerned about relative as well as absolute gains. Much of the debate has centered on whether a model consistent with the core assumptions of realism must represent this concern with relative gains in the preference orderings or, equivalently, in the utility functions of the actors. Joseph Grieco argues that realism requires such a formulation:

> Realism expects a state's utility function to incorporate two distinct terms. It needs to include the state's individual payoff . . . reflecting the realist view that states are motivated by absolute gains. Yet it must also include a term integrating both the state's individual payoff . . . and the partner's payoff . . . in such a way that gaps favoring the state add to its utility while, more importantly, gaps favoring the partner detract from it. (Grieco 1988a, 500)

Others argue that the assumption of absolute-gains maximization is entirely consistent with realism and offer models to show that actors can still be concerned with relative gains even though they are trying to maximize their absolute gains (e.g., Powell 1991, 1993).

The existence of this debate is both symptomatic of the weakness of realism's microfoundations and underscores the importance of specifying clearly the causal connections from realism's assumptions about the strategic environment to the outcomes that follow from these assumptions. First, the mere fact that what realism assumes about state preferences could be the subject of a major debate suggests that these assumptions are poorly specified. Second, this debate is based on the claim that a concern for relative gains implies that a state's utility must be, at least in part, a function of relative gains. In other words, the only way one can obtain an outcome in which the actors exhibit a concern for relative gains is for their utilities to be a function of each other's payoffs. It is easy to find formal counterexamples to this claim, that is, models in which the actors are trying to maximize their absolute gains but in a strategic setting in which their interaction induces a concern for relative gains.[21] These counterexamples show that the claim is wrong. But the fact that the claim was made illustrates the difficulty of correctly inferring outcomes when the underlying microfoundations are poorly specified.

---

[20] See Baldwin 1993 and Powell 1994 for reviews of this debate. For individual contributions, see Gowa 1986; Grieco 1988a, 1988b, 1990, 1993; Keohane 1984, 1993; Lomborg 1993; Powell 1991, 1993; and Snidal 1991a, 1991b.

[21] One may also assume that actors seek to maximize relative gains and to identify strategic settings in which they are induced to act so as to maximize their absolute gains. See Snidal 1991a, 1991b.

A second, related debate about the implications of anarchy also shows that existing theories often offer only weak and problematic causal arguments linking assumptions about the strategic environment to outcomes. Structural realism makes two fundamental assumptions. First, states at a minimum want to survive, and, second, the international system is anarchic (Waltz 1979, 88, 91). The first assumption characterizes the actors' preferences: States prefer survival to extinction. The second assumption characterizes the actions available to the actors, albeit vaguely: In an anarchic setting, with no higher authority or common government to enforce agreements, states are unable to make binding threats, promises, or commitments to restrain themselves from actions they might otherwise take; in short, under anarchy, states can do anything they are physically capable of doing.[22]

At least two conclusions are said to follow from these assumptions, but both are problematic. First, anarchic systems are generally conflictual and cooperation is unlikely (Grieco 1988a; Waltz 1979, 105–6). Keohane (1984, 6) argues, however, that anarchy does not preclude cooperation as long as states are on "friendly political terms." More recently Glaser (1994–95, 51) has suggested that anarchy does not imply a lack of cooperation even when states are on unfriendly political terms and there are significant political-military divisions among them:

> The strong general propensity for states to compete does not follow *deductively* from structural realism's basic assumptions. On the contrary, under a wide variety of conditions, structural realism predicts that states can best achieve their security goals through cooperative policies, not competitive ones and, therefore, should choose cooperation. (emphasis added)

These two challenges suggest that the assumptions of anarchy and the desire to survive do not necessarily imply that cooperation is unlikely. At the very least, the causal link imputed by structural realism between these assumptions and the claimed lack of cooperation is problematic.

Second, structural realism also asserts that these two assumptions imply balance-of-power politics; that is, actors will tend to balance in any system that is anarchic and in which the actors seek to survive. As Kenneth Waltz (1979, 121) clearly predicts, "balance-of-power politics prevail whenever two, and only two, requirements are met: that the order [of the system] be anarchic and that it be populated by units wishing to survive." But this, too, is problematic.

The folk theorem for repeated games demonstrates that the claim that these two assumptions imply balancing is formally incorrect. In a repeated

---

[22] For definitions of anarchy, see Art and Jervis 1992, 1; Axelrod and Keohane 1986, 226; Mearsheimer 1994–95; and Waltz 1979, 88–93.

game, essentially any division of benefits can be realized as an equilibrium outcome—in other words, for essentially any division of benefits, there exist strategies such that no actor has any incentive to deviate from its strategy and these strategies, when followed, yield that allocation of benefits. Furthermore, the strategies that support this outcome entail no balancing. Rather, they bear a striking resemblance to a collective security regime reminiscent of the ideal of the League of Nations. Should any actor deviate from the agreed division of benefits, all the other actors punish the deviator severely enough that the costs of being punished outweigh the gains. The threat to carry out this punishment therefore deters an actor from deviating as long as the threat is credible, and the folk theorem shows that these threats are credible—in that it is in each actor's self-interest to participate in punishing a deviator.[23] In sum, there is no balancing in these equilibria, yet the actors wish to survive. The strategic setting is also anarchic in that the threats on which these equilibria are based are self-enforcing and, accordingly, do not require a common government to police them. Thus the assumptions of anarchy and that states seek to survive do not in themselves imply balancing.

That these two assumptions do not imply balancing in repeated games must be interpreted carefully. It does not say that balancing does not characterize much of international politics (although the diplomatic historian Paul Schroeder (1994), for one, believes that bandwagoning is more prevalent than balancing). It does say that the causal chain from anarchy and the desire to survive to balancing behavior is incomplete. If this chain is to be completed, other assumptions about the strategic setting have to be made. Even interpreted cautiously, however, this fact does have important implications for past "tests" of neorealist theory. Although there has been a lively debate whether states "balance" or "bandwagon" in international politics, the empirical results are largely irrelevant to the theory because the theory itself is underspecified.[24] Even if states do balance, this cannot confirm neorealist theory as the prediction does not follow deductively from the assumptions. The vigorous empirical debate has revealed important patterns and inductive insights into the actual behavior of states, but analysts—both pro and con—have actually shed little light on the explanatory power of neorealism.

While we have focused above on neorealism, similar problems of inadequately specified microfoundations also arise in other theories of international relations. In his original treatment of the Great Depression that laid the foundation for the so-called theory of hegemonic stability, Charles

---

[23] See Benoit and Krishna 1985 and Fudenberg and Maskin 1986 for formal statements of the folk theorem.

[24] See Walt 1987; Schroeder 1994.

Kindleberger argued "that for the world economy to be stabilized, there has to be a stabilizer, one stabilizer" (1973, 305). This view initially gained wide acceptance and sparked a decade of creative theorizing and research.[25] Focusing on the strategic interactions of states within an anarchic international environment, however, subsequent research challenged this view and demonstrated that k-groups of more than one state are indeed possible (Snidal 1985) and that hegemony is neither necessary nor sufficient for stability to arise (Lake 1988, 1993). Likewise, the limitations and logical indeterminacies of Graham Allison's (1971) three models of foreign-policy decision making are clearly revealed when examined through the lens of strategic interaction (Bendor and Hammond 1992). Again, while both sets of theories here have generated large empirical literatures, their underspecification limits the implications and importance of these tests. Incompletely specified theories can neither be confirmed nor disconfirmed by empirical evidence.

In sum, existing theories in international relations often lack secure microfoundations. Too little attention has been paid to specifying the strategic setting and the causal chain linking assumptions to outcomes. Weak microfoundations, in turn, make it difficult to trace the effects that changes in the strategic setting have on outcomes. To redress this weakness, it is necessary to emphasize a more careful elaboration of the strategic problem facing a group of actors. By identifying the parts of a strategic setting, as well as the sorts of conceptual experiments that can be conducted within a given model, the strategic-choice approach can lead analysts to a fuller specification of the relevant microfoundations. This is a necessary first step prior to empirical testing. In turn, explicating full microfoundations may open the way for more productive empirical and theoretical work.

Beyond Traditional Distinctions

One of the most important functions of a theoretical framework is to show how phenomenon are related, connected, or similar. Theoretical frameworks help us see patterns and regularities in the confusion of empirical and historical experience. Theoretical approaches help us organize. International relations scholars have tended to organize the study of international politics in three major ways. First, following Waltz (1959, 1979), explanations are grouped according to the level at which they locate causes. In this levels-of-analysis approach, individual-level or first-image

[25] See, among others, Krasner 1976; Gilpin 1975, 1981; Keohane 1980; 1984. For critiques, see Conybeare 1984; Gowa 1989; McKeown 1983; Russett 1985; and Stein 1984.

arguments explain outcomes in terms of the attributes or characteristics of human beings (either separately, as in "great men"-of-history theories, or collectively); state-level or second-image arguments explain outcomes in terms of the attributes or characteristics of states; and structural or third-image arguments explain outcomes in terms of the attributes and characteristics of the international system (most commonly, system structure). Second, international relations scholars divide their field in terms of what is to be explained. Although this division has long been questioned (see Bergsten, Keohane, and Nye 1975; Cooper 1972–73), the high politics of war, peace, and security is assumed to be different from the low politics of money, trade, and finance, and thus each type of politics requires its own theoretical approach. For example, realism, which is usually associated with the study of the causes of war, and institutionalism, which is generally associated with issues in international political economy, are said to be based on different sets of core assumptions (see above). Finally, international relations theorists have used the notion of anarchy—which is the absence of a supranational authority that can ensure states honor their commitments—to define the domain of their field and separate it from other political arenas. Indeed, anarchy is often taken to be the fundamental fact of international relations, one "that distinguishes international politics from ordinary politics" (Wight 1978, 102). By emphasizing the strategic problem actors face, however, the strategic-choice approach transcends the levels-of-analysis distinction, spans the divide between security studies and international political economy, and serves as an analytic bridge between international relations theory and other fields of political science. Focusing on strategic interactions shows that actors at different levels often face similar strategic problems in different issue areas and in both domestic and international politics.

Three examples illustrate the bridging potential of focusing on strategic interaction. In *The Evolution of Cooperation* (1984), Robert Axelrod uses the repeated Prisoner's Dilemma to examine the ability of self-interested actors to sustain cooperation when each of them has short-run incentives to exploit the other. He suggests that the repeated Prisoner's Dilemma can serve as a model or at least a metaphor for situations as diverse as legislative behavior in the United States Senate, international trade, and trench warfare in the World War I. This suggestion is developed further in *Cooperation under Anarchy* (Oye 1986a) where the repeated Prisoner's Dilemma is used to study the Concert of Europe, the failure of cooperation in the July 1914 crisis, arms races, trade wars, and international banking. The repeated Prisoner's Dilemma is now widely used in international relations theory to model the security dilemma (Jervis 1978), alliance competition (G. Snyder 1984), arms races (Downs and Rocke 1990), the effect of alliances on trade (Gowa and Mansfield 1993;

Gowa 1994), and trade agreements (Yarbrough and Yarbrough 1992). Describing this wide range of issues in terms of the general strategic problem actors face rather than in terms of the specific details of a trade or security issue reveals a fundamental similarity between these issues that might otherwise not have been appreciated.

Of course, the repeated Prisoner's Dilemma is a very simple game that may not capture important aspects of particular problems. In a repeated game, for instance, the players face the same situation over and over again; regardless of what the players do in one round, they face the same situation in the next. Repeated games are therefore a poor model for situations in which the nature of the interaction changes over time because the actors can take actions, such as the launching of what Robert Gilpin (1981) calls hegemonic war, that transform the strategic setting.[26] The point here, however, is not the adequacy of the repeated Prisoner's Dilemma as a model for specific issues in international relations. It is, rather, that focusing on the strategic problems inherent in these situations—perhaps by initially characterizing them as repeated games and then asking what this formulation leaves out—reveals important similarities and differences that other analytic perspectives would miss.

The repeated Prisoner's Dilemma is now so widely used and its properties so well known that the conclusions derived from it may seem obvious. James Fearon's (1993) analysis of ethnic conflict offers a more subtle example of the potential advantages of focusing on strategic problems and of the way that this focus can transcend the levels of analysis.[27] He argues that an important cause of communal conflict may be the inability of a majority ethnic group to commit itself not to exploit a minority group. A minority group may face a dilemma during a period of transition, such as that which occurred throughout much of Eastern Europe and the republics of the former Soviet Union following the retreat and subsequent collapse of the Soviet Union. There may be agreements about respecting minority rights, which both the majority and minority groups prefer to violence given the cost of war and the existing distribution of power between the groups. This may suggest that neither group will fight, and they will escape civil war. Unfortunately the minority group may still fight if the majority is unable to commit itself to honoring a mutually preferred agreement. As the majority group consolidates its authority during the transition, it is likely to become more powerful relative to the minority. Once it is stronger, the majority may seek to "renegotiate" the agreement

---

[26] See Powell 1991, 1309–10 for an elaboration of this criticism of repeated games.

[27] Fearon examines the particular case of Croatia, but he constructs a more general argument. For a published paper that reproduces much of the original model, see Fearon 1998. For a discussion of the range of strategic dilemmas inherent in ethnic conflict, see Lake and Rothchild 1996.

with the minority. Anticipating these changes, the dilemma confronting the minority group is either to fight now when it is relatively stronger, fight later when relatively weaker, or ultimately accept the deal the majority offers after negotiating. Fearon shows that the minority often prefers fighting now, when it is stronger.

Fearon also points out that the strategic problem facing ethnic groups is akin to the problem of preventive war facing states in the international system (see also Fearon 1995). Using force is generally costly, and frequently agreements are made about the distribution of benefits, which all states prefer to fighting. But if the balance of power is shifting against a state and if nothing prevents the stronger state from using its improved position to "renegotiate" an agreement, then a state may find that its best alternative is to launch a preventive war. Fearon's analysis centers on the strategic problem actors confront. The approach reveals a fundamental similarity between some of the incentives leading to ethnic conflict and some of those leading to preventive war. It is doubtful that a focus that locates the problem of ethnic conflict at the level of domestic politics and that of preventive war at the level of the international system would have suggested this similarity.

Bargaining in the shadow of power offers a third example of the potential advantages of focusing on strategic problems. Suppose two states are bargaining about revising the territorial status quo. The states make offers and counteroffers until they reach an agreement or until one of them becomes so pessimistic about the prospects of an agreement that it uses force to impose a settlement. This strategic issue bears a striking resemblance to the strategic problem confronting potential litigants bargaining about the terms of a settlement in the shadow of the law.[28] These parties make offers and counteroffers until they reach agreement or until one of them becomes sufficiently pessimistic about the likelihood of reaching a mutually acceptable settlement that it takes the dispute to court. Schweizer (1989), for instance, studies a model in which the defendant and the plaintiff have private information about the strength of their cases. In light of this information, the defendant makes a take-it-or-leave-it offer which the plaintiff can either accept or reject by taking the case to trial.[29] If Schweizer's formulation were reinterpreted by taking the defendant and the plaintiff to be a status quo state and a dissatisfied state, respectively, and if the probability of winning in court were taken to be the probability of win-

[28] For a review of the literature on legal bargaining, see Cooter and Rubinfeld 1989 and Kennan and Wilson 1993, 76–79.

[29] Although only one offer can be made in this model, that both actors have private information makes the game technically difficult to analyze. See Powell 1996a for a model in which actors can make as many offers as they wish and in which they agree on the distribution of power.

ning a war, then Schweizer's model would be one of the best formal models we have of bargaining in international relations (see Morrow 1989, for another example). Indeed, the feature his model highlights, namely, that each actor has private information about its strength and thus is uncertain of its probability of prevailing, is central to many theories of the causes of war. Blainey (1988), for example, argues that wars result from the uncertainty of states about the distribution of power and the probability that they will prevail.[30]

Once again, a focus on strategic problems suggests a similarity that would not otherwise have been apparent. This similarity is especially striking because it transcends the distinction between anarchy and hierarchy on which so much of international relations theory has been built. No domain could be more hierarchic than that of two litigants bargaining in the shadow of a court that can impose a settlement. Yet, the strategic problem facing these litigants parallels that facing states in an anarchic international system, at least to a first approximation. Eventually, of course, a focus on these strategic problems may also reveal important differences, which will deepen our understanding of both problems. This, too, is part of the promise of focusing on strategic interactions.

The advantages of moving beyond traditional distinctions are twofold. First, seeing similarities where none were appreciated before may open new avenues for empirical testing. New sources or kinds of evidence may be brought to bear on old problems. Second, a sharper understanding of the similarities between two issues may also provide a deeper and more subtle understanding of how they differ. Paradoxically, breaking down traditional distinctions between the levels of analysis, security studies and international political economy, and international relations and other areas of political science may ultimately reveal new, more refined distinctions.

ALTERNATIVE APPROACHES

Many comparisons between the strategic-choice approach and extant theories of international politics have already been addressed above. Although realism and liberalism do not treat strategic interaction as their focus and unit of analysis, these two principal paradigms, with their numerous variants, and many second- and third-image theories typically share a concern with strategic interaction. As such, these other paradigms are generally compatible with the strategic-choice approach. This compat-

---

[30] For other game-theoretic models of legal bargaining with private information, see Nalebuff 1987; Reinganum and Wilde 1986; and Spier 1992.

ibility, of course, does not dissolve the important differences that distinguish one paradigm or theory from another. Indeed, bringing these paradigms and theories within a common framework that emphasizes strategic interaction highlights both their commonalities and differences. This common framework also allows us to probe better when the apparent differences matter: when selected assumptions are more fruitful or appropriate than others or when particular variables play a greater or lesser explanatory role. This analysis opens up new research opportunities and avenues of inquiry, not new divisions in the field. The resolution of the debate on absolute gains versus relative gains, such as it is, is exemplary in this regard (Grieco 1993; Keohane 1993). Having demonstrated that the behaviors central to each perspective can be derived as special conditions from models based on the assumptions of the other theory (see Snidal 1991a; Powell 1991), the debate is being transformed into a research program intended to assess the magnitude of critical variables and to estimate their causal importance. This demonstrates clearly the value of integrating seemingly disparate paradigms into a common framework that emphasizes strategic interaction.

Although many theories and approaches in international relations share this common emphasis on strategic interaction, not all do. The most general and influential alternatives to the strategic-choice approach are the cognitive and constructivist approaches to international relations. This section contrasts these two perspectives with the strategic-choice approach.

Cognitive approaches to international relations posit that individuals—and, by implication, other types of actors—are "nonrational," that is, they fail to respond to their environment through a relatively coherent, means-ends calculus. Cognitive limitations (such as bounded rationality), motivated biases (some of which are central to "prospect theory"), false consciousness (particularly the roles of ideas and ideology), and unmotivated biases and misperceptions all intervene to bias the way actors process or interpret information about the world around them.[31] These distortions produce observable behaviors that differ in some significant way from those predicted by other, more "rationalist" theories. In our terms, cognitive theories predict that actors with the same available actions, information, preferences, and beliefs will choose different strategies because of cognitive differences, and these strategies will produce different outcomes. In short, cognitivists make a methodological bet that they can explain politically relevant behaviors and outcomes by focusing on how actors process and interpret information. By analyzing how actors

---

[31] See Jervis 1976; Larson 1985; Khong 1992; and Farnham 1994. The literature on learning is reviewed in Levy 1994.

perceive or misperceive their environment, they seek to explain important patterns in world politics.

The strategic-choice approach makes a different bet, namely, that we can explain many important and interesting aspects of world politics by focusing on information asymmetries between actors, the actions available to them, their preferences, and so on. By analyzing the strategic setting in which individuals must make choices, rather than how they process information, the strategic-choice approach seeks to account more successfully and parsimoniously for many of the same patterns. As noted above, the strategic-choice approach begins from the fundamental assumption that actors are, at any level of aggregation, purposive; that is, actors have preferences over different states of the world and they pursue these preferences as best they can given the strategic situation they face. This does not imply that they obtain their most preferred outcome. Nor does it require that individuals (or more aggregated actors) possess unlimited powers of calculation. The pragmatic version of the strategic-choice approach advanced here merely posits that actors are purposive, that they choose strategies in light of the strategic setting as they understand it. To the extent that a given theory does not predict the observed behavior, the analyst generally questions his or her theory, not the actor's cognitive abilities.

Moreover, recent theoretical innovations, especially in game theory, now allow strategic-choice theorists to address at least some of the behaviors that gave rise to the cognitive approach in the first place. As Morrow discusses in chapter 3, early game theoretic models assumed that actors possessed complete information about other actors' preferences. Critics of these theories correctly recognized that actors often did not know other actors' goals. This led directly to studies of misperception—that is, when actors do not interpret objective reality correctly, at least according to the designs of the theory—and its sources (see Snyder and Diesing 1977; Jervis 1976). Games of incomplete information, however, now allow strategic-choice theorists to address these same issues in a systematic fashion. Rather than assuming that actors know the preferences of others, analysts can now posit that actors possess probability distributions over these variables, and they can examine how actors choose different strategies as their beliefs change. Moreover, analysts can now also apply Baye's rule to capture how actors update their probability estimates by observing the choices of others as the games unfold and, in this way, learn from their environment.[32]

Constructivism has recently posed a self-proclaimed challenge to "mainstream" theories of international relations, many of which share a

---

[32] On Baye's rule, see Morrow 1994a.

strategic-choice approach (see Katzenstein 1996a). More often stated as a critique rather than a positive theory, at least in its early stages of development, constructivists nonetheless emphasize that actors and their environments are mutually constitutive and are generally unwilling to separate actors from their environments even for analytic purposes. For constructivists, states are not primordially given or fixed, for instance, but are the product of self-affirming interactions with other similarly constituted states. Change the nature of states or their interaction, constructivists suggest, and their "identities" and "practice" will change as well (Wendt 1992). In short, constructivists are methodological "wholists" who maintain that actors cannot be studied independently from their social settings, and vice versa.

Despite criticisms to the contrary, the strategic-choice approach is also "wholist" but in a slightly different way than constructivism. Any equilibrium is the joint product of actions, information, preferences, and beliefs. A strategic setting is defined by all four features, and if any characteristic is left unspecified, outcomes cannot be fully explained. The strategic-choice approach posits that intellectual progress and explanation comes from varying one characteristic at a time and deducing and assessing its effects while holding the others constant, but this does not mean that a single characteristic "explains" any given outcome. A change in the information available to the actors, for instance, may affect their strategies and, in turn, outcomes, but only contingent on some set of preferences, beliefs, and actions. Similarly, every equilibrium reflects a shared understanding or common conjecture about how actors will behave in that setting. Outcomes depend on the mutual expectations of the actors as to their actions, information, preferences, and beliefs. Just as for constructivists, the strategic-choice approach sees international relations as a "social realm" in which all characteristics matter and shared understandings are important.

Constructivists make a methodological bet that by focusing on processes of socialization, in which agents and structures are mutually constituted, they can explain important patterns and features of international politics. This bet may be most rewarding, and perhaps essential, for processes that unfold over the long term. Yet, even recognizing its strengths, this methodological bet is not without its shortcomings. In denying the possibility of conducting the types of conceptual experiments that lie at the center of the strategic-choice approach, constructivists advance an intellectual position where everything is "endogenous," or dependent on everything else. This may actually be a correct description of the "real world." Nonetheless, with their insistence on the mutually constitutive nature of actors, environments, and behaviors, constructivists risk falling into the trap of, in mathematical terms, "too many unknowns." In this trap, the number of variables is greater than the number of equations, and thus more than one possible "solution" may exist.[33] With all key variables endogenous, constructivists can argue correctly that, in fact, different combinations of factors are possible that would produce a state of affairs different from that which we observe—realpolitik is not the only logical result of anarchy (Wendt 1992). Nonetheless, faced with too many unknowns, constructivists can only speculate about the possibility of this alternative state of affairs actually occurring. Multiple solutions are possible, but, in their self-contained logic, constructivists cannot explain why any particular solution emerges. Reflecting this problem, and as Paul Kowert and Jeffrey Legro (1996) point out, constructivists typically take "norms," a key independent variable, as exogenous, or given, when conducting empirical research. Constructivists thereby violate their own assumption that actors and environments are mutually constitutive.[34]

The strategic-choice approach makes an alternative bet, namely, that the processes of socialization remain constant over a single "round" of interaction. This is reflected in the assumptions noted above that actors' preferences, their beliefs, and so on—the stuff "inside" a particular "box"—remain the same in any given interaction. The bet is that for many important issues in international politics, the features of the strategic setting can usefully be treated as fixed, at least in the short term or for a single interaction. The strategic-choice approach recognizes the limits of this bet, however, and deals with its consequences in one of two ways.

First, as noted above, research within the strategic-choice approach views problems as boxes within boxes and proceeds by transforming the independent variables of one theory into the dependent variables of others. What is exogenous in one formulation becomes something to be explained in another. If the preferences of an actor cannot reasonably be taken as given even within a single interaction, then one possible response is to break this actor down into a more basic set of actors whose preferences can be usefully assumed to be independent of the environmental variations being considered. For example, systemic theories assume states to be unitary actors and take their preferences as given, but the central concern of other theories is to explain why states have the preferences they do by looking to the behavior and interaction of substate actors. Endogenizing preferences in this way is an important part of the strategic-choice approach.

Second, in a longer-term perspective, strategic-choice analysts recognize that features of a strategic setting cannot be held constant and may be affected by the outcomes of strategic interaction. This requires speci-

---

[33] For example, the equation $x + 1 = y$ has an infinite number of solutions.

[34] This is analytically equivalent to taking "preferences" as exogenous in more rationalist approaches.

fying how actors and their environments affect each other. Although work in this area is still in its infancy, the strategic-choice approach is currently looking to evolutionary models and processes of selection, discussed by Miles Kahler in chapter 6, to capture and explain long-term processes of change in the features of strategic settings.

Cognitivists remind us of the possibility of biased decision making. Constructivists have usefully called attention to and rendered problematic many of the theoretical primitives now widely accepted and employed in the field of international relations. These are important contributions. Strategic-choice theorists have just recently begun to take up the challenge posed by these alternatives. The differences between the approaches, however, lie more in the methodological bets they make than in their views on the nature of politics in the "real world." Which set of methodological bets ultimately proves most useful is an open question—and likely to be a source of continuing research and debate in the years ahead.

ELABORATING THE PARTS

In summary, the strategic-choice approach, like most rational-choice approaches, assumes that actors are purposive and that they can be usefully separated, at least analytically, from their environment. The approach organizes inquiry through conceptual experiments that recur at all levels of interaction; most broadly, these experiments vary the actors and environments and, more specifically, they vary the actions and information available to actors as well as their preferences and beliefs.

Pragmatism is at the heart of the strategic-choice approach. It does not, for instance, privilege one group of actors over another. Which actors are relevant and must be included in the analysis of a specific problem depends on the question at hand. Even so, there is no a priori way to know which actors to include. Choosing the actors in a theory is a pragmatic judgment the researcher makes about what is likely to prove a fruitful way to analyze the issue at hand. Similarly, the strategic-choice approach is based on the assumption or hope that international relations research can make progress by cutting into problems in many different areas. In this partial-equilibrium orientation, what is assumed in one analysis may very well be what another tries to explain. Once we understand the separate issues, the ultimate goal is to integrate them into a more general formulation. This partial-equilibrium perspective gives rise to an image of politics as a kind of boxes-within-boxes puzzle in which more basic actors interact and, through this interaction, constitute larger actors that, in turn, interact with other actors.

In the end, the strategic-choice approach must be judged in terms of its empirical payoff. Does it point to interesting research questions, and does it help us answer those questions? An important intermediate payoff, however, is that it can help tighten and sharpen the logic of our theories and thereby help us to decide which are worth the effort it takes to evaluate them empirically. This intermediate payoff derives from two characteristics of the strategic-choice approach: its emphasis on microfoundations, that is, the link from actors and their environments to outcomes, and the breaking down of traditional distinctions between levels of analysis, between the low politics of international political economy and the high politics of war and peace, and between international relations and other areas of politics.

The following chapters address selected dimensions of the strategic-choice approach. The first two highlight issues where there has been substantial confusion in the existing literature, as, for example, with preferences (see Frieden, chapter 2), or where there has been significant but perhaps unappreciated progress, as, for example, with asymmetric information and the analysis of dynamic interactions (see Morrow, chapter 3). The next two essays focus on the aggregation of the preferences of basic actors into "higher-level" actors, first within a context of established political institutions, an area where substantial progress has also been made (see Rogowski, chapter 4), and then within a context of weak or nonexistent institutions, where our understanding is still quite tentative (see Gourevitch, chapter 5). Finally, chapters 6 and 7 consider some of the limitations of the strategic-choice approach and directions for future research.

In chapter 2, Jeffry Frieden examines the problem of preferences. He argues, first, that distinguishing between preferences and other elements of the strategic environment is essential and that failing to do so has led to much theoretical and empirical confusion in the study of international relations. He then outlines three ways in which preferences can be specified—by assumption, observation, or deduction—and discusses the strengths and weaknesses of each alternative. He concludes that deriving preferences from a prior theory is generally (but not always) the most satisfying method.

James Morrow focuses on strategic interaction in chapter 3, and particularly the problems of asymmetric information and dynamic interactions. Three important features characterize many interactions in various political settings. First, the actors may not be able to bind or commit themselves to follow through on their threats or promises. In international politics, for example, anarchy makes it impossible for a state to commit itself to carrying out a pledge if, when the time comes to do so, following through no longer appears to be in that state's own self-interest. In American politics, no Congress can bind another. And within a Congress, agreements between members to trade votes cannot be enforced. One member of Congress cannot sue another for failing to live up to his or her part of a log roll. Second, actors—be they substate actors or states—are often unsure of the motivations, interests, or preferences of other actors. In a crisis, for example, a state may be unsure how much risk of war another state is willing to run. Third, actors often have an incentive to try to exploit other actors' uncertainty by bluffing, lying, or otherwise misrepresenting their true preferences. These features create many problems, and Morrow discusses three of the most important that arise in international relations: signaling, commitment, and bargaining. He shows how the insights derived from the game-theoretic analysis of these problems is reshaping our understanding of important areas in international relations, including those of alliances and crisis bargaining.

Chapters 2 and 3 center on actors' attributes and their environments. Chapters 4 and 5 elaborate on the way strategic interactions are organized and on the insights that begin to emerge from this interaction. As outlined above, the strategic-choice approach often assumes that more basic substate actors interact and, through this interaction, aggregate into states that interact in the international arena. The role institutions play in shaping actors' behavior has been the subject of much work and debate. In domestic politics, actors often take their institutional environment for granted and act within it. Domestic institutions often serve as constraints that partly define the strategic arena in which domestic actors interact, and, arguably, international institutions sometimes also constrain and shape state behavior.[35] Chapters 4 and 5 pay particular attention to institutions.

In chapter 4, Ronald Rogowski uses the second type of conceptual experiment described above to examine how different institutional environments affect actors' interactions and the aggregation of their preferences. In particular, he investigates the effects that changes in the institutional features of a democratic state have on the character of its foreign policy. He does this by positing that the basic preferences of the substate actors remain constant but the institutional setting in which these actors pursue their ends varies along three dimensions—the scope of the franchise, the

---

[35] Indeed, whether international institutions constrain state behavior or merely reflect the distribution of power is at the center of the heated argument between neorealism and institutionalism. We take a middle ground. It seems evident that international institutions are less constraining than domestic institutions. But it also seems extreme to claim they have no effect. The real issue, it seems to us, is to explain why the constraining effects of institutions vary between domestic and international politics, across issues in international politics, and across domestic politics as well. On important problems of selection bias in the study of international institutions, see Downs, Rocke, and Barsoom 1996 and Lake 1999.

nature of representation, and the decision-making rules within a government. In a wide-ranging empirical survey, Rogowski shows how changes along these three dimensions affect the bias, credibility, and coherence of a state's foreign policy, its ability to mobilize resources in pursuit of that policy, and the strategic environment of domestic actors. Rogowski then generalizes the insights derived from his study of domestic institutions to the international arena.

Rogowski's treatment of institutions in chapter 4 and Peter Gourevitch's treatment of them in chapter 5 illustrate the partial-equilibrium orientation of the strategic-choice approach. Rogowski considers situations in which actors take for granted the institutional structures that govern them. There are times, however, when the institutions themselves are at issue. In these governance problems, the actors may be bargaining about how to set up or change the institutions that will structure their subsequent interaction. Gourevitch explores the politics of governance problems by distinguishing two types of situations.[36] When the cost of changing institutions is low, Gourevitch argues that institutions are largely epiphenomenal and have little influence over actors' behavior. Actors choose those institutions that produce the outcomes they prefer. When the cost of institutional change is high, institutions are likely to shape the actors' behavior and the policy outcome. Gourevitch's distinction alone advances the debate between neorealists and institutionalists about the constraining effects of institutions. If the cost of institutional investment is low, we obtain the neorealist image of international relations in which international institutions are epiphenomenal and merely reflect the distribution of power. If the cost is high, then the institutions have important constraining effects and will influence state behavior, as institutionalists believe. Gourevitch's distinction moves us beyond competing claims about institutions' different effects by focusing our attention on factors that determine the degree to which institutions shape behavior among states as well as other types of actors. Gourevitch then goes on to examine how governance disputes are resolved.

Chapters 6 and 7 consider limitations of the strategic-choice approach. The payoff to the methodological bet of decomposing strategic interactions into analytically separate components of actors and environments is likely to be smallest when it is used to study what might be called evolutionary situations, that is, situations in which actors and their environment shape each other. In these situations, one cannot conduct the two

---

[36] This distinction is reminiscent of Keohane and Nye's (1989) work on regime theory and what they called vulnerability interdependence. If the cost of changing a regime were low, the situation was one of low vulnerability. If the cost was high, the actors were vulnerable.

conceptual experiments discussed above. If, for example, actors and the environment influence each other, then one cannot imagine the same set of actors in a different environment. For if the environment were different, this would have had an effect on the actors and they, too, would be different. However, even when actors and the environment codetermine each other, one nevertheless can imagine that the actors are still striving to further their interests. These kinds of situations are just more difficult to study. In chapter 6, Miles Kahler looks to evolutionary theories, which necessarily deal with situations in which actors and the environment shape each other, and discusses what these theories might contribute to the study of international relations.

Finally, Arthur Stein in chapter 7 shows that some of the most frequent criticisms of the strategic-choice approach often pertain to specific modeling choices and not to the approach itself. He then turns to fundamental criticisms and limitations of the strategic-choice approach, emphasizing the incomplete nature of theory. By surveying the weaknesses and limitations of the strategic-choice approach, both Kahler and Stein trace the boundaries within which the methodological bets made in this approach will be rewarding.

CHAPTER TWO

Actors and Preferences in International Relations

JEFFRY A. FRIEDEN

INTERESTS are central to the study of international politics. To understand relations among countries we must take into account their interests, just as to analyze national foreign policy making requires due attention to the interests of groups, bureaucracies, and other participants in national debates.

Yet, scholarly attention to the sources of national or subnational interests—or, as we call them, preferences—is wrought with confusion. Even definitions of preferences vary greatly within the study of international relations, and the analytical use to which they are put varies even more.

This essay makes two principal points about the role of preferences in explaining international politics. First, for most analytical purposes, preferences must be kept separate from other things—most important, from characteristics of the strategic setting. Otherwise, we are unable to distinguish between the causal role of actors' interests and that of their environment. Second, scholars need to be explicit about how they determine the preferences of relevant social actors. Whether preferences are variables of interest or control variables, it is essential that they be derived clearly and unambiguously.

This chapter is intricately linked to the next. I highlight the need for careful consideration of actor preferences in the analysis of international politics, while James Morrow emphasizes the role of the strategic setting. The two are essential components of the strategic-choice approach.

The analytical need to set preferences apart from other things, and to determine them explicitly, applies to theoretical issues, to explanatory questions, and to investigations of particular cases. For example, at the theoretical level, debates over the extent to which wars are caused by features of the international system or by conflicts of state interests need to be able to assign preferences to states. Otherwise, we could not tell whether wars were the result of bellicose aims of governments, in which

The author acknowledges helpful comments and suggestions from other members of the IGCC project on Strategic Choice in International Relations, especially David Lake and Robert Powell, and from William Clark, Jack Hirshleifer, Jeffrey Legro, Lisa Martin, Jack Snyder, and Michael Wallerstein.

case explanation rests on assertions about their preferences, or of a hostile and uncertain environment, in which case even the best of intentions would be overwhelmed by the setting.

At a less abstract level, the hypothesis that, for instance, countries are more likely to cooperate the more similar their interests are requires some way of determining their interests independently of their cooperative actions. By the same token, the hypothesis that a small group of countries is more likely to cooperate than a large group of countries needs to be able to control for differences in the degree to which the countries in question have similar interests.

The same is true for evaluations of specific episodes. Just as participants' views of the actions of Germany in the 1930s depended on their beliefs about Germany's goals (preferences), in ways detailed in the following chapter, so, too, do scholarly interpretations of German actions. It is plausible that Germany responded to the European power balance in much the same way as other countries might have—even those with very different ideological and other preferences. But it is also plausible that German actions primarily flowed from the unique, perhaps uniquely aggressive, preferences of the country and its leaders. The two interpretations require some prior notion of what, in fact, German preferences were, in order to investigate their effects on German policy.

The issue is especially important because although preferences are part of all explanations, they are not directly observable. Like participants, scholars of international politics observe only the behavior of states and their leaders; we cannot know their true motivations. And while the observed behavior might perfectly reflect an actor's preferences, it might just as well be powerfully affected by uncertainty, institutions, and other features of the strategic setting. This, then, requires careful attention to the independent impact and sources of actor preferences.

This chapter clarifies the role that preferences play in the study of international relations. It points to common errors, insists on the need for a clear demarcation between preferences and other factors, and explores different approaches to the derivation of preferences. The essay is meant not as an original contribution but rather as a summary and distillation of scholarly "best practice." The motivation is a practical concern for a common language that allows the work of scholars to contribute to the cumulation of knowledge rather than debates based on misunderstanding and misconception.

The first section presents definitions used to discuss preferences and preference formation. For this volume, actors are regarded as having preferences for outcomes, such as for wealth or territory; these preferences lead them to strategies, such as free trade and military offensives. The next section discusses the need for precision in evaluating preferences, and in using them to explain other matters. It presents three common sets of errors made with regard to preferences: confusing them with strategies in a single interaction, focusing solely on preferences and ignoring their context, or focusing solely on the context and ignoring preferences.

In the third section I turn to the ways that analysts try to establish preferences for the purpose of analysis. Whether the units in question are individuals, bureaucratic agencies, interest groups, or nation-states, their actions cannot usefully be analyzed without some prior sense of their aims. These preferences can be assumed by the analyst, either by convention or by choice. Preferences can themselves be investigated empirically. Or—in what I argue is the most satisfying but in some ways the most difficult research strategy—actors' preferences can be deduced from prior theoretical principles.

The fourth and final section gives examples of how the approach suggested here might assist scholars. I argue that explicit attention to preferences helps illuminate enduring issues in international relations, both at the theoretical level and in empirical applications.

DEFINITIONS: PREFERENCES AND STRATEGIES

The words *preference* and *strategy*, and others equivalent to them, are used continually in the social sciences but are often invested with different meanings. Here we adopt simple definitions, recognizing that there is no universally accepted set of terms and that they are not a matter of principle.

The essential point is that in any given setting, an actor *prefers* some outcomes to others and pursues a *strategy* to achieve its most preferred possible outcome. As indicated in chapter 1 of this volume, an actor's preferences rank the outcomes possible in a given environment. The actor's strategy is its attempt to come as close as possible to the outcome it most prefers.

These definitions refer to a particular interaction—one box, which may well be inside other boxes, to use the first chapter's metaphor. An interaction in this sense could last a long time, such as Anglo-German relations from the 1870s until World War II, or a short time, such as Anglo-German relations in the 1938 Czech crisis. The distinction is complicated because what are considered preferences in one "box" might be strategies in another. However, within any given interaction, preferences and strategies must be distinct, and preferences need to be held constant for the given interaction.

Preferences

An actor's preferences are the way it orders the possible outcomes of an interaction. If, as in most instances of interest to us here, the environment is one of strategic interaction (a game), this involves ranking the terminal nodes of a game tree.

Preferences are taken as given in one defined interaction and used to analyze other factors. A firm's preference for trade protection is usually used to explain something else, such as its lobbying behavior. For example, a firm might face a choice of whether to ask the government for a tariff or for a quota or to seek no protection at all. Illustrated in Figure 2.1 is a firm that prefers a quota to a tariff to no protection, a pattern of preferences that is taken as given and unchanging for this interaction. In this figure, government responses to the firm's lobbying efforts are also represented. If the firm seeks a quota and the government complies, the firm obtains its most preferred outcome which has a payoff of, say, 2. The firm secures its next best outcome if it seeks a tariff and the government agrees. This brings the firm a lower payoff of, say, 1. Finally, the firm gets its worst outcome and lowest payoff if it does not seek any protection or if the government rebuffs its lobbying efforts.

Suppose further that the firm knows there is a conflict of interest between it and the government. In this very simple example, the government prefers free trade to other alternatives, mildly dislikes tariffs, and abhors quotas, but it also wishes to meet constituents' demands. Therefore it prefers no trade barriers (when none are demanded) to granting a tariff, in turn prefers granting a tariff to denying a constituent demand, but prefers to deny a constituent rather than grant a quota.[1]

Given these preferences and this simple strategic setting, the firm's best course of action is to lobby for a tariff even though its most preferred outcome is a quota. If the firm seeks a tariff, the government will yield to its lobbying efforts and the firm will obtain a payoff of 1. If, by contrast, the firm pushes for a quota or does not lobby at all, it will not receive any protection and will be left with a payoff of 0.

Although this example is extremely simple (chapter 3 considers more complex strategic interactions), it makes an important point about preferences. The firm has preferences that determine how it orders possible outcomes: quotas over tariffs over no protection. In this particular interaction, it receives its most preferred outcome, its highest possible payoff,

---

[1] This highly stylized example assumes that firms cannot bluff or oversell their case and that the government will only provide something a firm demanded. In a more complex—and perhaps more realistic—setup, it might be the case that demanding a quota would be a good strategy to obtain a tariff. But we are purposely keeping the interaction simple for the sake of argument.

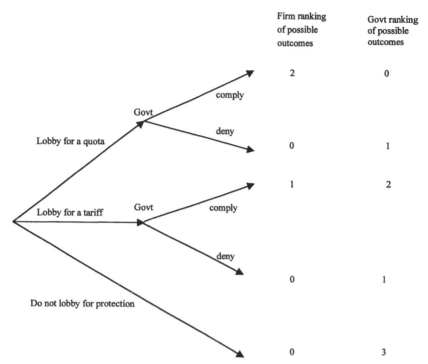

Figure 2.1. A firm's preferences for one interaction may be used to analyze other actions. In this example, a firm's preference for trade protection is used to explain its lobbying behavior.

if it pursues the strategy of lobbying for a tariff, which the government grants. It obtains a worse outcome and a lower payoff if it lobbies for a quota, which the government denies—even though, in the abstract, it prefers a quota to a tariff.

This simple example shows how the seemingly straightforward notion of preferences as a ranking over possible outcomes can obscure important subtleties. Preferences depend on the specification of the problem, and this points toward the hard questions that are the subject of this essay.

Rather than look further at the interaction illustrated in Figure 2.1, we can open the "box" containing this situation to ask, for example, why, in fact, the firm prefers a quota to a tariff—both of which, after all, are themselves presumably means to more basic ends. For the analysis in this box, again we need to fix preferences, here for more protectionist rents over less protectionist rents. The firm's counterpart now is, say, a foreign producer (in a two-country, two-firm world market). The options available involve the foreign and home countries' trade policies. If both firms obtain quotas in their home markets, rents are maximized (foreign and domestic producers split the rents from a quota, while domestic producers and the domestic government split the rents from a tariff).[2] The home firm knows that if it obtains a tariff, the foreign firm will also do so, and bilateral tariffs produce less protectionist rents than bilateral quotas produce. So the firm's preference for more protectionist rents over less, which is given and unchanging for this interaction, means that the terminal node that involves bilateral quotas is ranked above that involving bilateral tariffs.

We could continue to probe, on into the next box, perhaps asking why this firm prefers to seek policy-induced rents rather than concentrate entirely on market activity. In this box we fix the firm's preferences as for more profits over less (to maximize profits). Then we examine the environment within which the firm operates to see what it implies for the desirability of rent seeking. For a particularly dynamic firm, the opportunity cost of political lobbying might be too high to justify diverting precious managerial time from its extremely productive alternative uses. Or it might be—to take us back to the boxes discussed above—that for a troubled firm, the energy of otherwise unproductive managers is most profitably spent trying to get the government to provide rents. In this box, then, profit-maximizing preferences lead the firm to engage in the pursuit of protectionist rents.

Within a particular "box," political scientists are not usually interested in the preferences themselves but rather in how these preferences affect choices. Most commonly, preferences are of interest because of the behavior they engender. This is not to say that preferences are not to be explained, and indeed much of social science involves explaining differences in the preferences of firms, states, and other units. The point, from the pragmatic standpoint of making analysis possible, is only that within the interaction in question, preferences are taken as given and held constant. This is not meant as a description of reality but as an analytically useful bounding of the problem to be examined.

Often this notion is called *preferences over outcomes*. As expressed in chapter 1, actors' preferences are how they value different possible results

---

[2] The tariff is a border tax that raises domestic prices by the amount of the tariff: Domestic producers get the difference on their output sold domestically; the government gets the difference on foreign products imported and sold domestically. (This is why it is realistic to assume that the government strongly prefers tariffs to quotas.) A quota is a quantitative restriction that raises domestic prices; both foreign and domestic producers get the difference between the world market price and the domestic price. It is commonly argued that this helps explain why quotas—such as "voluntary" export restraints—give rise to less international conflict than do tariffs (see Hillman and Ursprung 1988 and Rosendorff 1996). In this instance, with bilateral quotas the home firm would get rents both at home and abroad, whereas with bilateral tariffs the home firm would only get rents at home. The example assumes a quota and a tariff with equivalent price effects.

of their actions and those of others. Actors do not have independent preferences over the means to achieve these results, only over the results.[3]

We can return to our trade-policy example, reversing the order in which the cases were presented above to accord more fully with the logic of the example. In the first instance, it is given that the firm prefers more profits to less, and within this setting the firm determines that protectionist rents are worth pursuing. In the second instance, it is given that the firm prefers more protectionist rents to less, and within this setting it determines that the best available result involves bilateral quotas. In the third instance, it is given that the firm prefers quotas to tariffs to nothing, and within this setting it ends up asking for tariffs because asking for quotas would yield an even worse outcome, nothing.

Preferences are not directly observable. The actor's preferences lead to its behavior but in ways that are contingent on the environment. As discussed in detail in the next chapter, the strategic setting can fundamentally affect the behavior of people, firms, and states. So without more information about the strategic setting and/or about the process of preference formation, it is impossible to know how the behavior maps back to the preference. A particular public trade bargaining position is conceivably consonant with a wide range of preferences. In the above example we observe only that the firm asked the government for a tariff; it would be incorrect, in this case, to infer that the firm preferred tariffs to a quota.

Strategies

States, groups, or individuals require ways to obtain their goals, paths to their preferences. These paths must take into account the environment— other actors and their expected behavior, available information, power disparities. Given this *strategic setting*, strategies are tools the agent uses to get as close to its preferences as possible.

Strategies imply particular means to an end. As such, the unit in question has no *independent* predilection for one set of strategies or another; it wants only the best means to the desired end. Strategies are derived from preferences; they are ways to achieve goals given the anticipated actions of others, differential capabilities, knowledge and information,

---

[3] This somewhat elastic definition of preferences is not universally accepted. Some (such as Hirshleifer 1995, 264–67) define preferences only in terms of primitive preferences, referring to such broad concerns as personal or national security or wealth maximization. In these terms, everything else is a series of strategies. But this seems too restrictive for our purposes.

and other features of the setting; some of the most important informational features are dealt with by James Morrow in chapter 3.[4]

The direct unobservability of preferences has its parallel with regard to strategies. It is never inherently obvious whether action is the result of preferences or strategies, underlying interests, or the environment in which they play themselves out.

In any *given* setting preferences are fixed, and strategies derive from them. However, by the "boxes within boxes" standard, a preference in one box may well be the strategy from a previous box. Returning to trade policy, in one interaction the preference to maximize profits led to a strategy of rent seeking; in the next interaction, the preference for maximal rents led to a strategy of bilateral quotas; in the final interaction, the preference for quotas over tariffs over nothing led to a strategy of demanding a tariff.

A progression is implied by the terms. Given its preferences, an actor forms strategies based on the possibilities presented by the environment. In a subsequent interaction, which must be analytically separated, the strategies of the first instance can be seen as preferences, toward the achievement of which the actor develops strategies, again based on the constraints of circumstance. Each step in this progression involves a preference, then an evaluation of the setting within which this preference is to be pursued, and finally a derived strategy to obtain the preference. Preferences, in a determined environment, give rise to strategies.

The desirability of a clear progression from exogenously given preferences to strategies does not rule out attempts to explain preferences themselves. What is taken as exogenous in one context might be "problematized" and investigated in another. In some settings it is useful to start with a firm's preference for trade protection and investigate how this affects the firm's lobbying behavior; in other settings it is useful to try to determine the source of the firm's trade-policy preferences.

Important as it is to question the origin of national or other preferences, it is desirable to hold them constant for one "round" of analysis. If we are interested in diplomatic relations between two countries, it does little for our analysis simply to assert that one of the countries' preferences changed in the middle of the interaction. Of course, this may well have been the case—governments are overthrown or voted out of office and replaced by others with different preferences—but this is better regarded as changing the character of the interaction so that it is another round or game.

---

[4] It is not uncommon to see strategies referred to as "policy preferences." This is because the actor's preference is for an outcome, and policy is often a direct means toward that end. A firm that prefers maximum rents may have a strategy that involves a policy of a quota toward this end. The distinction between preferences and policy preferences, like that be-

To summarize this section, for the purposes of this volume a preference represents the most desired outcome of an interaction. The preference, in a particular setting, leads the agent to devise a strategy. In one interaction, preferences (ends) within the given setting determine the choice of strategies (means). It is practically and analytically important to separate the preferences of states, groups, and individuals, from the strategic environment they face. By the same token, it is practically and analytically important to hold preferences constant for one round of interaction. This allows us to explore how different preferences and environments affect outcomes.

Scholars disagree about the appropriate preferences to assign to countries, groups, firms, or individuals. But the pursuit of legitimate disagreement is only hampered by unclear definitions; in this light, we propose a common language within which to carry out theoretical and empirical debates. In what follows, I move on to discuss how preferences can be assumed, examined, or deduced, and how this derivation of preferences affects analysis. First, however, it is useful to point out some of the problems associated with the concept of preferences and its usage in international relations.

PROBLEMS WITH PREFERENCES

The preference-strategy-outcome distinctions seem straightforward, yet the role of preferences in explanation is often glossed over with easy assertions or muddled with ambiguity. Indeed, a great deal of confusion in international relations can be traced to imprecision in the definition and use of preferences and strategies as analytical concepts.

Typically the goal of social-scientific inquiry is to explain *outcomes*, observed trends or events. Analyzing outcomes usually involves comparative statics, the "conceptual experiments" discussed in chapter 1. We can ask, for example, how an outcome might be affected by changes in the preferences of one actor or by changes in the strategic setting. James Morrow, in the next chapter, gives many examples of how changes in the strategic setting can affect outcomes; Ronald Rogowski, in chapter 4, provides many examples of how changes in one particular component of the strategic setting—the institutional environment—can affect outcomes. Much of social science has to do with conceptual experiments in which changes in one or another such ingredient affects events.

In fact, analysts of international relations have long debated how preferences and the strategic environment affect outcomes, jointly and sepa-

---

tween "preferences over outcomes" and "preferences over strategies (policies)," is analogous to the preferences-strategy distinction.

rately.[5] Many debates in the field have to do with whether outcomes are primarily the result of the constraints of the international system or of differences among national preferences. A strong variant of realism, for example, implies that state preferences are so swamped by the pressures of interstate competition that all states must pursue essentially identical strategies. A strong domestic-dominance perspective might, on the other hand, argue that different state strategies flow primarily from different national characteristics and preferences.[6] Assessment of the explanatory effects of variations in national interests and international constraints—preferences and the strategic setting—is central to the study of international relations, and it requires clear analytical separation of the two.

We cannot carry out the conceptual experiments necessary to evaluate these contrasting positions without clearly separating preferences, strategies, the environment, and other factors whose impact we want to evaluate. Specifically, we cannot determine exactly how preferences and the environment interact to affect outcomes by observation alone. Preferences are unobservable independent of outcomes; it may, in fact, be the case that the actors' interests explain an event, but it is rarely self-evident whether an effect was caused by the untrammeled intentional action of a group or individual, or whether it was the result of interactions among groups and individuals, in a changing environment. In evaluating such possibilities, a clear prior picture of the agents' preferences is crucial.[7]

In other words, where actors are strategic, we cannot infer the cause of their behavior directly from their behavior. We need to take into account both their underlying preferences and the strategic setting within which they design their actions. If a policy affects only one actor in a completely unambiguous way, the translation from preferences to behavior and outcomes might be simple. Where more than one actor (or group of actors) is involved, the possibility of strategic interplay among them arises. If the informational environment is problematic—there is uncertainty about the true characteristics of the world or of others—the arrow from desire to action to effect becomes harder to draw. As the next chapter points out, much of politics can be described in these terms, so, for a wide range of problems of interest to us, neither a simple knowledge of preferences nor a simple knowledge of the strategic environment is sufficient to understand political causes and effects.

---

[5] For four examples, see Bueno de Mesquita and Lalman 1992; Levy 1990–91; Rhodes 1989; and Stein 1990. Snyder and Diesing (1977, 471–80) make an analogous distinction between structure, pattern of relations, interactions, and internal characteristics.

[6] Bueno de Mesquita and Lalman (1992) indeed evaluate these two perspectives empirically and find for the latter, but the issue is by no means settled.

[7] The presentation here closely parallels the exceptionally clear discussion of payoffs in Snidal 1986, 40–44. For another articulate statement of the importance of preferences and an argument that their derivation is central to "liberal" approaches to international rela-

In our trade-policy example, the government granted a firm tariff protection. Analysis of this outcome would presumably focus on attempting to understand how firm preferences, the preferences of other actors, and the strategic setting interacted to lead to the observed policy. Melding preferences and strategies might lead the analyst to conclude that the government preferred tariffs to other policies—after all, that is what it implemented. It might also lead the analyst to conclude that the firm preferred tariffs to quotas—after all, that is what it demanded from the government. Both conclusions would be incorrect; in our setup, the government preferred no trade protection to tariffs, and the firm preferred quotas to tariffs.

Only a more complex research design, or series of conceptual experiments, could establish the true chain of causation. First, we need a clear separation of preferences from strategies and careful consideration of the action of both. Second, we require some prior way of establishing which firms are expected to hold which preferences. I return to the latter problem (determining preferences) in the next section and focus here on the pitfalls of inadequate attention to the former problem.

Political science and international relations are rife with violations of the principles of clear separation between preferences and the environment, and careful consideration of the possible impact of each on the outcome. These violations typically fall into three categories, which I call sins of confusion, of commission, and of omission.

The first, *sins of confusion*, mixes preferences and the strategic setting in ways that do not allow their independent effects to be examined. This confusion has infused one of the oldest and least fruitful debates in international relations: the debate over the preferences of nation-states in "realist" approaches.[8] Many early realists argued—as some still do—that states maximize power or the probability of survival. Both are positional and analogous to maximizing "relative gains" (I take the two as analogous although they are somewhat different).

The most direct interpretation of this assertion is that the desire for power is an actual preference of states, and indeed this is often stated explicitly: Power or survival are in states' utility functions. This implies that states value power for its own sake and would be willing to subjugate all other goals to power, no matter what the setting.

This is almost certainly not what most realists have in mind; indeed, they often make explicit that it is the international system that forces

---

tions, see Moravcsik 1997. Legro (1996) emphasizes nonmaterial aspects of preference formation.

   [8] For examples of this long controversy, see Waltz 1979; Grieco 1988a; Powell 1991; Snidal 1991a; and Niou and Ordeshook 1994. In my view, the articles by Powell, Snidal, and Niou and Ordeshook essentially ended the debate. I use the term *realist* to encompass both classical realist and "neorealist" writing on these issues.

states to maximize power or survival probability.[9] If so, then power maximization is not a preference but a strategy. This means that state preferences are not defined by realists, which makes their analysis inherently incomplete.

One possible interpretation is that realists believe (and therefore assume) that the international environment is so powerful that it forces all states, no matter the differences in their preferences and in the environments they face, to pursue identical strategies of power maximization. This means that size, shape, socioeconomic and political makeup, and the international setting have no effect on the power-maximizing strategies of states.

The logic of the realist position, then, is that national preferences are irrelevant in international politics. This is so because systemic constraints are so tight that all states must pursue identical power-driven strategies. The implications of this extremely strong assertion are not always appreciated.

This illustrates the importance of clear definitions. At least some theoretical confusion in international relations has been caused by the use of such terms as *preferences* and *strategies* in a variety of ways, often with very different meanings.

For example, it is common in international relations to combine interests and geopolitical conditions into one overarching explanatory variable. To take one instance, Steve Walt (1987) proposes a revision of balance-of-power analysis that he calls "balance of threat." By this he means that countries respond not only to the power ratios they face but also to perceived threats posed by other countries. The perception of threat incorporates such considerations as aggressive intentions, geographical proximity, and ideology. Walt clearly has in mind characteristics that include the preferences of the states involved, for example, the degree to which there are inherent "conflicts of interest." This blends national preferences, strategies, and the environment into a single factor: not only how powerful the actor is, but what it wants, how it proposes to get it, and the setting in which this takes place.

It is not surprising that this blend of preferences and strategies outperforms a simple focus on power (i.e., strategies that flow from a nation's relative position) itself, for it expands the range of explanatory factors. Walt's empirical application to the formation of alliances (see also Walt [1991]) indeed combines several factors into what he calls one: the preferences of a state, plus the strategies it pursues given both its preferences and characteristics of the environment (such as its power).

---

[9] It should be noted that contrary to common assertions, this view is not analogous to the relationship of firm preferences to competition in the marketplace: It is not product

The problem is that this approach makes it *impossible* to know how outcomes were affected by international power relations, by different national interests, and by other features of the environment that are bundled together as the perceived threat. First, the slurring of several potential causal variables makes it hard to see the logic of the argument in full—whether and how, for example, conflicts of interest affect the strategies of states or are themselves affected by power disparities or are affected by the intentions of other states. The logic of the theory would be stronger were a state's preferences—perhaps as a function of its ideology—analytically separated from its strategies—that is, the "aggressiveness" of its actions. Second, empirically it is impossible to disentangle how national policy and outcomes might respond to changes in preferences, the environment, and other factors. The aggressiveness of intentions might be affected by geographical proximity, ideology, or power differentials, and the inability to hold one or the other constant makes impossible the conceptual experiments that most have in mind in trying to explain alliance patterns: How would alliances be altered by more similar preferences among states, by better information, or by smaller power disparities?

The entangling of preferences and strategies also causes theoretical confusion. Walt appears to regard his argument as a slight amendment to an emphasis on power (the strategic environment). But this is incorrect: he insists, in fact, on the significance of both preferences and the strategic setting, in contradistinction to realists' belief in the predominance of systemic constraints.

Attention to both preferences and strategies is certainly an advance over focusing on only one or the other. However, the inclusion of both makes it that much more important to ensure that they are separated analytically. Failure to do so serves to confuse, not clarify, explanation; it also confounds careful consideration of the theoretical implications of the arguments and evidence so presented.

Beyond confusion, that preferences are not directly observable independently of outcomes makes two other sorts of mistakes common, and damaging. One, which I call sins of commission, is to assert that variation in outcomes is *solely* owing to variation in preferences. The other, which I call sins of omission, is to assert that variation in outcomes has *nothing* to do with variation in preferences. Each sin involves the failure to carry out one of the conceptual experiments discussed in chapter 1. The first set of sins neglects the comparative statics exercise of holding the properties of actors constant while varying the environment; the second neglects

---

market competition that leads firms to prefer profit maximization but the preferences of firm owners.

the exercise of holding the environment constant while varying the properties of actors.

Sins of commission arise when analysts observe an outcome and draw a direct line from it back to the preferences of actors. Typically such analyses assert that because the result benefited some actors, they and only they caused it. This commits the logical fallacy of asserting that the preferences of those most favored by an outcome must have determined the outcome itself, ignoring the possibility that strategic interaction might have fundamentally transformed the process and its end point. Indeed, such arguments are often doubly circular: They infer powerful actors' motivations from the outcome, then go on to argue that the outcome was determined by the powerful actors.

Such sins of commission, then, ascribe outcomes to preferences without careful attention to strategic interaction and other factors besides actors' preferences. It may well be the case, as is commonly asserted, that the causes of interstate conflict must be sought in the belligerent nature of particular nations, or that trade protection is adopted because of the influence of those who stand to gain from it. However, we cannot know whether these views are accurate without assessing the potential effects of factors other than preferences themselves. In the next chapter James Morrow gives both general guidelines and specific examples about the impact of the strategic setting on behavior.

A common variant of this lapse is to explain changes in interstate relations simply by *asserting* that national preferences changed.[10] Careful attention to the interaction in question is required before we rule out the possibility that an altered outcome was owing to modification in the strategic environment, such as increased information or changed bargaining conditions. Too many analysts, faced with a change in relations among states, surrender to the temptation to explain this by invoking a change in states' preferences themselves. While this may often be the case, assessment of the argument requires rejection of the possibility that preferences remained constant while the environment—things that alter the character and results of strategic interaction among a fixed group of governments—might have changed. For explanatory purposes, the direct translation of preferences into outcomes cannot be taken for granted.

On the other hand, *sins of omission* involve assertions about the impact of strategic interaction and other environmental factors without controlling for actors' preferences. This is especially common among those scholars who emphasize the importance of the setting within which the

---

[10] To avoid giving too much offense, I can cite my own work (especially Frieden 1988) as an example of this shortcoming. Even one of the most careful studies in this mode, Conybeare 1987, sometimes slips into ascribing changes in results to changes in preferences in a somewhat ad hoc manner.

behavior in question takes place—such as great uncertainty or the absence of a third-party enforcement mechanism (such as the "anarchy" of international politics). This often leads analysts to ascribe outcomes to strategic interaction itself, without paying careful attention to the actors' underlying preferences. Disagreements among states might be owing to the difficulty of sustaining cooperation in an uncertain and information-poor world that lacks third-party enforcement; or they might, in fact, occur because of inherently antagonistic goals of two or more states. Trade protection could be the result of a breakdown of cooperation or of a simple desire on the part of both countries to reduce their imports—for whatever domestically derived reason.

Kenneth Oye (1986b, 6–9) gives a particularly clear argument for why careful attention to preferences is analytically important. He notes that many instances of international conflict or cooperation are ascribed to structural factors when, in fact, they might more accurately be attributed either to irreconcilable or to harmonious national preferences, which makes attention to environmental constraints superfluous. One cannot assert that the strategic setting led to cooperation among states without first establishing that there might otherwise have been some reason for disagreement, and vice versa. Martin (1992b) thus distinguishes among interstate interactions in which preferences are essentially harmonious and those in which there is, in fact, a real or potential conflict of interest. This avoids sins of omission, in which the strategic setting is taken to determine outcomes without adequate attention to preferences.

A full understanding of the sources of international political outcomes requires careful attention to both preferences and the strategic environment. It also requires a careful delineation of the two, as well as careful theoretical and empirical consideration of the explanatory importance of each.

However, this requires first and foremost some way of determining actors' preferences. As discussed above, preferences are not directly observable; this means that it is not easy to "assign" preferences to particular individuals, groups, or nations. Indeed, one of the most daunting problems in the social sciences, and in international relations, is determining agents' preferences. It is to this problem I now turn.

PREFERENCES ASSUMED, OBSERVED, AND DEDUCED

Because preferences are so important to analysis, it is crucial to have some way to know these preferences. Scholars typically specify preferences in one of three ways: by assumption, by observation, and by deduction. These methods are not mutually exclusive, but they are different.

Each method has advantages and disadvantages. I believe, however, that the most analytically satisfying route is to deduce preferences on the basis of prior theory.[11] However, when analysis requires *national* preferences, it must be admitted that we have few theories of preferences at the national level—that is, ways of determining what a nation's preferences will be solely on the basis of the nation's properties. This means that "national preferences" are best deduced from theories of the preferences of subnational units—especially individuals, firms, and groups—along with theories of preference aggregation at the national level. This is a daunting path, but it is the most promising one. Partly because of the difficulties of the option for which I argue, it is worthwhile to explore alternatives. These include assuming and observing preferences.

Assumption

It is easiest to assume preferences. In the principal application in international relations to the preferences of nation-states, the simplest assumption might be that states attempt to maximize national welfare. But this is either vacuous, leaving open how national welfare is defined, or implausible, assuming that governments accurately reflect their citizens' preferences by some simple criterion.

We might assume that states prefer to maximize national wealth or size. Niou, Ordeshook, and Rose (1989, 49), for example, assume that states maximize national resources.[12] In principle, any set of goals can be assumed for states and other units of analysis. Indeed, assuming preferences is the method most similar to that used in economics, and, despite long debates, it seems appropriate there.

However, there are problems with assuming national preferences. It is no accident that contentious discussions of preferences in international relations contrast with the relatively straightforward way that preferences are used in economics. A comparison of the two realms, in fact, helps clarify why assuming preferences can be so problematic in international political analysis.

---

[11] Again, this point closely follows Snidal (1986, 40–44).

[12] Even here, the authors fold strategic considerations into preferences by making the preference for resource maximization conditional upon the survival of the state. While this may be technically necessary, it is difficult to see an analytical basis for it. Indeed, it is interesting and potentially important to note that solely a preference for resource maximization cannot lead to anything approaching power balance: At some margin, states will find it more attractive to be absorbed by other states rather than to maintain their sovereignty.

In economics, it is typically assumed that individuals and firms are wealth- (or profit-) maximizing.[13] Most economists accept that this is not an accurate description of reality, simply a useful one for economic analysis. They posit preferences for wealth or profit maximization, and, on this basis, build models of how individuals and firms act within different circumstances to maximize their income.

In this context, all actors have essentially identical wealth-maximization preferences, and everything that flows from these preferences is a strategy.[14] Variation in outcomes is the result of firms and individuals with identical preferences finding themselves in different settings. Prices are different in competitive than in oligopolistic markets because of the market structure, which is exogenous to any one firm, not because of the preferences of firms. The behavior of firms in competitive markets is different from that in oligopolistic markets, not because of variation in preferences—all are profit maximizers—but because they face different settings. Different outcomes (prices, quantities) or different behaviors (marketing or investment strategies) are not the result of different preferences—some firms for wealth maximization, others for security—but of different conditions.[15]

The situation is not quite so simple, to be sure. A large body of literature in economics is devoted to "problematizing" the preferences of firms, in the sense that it starts with the individuals who make up a firm and then attempts to see how relations among these individuals affect the firm's goals. The notion that firms are not pure profit maximizers but, rather,

[13] To be completely accurate, the basic assumption is that individuals are utility maximizers, that wealth is translatable into utility, and, in fact, that wealth maximization is a strategy to achieve maximum utility. Of course, utility is unmeasurable so this step is somewhat superfluous for all purposes except those of logical completeness.

[14] Some strategies, to be sure, are not strategic in the usual sense. In competitive markets, actors need not take the actions of other individuals into account: They are price takers rather than price makers. A wheat farmer does not strategize about his planting decisions, as he knows that his actions will have no impact on the price of wheat. Technically, however, not strategizing is also a strategy. The wheat farmer can best maximize his income by not wasting energy strategizing where it can make no difference. This is the distinction between decision- and game-theoretic analyses, both of which make important contributions. When numbers are small enough, and there is some reason to try to anticipate the reactions of others, actors are strategic in the traditional (game-theoretic) sense. There are indeed few enough television producers or automobile manufacturers or major investment banks in the world that they may act strategically in designing their company investment, production, marketing, labor, and pricing policies.

[15] This highlights, to repeat, the confusion of Waltz (1979) and many other realists, despite their invocation of oligopolistic markets as analogues to international politics. In economic models, firm preferences are all the same and their strategies vary according to market structure; in the Waltzian mistranslation, state preferences may all vary, but their strategies are all the same because of the international political structure.

reflect the wealth maximization motives of the individuals who constitute the firm is, in fact, widely accepted, and many economists have explored how firms are constructed out of large numbers of individuals.[16] (The parallel to political scientists' attempts to specify nations' preferences by looking at those who constitute them is obvious.) Nonetheless, this has not kept most economists, most of the time, from using the simplifying assumption of profit-maximizing firms.[17]

Three characteristics of the study of international politics make the simple assumption of national preferences more difficult than the assumption of preferences in economics. First, in economics there is limited variation in the cast of characters, namely, firms and individuals. It seems reasonable that, with regard to market transactions, firms have relatively similar preferences to one another, as do individuals, and, indeed, that the two sorts of preferences are analogous: profit maximization for firms, wealth maximization for individuals. But international politics involves individuals, firms, groups, nation-states, international organizations, transnational actors, and perhaps others. And there is little reason to expect all these varied actors to have analogous preferences, or even for the preferences of the same kinds of actors (states, groups, international organizations) to be homogeneous.

Second, even if we could agree on some principal homogeneous actors in international politics, there is no unambiguous preference we could assume for these actors. Scholars who use models in which nation-states are purposive unitary actors do not agree about what purpose (preference) should be assumed for them. In other words, economics-like consensus on a generally accepted assumption, and on a generalized equivalence of actor preferences, is lacking.

Third, international relations deals with a multiplicity of issues on many dimensions. Economics is primarily about interactions within markets, and, although it is common that market actors have to deal with more than one concern (price, quantity, and quality, for example), this pales in comparison to the complexity of international politics. States, or whatever else may be the relevant units of international political analysis, are likely to have preferences about, and strategies toward, a wide range

[16] The literature is too vast to cite in detail; Williamson 1985 is a standard summary, while Grossman and Hart 1986 is a particularly influential example of attempts to understand the problem.

[17] Nor is the distinction between preferences and strategies quite so clear, even in economics. Sometimes analysts take the strategy, derived from the firm's profit-maximizing preference, as a given. They then use this strategy as a preference in a subsequent interaction. For example, firms in oligopolistic industries might be asserted to have a preference for greater market share; scholars would then go on to examine how different strategies (limit pricing, advertising) might increase a firm's market share. But it is understood that greater market share itself is desired only as a means to profit maximization.

of concerns: trade, money, and national defense, to be sure, but also cultural and linguistic ties, cross-border pollution, immigration, human rights, ideology, and ethnicity. It is not hard to imagine how to derive a profit-maximizing firm's strategies toward price, quantity, and quality, but it is difficult to see how to assume preferences that would be both nontrivial and useful to analyze the international components of French cultural policy, British immigration policy, Iranian religious policy, or American drug policy.

For all these reasons, the simple assumption of preferences common in economics is often dissatisfying in international relations. While economists typically begin their analysis with an unproblematically profit-maximizing firm, scholars of international politics must pay much more attention to the preferences of the actors.

This is not to deny that valuable analyses can be performed with assumed state preferences. As in much else, this is likely to be where we have some reason to believe that the assumption is realistic—perhaps by working backward, unpacking boxes within boxes, until we get to a level at which it seems relatively clear what we need to assume. This might be the case of international public goods with few obvious distributional consequences, such as preventing global warming or controlling infectious diseases. A preference for reducing these threats at the lowest possible cost to the country is not far-fetched. Relatively unproblematic preferences might also be assumed where the interaction is limited to a one-dimensional realm. It seems reasonable that in a major crisis nuclear powers might have similar preferences for victory without war over victory with war over defeat without war over defeat with war. Similarly, in negotiations between creditor and debtor countries over debt repayment, it seems reasonable to assume that debtors want to pay as little as possible and creditors want to be paid as much as possible.

In fact, even this begs the question. To say we feel comfortable about assuming preferences that "seem reasonable" simply hides the underlying theoretical or empirical arguments about those preferences. It would make more sense to pay explicit attention to what it is that makes some preferences seem more reasonable than others. So, while practical analysis often requires an assumption of exogenously determined national preferences, we have reason to want more.

Observation

A second method used to fix the preferences of nation-states in the international arena is by observation (or, as it is sometimes called, induction). In this case, the scholar attempts to determine the national preference by investigating the country's behavior. These observed (or "revealed") preferences are then used to analyze interaction among states or between state and nonstate actors.

A variety of examples exist; indeed, most investigations of enduring goals of nation-states fall into this category. Typically scholars study statements and actions of the nation and of its policy makers, and, on this basis, impute the functional equivalent of a national preference.

Broad-based national ideological conceptions are often presented as definitive of preferences. These include national identities (Larson, in Jervis and Snyder, 88–92) and widely shared beliefs about appropriate national goals. Charles Kupchan refers to this as "strategic culture," something that "provides a deeply embedded notion of what constitutes national security" (Kupchan 1994, 89). One examination of this type (Krasner 1978) studied American policy toward overseas raw materials investments and concluded that the American "national interest" was largely ideological.

National preferences are often traced, more narrowly, to the ideological perspectives of national elites. These are more specific than national cultural characteristics; Kupchan (1994) distinguishes between strategic culture, which inheres to the whole population, and strategic beliefs. The latter, in his account, are a matter for elites and include such things as "the relative weights assigned to military, economic, and reputational considerations in setting geographic priorities" (Kupchan 1994, 68).

The invocation of national grand strategy typically refers to goals defined by elites over a relatively long period but not so inherent as, say, ethnic identity.[18] Presumably cold war era American and Soviet commitments to capitalism and socialism, respectively, fall into this category. The same might be said of enduring features of national public opinion. These are all closely related to the invocation of ideological or other ideational sources of preferences that the observer determines by investigation.[19]

A step removed from identifying national preferences in and of themselves is asserting that these preferences are determined by enduring subnational interests that dominate the formation of national preferences. This typically involves "inducing" not the *nation's* preferences, but those of powerful actors, who then, it is argued, determine national goals. In other words, rather than looking for the revealed preferences of the na-

---

[18] Mearsheimer (1983), along these lines, invokes such broad national purposes in explaining choices about military strategies in the first years of World War II; see pages 77–79 on Britain, for example. Lake (1996, 1999) develops a notion of grand strategy that attempts to explain its origins. The articles in Rosecrance and Stein (1993) explore the impact of domestic factors on the evolution of national grand strategies.

[19] The articles in Goldstein and Keohane 1993 and Goldstein 1993 represent similar examples of attempts to understand how such ideational factors affect the behavior of groups or countries.

tion, scholars look for the revealed preferences of groups, parties, bureaucracies, or others, who, it is claimed, set national priorities.

Some, for example, focus on the enduring impact of important private or public groups for the definition of a country's "national" preferences. They argue that German or Japanese bureaucrats, for example, determine national goals and thus we can derive national motives from the interests of bureaucrats. Cain and Hopkins (1993a, 1993b) make a case for the centrality of the landed gentry and the financial sector in the formation of British international economic and political preferences from the mid-eighteenth century to the present. Within countries, some scholars associate different parties with different preferences with regard to the international choices they face; Eichenberg (1993) does so for Germany and the United States, and he uses these differences and their evolution to help explain the course of NATO policy toward the intermediate nuclear force between 1977 and 1988. Again, the actors' goals are determined by observation, but this variant also includes an argument about the impact of particular groups on national preferences.

Scholars also sometimes observe national preferences on the basis of temporary national political conditions. This is especially appealing if the matter to be explained is of short duration or limited scope. Issues of war and peace may involve broader concerns, but most international politics is not about such earth-shattering choices. We can explore national preferences in a more restricted realm, such as fisheries policy or human rights.

All these ways to pin down the preferences imputed to nation-states for use in further analysis share a major problem, common to the investigation of anything that cannot be directly observed. The attempt to "induce" preferences by observation risks confounding preferences with their effects. The behavior observed—policies, statements, responses to surveys—is used "inductively" as indicative of preferences. Yet, in all these instances it may well be that this behavior results only partially, perhaps misleadingly, from underlying preferences. Perhaps the environment within which the behavior takes place is responsible for it in important ways that make it impossible to "read back" from behavior to preferences. This problem is well understood by survey researchers, who spend a great deal of time trying to make sure that the observation (the answer) is as true a reflection as possible of the individual's beliefs (the opinion).[20] But the problem is more general.

The position of a government representative, politician, manager, lobbyist, or union leader typically embeds in it calculations of what the impact of this position might be. This is especially daunting if we are trying

---

[20] For an investigation of the problems of measuring and explaining public opinion, see Zaller 1992.

to read preferences back from the postures countries (or other actors) take in bargaining. We anticipate that public positions reflect both the actor's preferences and its expectation of how its stance will affect the actions of others. A country that prefers compromise over a territorial dispute could adopt an intransigent tone if it judged this most likely to induce movement toward a settlement. We would be misinterpreting the country's preferences if we were to impute to it belligerent or expansionist preferences on the basis of its behavior (including its statements). In other words, to repeat what has been stated above, an actor's behavior incorporates *both* its underlying preferences *and* its strategic response to the setting it faces. In no way can the two be separated by observation alone.

There is no avoiding this problem. Our observations are largely limited to the behavior of individuals, groups, or governments (including what they say), rather than to their underlying motives. Any attempt to infer a government's preferences from its actions runs the risk that these actions reflect both preferences and the environment. This is particularly disturbing when, as is very often the case, the attempt to establish preferences by observation is undertaken in order to be able to see how these preferences affected outcomes. If the observation, thus the preference inferred, includes other factors, the causal conclusion drawn will be incorrect.

For example, a scholar might set out to investigate the impact of German national goals (preferences) on the coming of World War II, as discussed in more detail in the next chapter. He might look at the actions and statements of German leaders in the years before the war and find a myriad of peace offerings and expressions of pacific sentiments. Like British and French policy makers at the time, the scholar would be remiss to conclude (or "induce") from this that German preferences were for the status quo and peace. German leaders may well have wanted expansion and even war but have downplayed their belligerence in the interest of lulling others into complacency or in an effort to obtain as much as possible without violence. So long as German actions and statements were colored by prior German calculations of their potential impact (as we would expect them to have been), we cannot use them to draw conclusions about German preferences nor can we use preferences thus arrived at to explain outcomes.

It is especially egregious to "induce" preferences from observed behavior and then use these preferences to explain this very behavior. If American bargaining positions toward Japan are used to "induce" an American preference for free trade, it is tautological to argue that these positions were the result of an American preference for free trade.

This is not to say that observation is useless in establishing actors' preferences. In many instances, it may be the best research strategy available. And although public statements and actions may be unreflective of preferences, scholars often have access to more accurate private information—from archives or interviews, for example. But the observational or inductive approach to determining preferences has serious shortcomings.

Deduction

The final way that preferences can be established is by deducing or deriving them on the basis of preexisting theory. In this case we know features of the actor, and theory predicts that in a determined context these will lead to a particular set of preferences.

This posits a prior theory of preferences. As an actor's features vary or the context varies, the actor's preferences vary in ways anticipated by theory. In other words, the preference used in the "box" of interest is deduced from a prior "box." If we want to know a firm's preferences over trade protection, we start one level up, in a bigger box, in which the firm's properties and environment are known, and which lead it to order its trade preferences. To take our earlier example, a very primitive theory of preferences might be that firms' preferences for protection increase as their profitability declines: The less profitable firms are, the more they prefer protection.[21] On the basis of this "theory," if we know the firm's profitability, we can infer its preferences for protection.

This applies preexisting theory to identifiable characteristics of the actor and the environment in order to derive the anticipated preferences of different actors. The smaller the country, the more favorable it is to trade liberalization; the more negative the industry's trade balance, the more favorable it is to trade protection; the better endowed the worker with human capital in a human capital-rich country, the more favorable he is to trade liberalization; the larger the country's net foreign assets, the stronger its preference for stable international property rights; and so on. These preferences of nations, groups, and individuals are then used in the analysis of the interaction in question.

This sort of comparative static exercise, using actors' features and the context to derive their preferences on the basis of theory, is analytically valuable for two reasons. First, the preference to be used in subsequent analysis is itself not assumed but derived. It should be clear that the prior preference (from which the preference to be used in analysis is derived) is, in fact, assumed or observed in precisely the ways described earlier.

[21] This extremely primitive example makes it possible to abstract from the difficulties of independently observing how competitive a firm is with imports or how dynamic it is. There are many ways of categorizing firms and industries so as to be able to derive trade-policy preferences, but to go into them in detail would introduce far more complexity than is desirable here.

The trade-policy example above did not derive the firm's preference for maximum profits; it assumed it and then went on to derive preferences over protection. *Something* is always exogenous. The choice is this: How far back do we push our search for theoretically based preferences? The deductive method described here takes as given, for example, firm profit maximization and derives firm preferences about trade protection on this basis.

Second, the preferences deduced in this way are expected to vary along with conditions that are more readily or "objectively" assessed than the preferences themselves. Typically the exercise is structured so that the features that determine the preferences to be derived are relatively easy to observe. The predicted preferences about trade discussed above are a function of the profitability of the firm, which is amenable to more direct measure than its trade preferences. To take other examples, inasmuch as geography and resource endowments are more or less readily evaluated, it is meaningful to deduce that similar countries in different geographical circumstances will hold different preferences or that similar countries with different resource endowments will hold different trade preferences. What these preferences might be, of course, depends on the geostrategic or political economy theory used.

This method can also be used to explain or predict changes in preferences. If an actor's characteristics change, its preferences are expected to change: A firm that becomes more profitable, in our simple example, prefers free trade more. As countries develop, their resource endowments change, which might be expected to affect preferences in predictable ways. If theories about preferences are accurate, they explain variation over time as well as across units.

There are many such "theories of preferences," most commonly related to individuals and firms. Theories of preferences are best developed in the realm of political economy, where scholars have long speculated about how the characteristics of nations, groups, firms, and individuals affect their interests. Preferences toward trade policy have been analyzed in great detail, although the relevant trade theories sometimes give rise to different expectations.[22] Analogous theories of preferences exist, in full or in part, with regard to foreign direct investment, immigration, financial liberalization, and many other international economic issues (see, for example, Froot and Yoffie 1993; Wong 1997; Goodman and Pauly 1993). The advanced state of these theories owes partly to the fact that economists have developed clear "maps" of the distributional implications of many economic outcomes, and it is easy to read these distributional impli-

[22] For surveys, see Hillman 1989 and Alt and Gilligan 1994.

cations back to the anticipated preferences of those expected to be affected by the policies.

While political economy has the best-developed theories of group preferences, largely because of its reliance on prior theories of the incidence of economic policies, other areas of international relations have also given rise to important work in this regard. A wide variety of scholars believe that military bureaucracies tend toward particular preferences: Mearsheimer (1983, 63–64) associates them with a desire for decisive victories, Posen (1984, 1991, 16–19) with a preference for the offense.[23] Typically such claims are based on some theoretically grounded idea of how military organizations stand to gain from particular outcomes, although it is sometimes the case that these assertions about preferences could stand to be more clearly deduced.

Theories of preferences can involve either variation in actor properties or their environment. Where actor characteristics remain the same, changes in the setting can lead to different preferences. New technologies can influence travel time or relative abilities to produce goods and services in such a way as to alter preferences.[24] Again, these comparative statics are feasible because the changes in question—such as the development of new technologies—are observable.

Technical advances that affect the ability of goods and capital to move across borders can alter the environment and thus the preferences of nations and groups (Frieden and Rogowski 1996). The railroad, steamship, and telegraph helped recast such countries as Argentina and Australia from backwaters into thriving agricultural exporters, and so transformed preferences. High levels of capital mobility in the last twenty years have, in many analyses, altered the preferences of groups, firms, and nation-states (Frieden 1991, 1994a; Goodman and Pauly 1993; Strange 1992).

It is frequently argued that in recent decades, advances in telecommunications and exponential increases in scale economies have changed the preferences of firms and industries. Firms once content to dominate domestic markets behind protective barriers are now driven by rapidly rising economies of scale to desire open markets at home and abroad.[25] The rise

---

[23] See also Snyder 1984a, 1984b; and Van Evera 1984; 1986, 95–99. The claim has not been universally accepted; see especially Sagan 1986.

[24] Again, in a prior box the actor has an exogenous preference, and, given this, technological or other change affects the strategy chosen—where the strategy is the preference we are interested in. So a firm with a preference for maximum profits might, given technological change, jettison its protectionist preferences in favor of free-trade preferences.

[25] The literature on strategic trade is based on the alleged importance of large-scale economies, and there is some evidence that firms and governments have responded to increased economies of scale by redefining their goals. See Milner and Yoffie 1989 and Richardson 1990 for examples, and Chase 1998 for an application to regional trade agreements.

of the multinational corporation, in great measure the result of technological change, has, in the view of many (e.g., Helleiner 1977; Milner 1988), transformed trade-policy preferences, typically moving them in the direction of greater desire for liberalization. In all these instances, characteristics of the actors and their environments lead to predictable preferences over trade, money, regulation, and a host of other things.

In addition to such forces as geography, resource endowments, and technology, other factors exogenous to the relationship under investigation can provide theoretical grounding for the derivation of preferences. For these purposes, many aspects of the global environment can be considered exogenous, even when they are not completely so.[26]

These theories provide useful comparative statics that we can bring to bear on further analysis. Differences among groups in their factor ownership, import and export competition, and scale economies, coupled with the national economic setting, lead to clear expectations about the economic preferences of groups. These different preferences can then be used for analyses of the domestic pressures on international economic policy making—or, more broadly, the determination of national preferences.

Whereas theories of firm and individual preferences are common, few true theories of national preferences exist, although some approaches push, or could be pushed, in this direction. Geography is widely expected to affect national preferences, although theories to this effect are rudimentary at best. From early geopolitics on, the fundamental difference between an island and an exposed plain has been central to security studies.[27] States with different geographical characteristics are expected to have different preferences: If the United Kingdom or Australia were not island nations, their geostrategic preferences would be very different.

Some theories also associate technological change with variation in national geostrategic preferences. Technical developments can alter the costs of military conflict or the relative attractions of offense or defense in ways that affect the preferences of nations. An island's geography has different implications for its geostrategic preferences in a world with airplanes than in a world without, and these preferences may be different still in a world with intercontinental ballistic missiles. The nuclear revolution may have fundamentally altered countries' preferences; so, too, may the develop-

---

[26] Of course, technology itself is not really exogenous. Indeed, advances in long-distance shipping and railroad transportation may have been the result, not the cause, of the opening up of extremely fertile land in the New World. After all, the invention and development of new technologies respond to economic opportunities just as much as the reverse. But for any one nation or group, technological progress can be assumed to be part of the environment, at least as a first approximation.

[27] For example, Walt 1987 incorporates proximity expressly into his evaluation of states' propensities to ally.

ment of long-distance delivery systems for weapons of mass destruction have reduced the value of holding territory, which could have a substantial impact on national preferences.

In most instances, however, national preferences do not emerge seamlessly from existing theories. Typically the application of theories of preferences to social collectivities requires a complementary theory of the aggregation of preferences, from individuals and firms up to groups, sectors, classes, and nations. The higher the level of aggregation, the more complicated the derivation of the "collective preference." Firms and individuals can constitute themselves into groups, regions, industries, or parties in many different ways, and in just as many different ways can these latter categories affect the formation of national preferences. It is not enough to determine the preferences of domestic actors; we must also show how these preferences are aggregated to the national level.

Preference aggregation is an age-old problem of the thorniest type, and I do not address it here. The goal, for our purposes, is to look for arguments that provide regularities in national preference formation. The range runs from patterns of group organization through broader social organization to characteristics of the political system. Chapters 4 and 5 in this volume—by Ron Rogowski and Peter Gourevitch, respectively— discuss these issues more fully. Theories of preference aggregation contribute to theories of national preferences inasmuch as they contend that institutional or other factors affect the formation of national preferences in predictable ways.

This, I believe, is the most compelling manner to deduce national preferences. Preexisting theories of individual and group preferences, and of the impact of individuals and groups on national politics, are used to establish the preferences of governments. This is all prior to the analysis of interest and provides the raw materials for this inquiry.

While the deductive approach to preferences may be the most theoretically satisfying, it is not without problems. First, the preferences deduced from preexisting theories are only as good as the theories themselves. Every theory of preferences mentioned here is controversial, and using one among these many requires choosing among alternatives in a way that may simply push the debate back to the original theory.

Second, while there are many theories of preferences, there is not a ready-made toolbox for all purposes. Scholars often analyze processes or events that have not yet given rise to substantial bodies of theories; indeed, this is often the attraction of the analysis. In such circumstances, the analyst has to provide his own prior theory of preferences, perhaps by analogy to some roughly similar problem. This at least doubles the work involved and similarly doubles the likelihood that others will disagree.

Nonetheless there are many reasons to use preexisting work that associates features of actors and the environment with actor preferences. This is the theoretically soundest method and is also the one that lends itself most obviously to a cumulation of theoretical and empirical knowledge.

Whichever of the three modes presented here may be chosen, the principal point is that there are ways of using preferences carefully for political analysis. Preferences can be assumed, examined, or deduced on the basis of the intrinsic features of the unit and the environment within which it operates. Based on this, we can analyze interstate (or domestic) interaction; but it is crucial to have some set of stable preferences as building blocks for further analysis.

ILLUSTRATIVE EXAMPLES: INTERNATIONAL TRADE RELATIONS AND IMPERIALISM

Many controversial issues in international relations are about the relative importance of interests (preferences). Often analysts disagree as to the preferences of relevant actors. At other times they disagree about the relative explanatory importance of actors' preferences, on the one hand, and the environment within which they operate, on the other.

For this reason it is important to have clear definitions, both of preferences and other things, to separate preferences from other things, and to make explicit the origins of the preferences used in analysis. But in too many cases, disagreements persist without an analytically sharp delineation of their character.

To illustrate this point, I discuss two broad debates of long standing among scholars of international politics. My goal is not by any means to be exhaustive with regard to the content of the debates but rather to show that explicit attention to preferences can help elucidate an issue and ways to analyze it.

The first topic has to do with explaining international trade relations, which I present as a positive example of how explicit attention to preferences has enriched our understanding. The second topic is explaining colonial imperialism in the nineteenth century, which I present more negatively, as an example of how confusion about preferences can impede scholarly progress.

Explaining International Trade Policy

Observers have long noted that there is a great deal of variation in trade policy. At the global level, the international economy appears to go through periods in which trade is very tightly controlled and those in which trade is relatively free. At the national level, countries vary substantially in how open or liberal their trade policies are. At the subnational level, there are major differences in the activities and industries that are protected. All three dimensions of variation in trade policy are of interest, and all have been discussed at great length by scholars.

The analysis of trade policy has been much enhanced by clear attention to the preferences of social actors and by the accurate use of these preferences in trying to explain outcomes. Indeed, this issue area serves as something of an example of clarity in the treatment of preferences. This may be because it is easier to establish preferences with regard to economic matters or because the area has simply attracted a great deal of analytical attention.[28]

The study of trade policies has, in fact, typically been organized by scholars with the three steps—the boxes within boxes—recommended here. First comes the theoretically grounded derivation of preferences at the domestic level. Then the aggregation of these interests to "national" preferences is considered. Finally, the interaction of national preferences and the international strategic environment is examined to explain outcomes. Although not all the literature follows this pattern, enough does so that substantial analytical progress has been made in the past twenty-five years. And a look at the trade-policy literature helps establish that clearer analysis does not mean the end of disagreement—only a better ability to understand and evaluate disagreements.

The first step, then, is to fix the trade-policy preferences of actors at the domestic level. The simplest view is a naive neoclassical one, for which all nations prefer free trade all the time (absent an optimal tariff). This is so simple-minded that it is not an entry in the literature, but it is an important presumptive baseline from which to start: Why, after all, might states not prefer a policy that increases aggregate national welfare? The typical answer to this question locates the origin of trade-policy goals in interest groups, especially firms, for which they provide redistributive opportunities.

Some of the earliest work on trade policy assumed simply, and not implausibly, that all firms preferred protection for their own products. This led to explanations of outcomes that emphasized the ability of firms to organize in order to achieve protection and consumers' inability to organize to counter protectionist pressures. The notion that trade policy could largely be understood as the result of firms with identical (protectionist) preferences having different capacities to influence policy, given the strategic setting, was central to Schattschneider's classic 1935 study

---

[28] It might be noted that the analysis of some other economic policies is also well developed; most prominent are international monetary relations, on which see Eichengreen 1989b, 1992.

of the Smoot-Hawley Tariff (Schattschneider 1935). It was made explicit in Gourevitch's classic analysis of responses to the Great Depression of 1873to 1896 (Gourevitch 1977). Even where researchers posited differences in trade-policy preferences, as both Gourevitch and Kindleberger (1951) did, these preferences were largely based either on observation of the statements of the principals or on assumption.

Further theory and analysis led scholars to move away from such simple notions of trade preferences, toward more theoretically grounded ones. The Heckscher-Ohlin approach and its Stolper-Samuelson extension emphasizes the impact of factor endowments on trade-policy preferences, with more locally scarce (abundant) factors more favorable to protection (free trade): In a capital-rich country, labor is protectionist and capital is free-trade.[29] The Ricardo-Viner approach focuses on factors specific to particular industries: Labor and capital in import-competing industries favor protection; labor and capital in exporting industries favor free trade.[30] Analyses of international trade with imperfectly competitive markets often emphasize the scale of industries or firms: In some variants, for example, smaller firms, or industries from smaller countries, will be more favorable to protection (Richardson 1990; Milner and Yoffie 1989; Chase 1998). Other approaches focus on the impact of domestic or international diversification, which weakens national sectoral attachments (Schonhardt-Bailey 1994; Milner 1988).

Greater attention to the preferences of individuals, firms, industries, and classes (factors) has not ended disagreement. Indeed, explicit consideration of preferences has led to heated debates over them. But this is all to the good: Clearly stated arguments have allowed for logical and empirical assessment of their claims.[31]

The trade preferences derived from these theories must be analyzed as they are mediated through the national strategic setting. This requires explicit assessment of the process of preference aggregation, from domestic actors to national policy. Of course numerous possible approaches to this exist. The simplest is that mentioned earlier, emphasizing the role of concentrated and diffuse interests: The more concentrated the interest, the more likely it is to be successful in organizing to achieve its goals. More recent work has brought into play features of the political system, such as the organization of interests and parties, and the effective size of the constituency being represented. Rogowski (1987) asserts that proportional representation predisposes governments toward freer trade; Loh-

---

[29] The best-known application of this approach to domestic and interstate politics is Rogowski 1989.

[30] Again, Hillman 1989 and Alt and Gilligan 1994 provide excellent surveys.

[31] As is done, for example, in Magee 1980; Ray 1981; Marvel and Ray 1983; Eichengreen 1989a; and Mansfield and Busch 1995.

mann and O'Halloran (1994) argue that the greater the influence of the American Congress, the more protectionist trade policy is likely to be (see also Alt and Gilligan 1994). Still others focus on ideological or other institutional characteristics of the political system (Kindleberger 1975; Goldstein 1993).

Institutional approaches of more general origin can be applied to the trade-policy arena. There is a common view, for example, that "corporatist" political economies allow decisions to be made in a bargained, consensual manner (Katzenstein 1985). This, it is said, leads socioeconomic actors to internalize the effects of policies adopted, so that more efficient policies are likely to be chosen—compensation over trade protection, for example. Tsebelis (1995) associates political systems with multiple "veto points," such as those involving divided powers or federal structures, with a bias toward the status quo; where trade-policy making requires changes in policies, this would have a systematic impact on outcomes as well.

The final step is to examine how these domestically derived preferences play themselves out in the global strategic setting. Some scholars emphasize aspects of the international environment that affect trade-policy *strategies*. For example, world macroeconomic conditions can alter a nation's policy even where its goals remain the same. The same country might pursue liberal trade relations in times of global growth but turn toward protection in times of crisis. In an analogous way, international monetary conditions are sometimes given as potential sources of trade policy: Stability is conducive to commercial liberalization, whereas breakdown and competitive devaluations encourage protection (Eichengreen 1989a, 1992). There might be several interpretations of this correlation, but a common one focuses on how such international instability shortens time horizons, increases uncertainty, and thus makes interstate cooperation more difficult.

The most prominent feature of the global strategic setting scholars invoke to translate preferences into outcomes are those imposed by differential national capabilities and bargaining—power, in a word. Some argue that hegemony, or more generally a concentration of power among a few states, makes trade liberalization more likely (Krasner 1976; for a more recent survey, see Lake 1993). Others argue that countries use liberal trade policies to reinforce preexisting alliances (Gowa 1989, 1994). All take as given national preferences and accent the causal significance of the strategic setting, typically characteristics of the global political or economic order.

It is easy to see the logical progression and empirical implications of the different arguments at all three steps, and to see how the steps might fit together. This, of course, does not mean scholars agree—only that most agree on how to formulate and evaluate their disagreements. Indeed, many differences of interpretation remain.

One axis of disagreement, as usual, is over the relative explanatory importance of preferences and the strategic setting. There is some affinity between preference-based explanations and domestic approaches to explaining trade policies and, similarly, between constraint-based views and "systemic" explanations. Partisans of the explanatory predominance of preferences point out that national governments often prefer unilateral protection to free trade and that exogenous conditions are irrelevant in the face of this.[32] Others argue that most of the explanatory power is given not by different preferences but by changing strategic conditions.[33]

Another axis of disagreement, as already described, is over the various theories of preference formation. This includes the determinants of individual, firm, and sectoral trade-policy preferences and how these preferences are aggregated. That the analytical debates are easy to state and that their comparative statics properties are simple to derive is an indication of how important careful definitions are to scholarly progress, including scholarly disputes.

It may well be, of course, that some factors are more important to some outcomes than others. It would not be surprising to find that features of the global environment are especially important in affecting trends in international levels of trade protection over time, whereas domestic factors predominate in determining the structure of protection among industries. Here, again, the careful structuring of the research questions and designs helps us to arrive at sounder conclusions.

Indeed, progress in the analysis of international trade (and monetary, financial, and investment) policies has brought forward new classes of questions. One of the more intriguing is the possibility that the international setting has an impact on domestic preference formation. This might be because changing global conditions come to alter the preferred policies of subnational groups or because they change domestic coalitional arrangements and strengths.[34]

An example of this can be drawn from Latin American economic policy. The massive terms of trade shocks of the 1930s, and the general inward turn of the developed world's trade policies in the 1930s and 1940s, was associated with a Latin American shift from free trade toward protectionism. By the same token, in the 1980s the debt crisis and the quickening of global financial and commercial integration was associated with a turn away from protection and toward trade liberalization. In both instances,

---

[32] For some examples, see Kindleberger 1951; and McKeown 1983, 1986.

[33] Conybeare 1987 is a good example, and Lake 1993 provides a good summary of one class of variants.

[34] The articles in Keohane and Milner 1996 attempt to clarify how this might work both theoretically and empirically.

a case can be made that the dramatic shifts in trade policies were the result of changes in the international strategic setting, with global closure in the former and "globalization" in the latter. Or the policy shifts might have been owing to changes in the dominant coalitions in Latin American countries: The collapse of commodity prices in the 1930s weakened free-trade commodity exporters, while the collapse of domestic markets in the 1980s weakened protectionist import-substituting industries. Or international conditions might have changed the policy preferences of domestic actors: Foreign markets looked much less attractive in 1935 than in 1895, much more attractive in 1995 than in 1955. Whether these assertions are correct, their consideration helps highlight the possibility of building both new conclusions and new questions on the basis of carefully structured debates.

Studies of international trade relations have benefited from clear statements of the explanatory importance assigned to trade-policy preferences, the domestic setting, and international conditions. Such studies are, in turn, most convincing inasmuch as scholars clearly state the preferences of the major actors—be they states, politicians, firms, groups, or individuals—and provide presumptive, empirical, or theoretical justifications for the preferences in question. This sort of clarity would help the long-standing debate on nineteenth-century European colonial imperialism.

Explaining Classical Imperialism

Debates over the causes of the rush for colonies by European countries (and Japan and the United States) in the late nineteenth century go back to the events themselves. Yet, disagreements remain as confused and confusing as they were then, and there is little sign of significant scholarly progress on many important issues. A great deal of this, I believe, is the result of confusion about the analytical role of preferences.

There are three particularly enduring, and enduringly contentious, explanatory issues in the literature. They are the importance of economic and noneconomic causes of imperial expansion, the relative impact of domestic and international sources of imperialism, and the causal importance of conditions in the underdeveloped regions themselves.[35]

The first question is the extent to which imperialism was driven by the prospect of financial gain, either to the colonizing nation or to groups

---

[35] Even the surveys in the literature are so numerous that only a few representatives can be mentioned here. They include Fieldhouse 1961; Landes 1961; Cohen 1973; Smith 1981; and Doyle 1986b. The three-way division used for convenience here is similar to that which motivates Doyle's categories of metropolitan dispositional, systemic, and peripheral approaches, respectively.

within it. The so-called economic theory of imperialism[36] is associated with the view that the search for imperial profits (more likely, rents) was a strong motive for colonialism. The most famous variant, that of Lenin and Hobson, asserts that the maximization of returns to financial capitalists was the goal of the imperial powers.[37] Opponents insist that economic motives were not a major source of colonial imperialism. They posit principal causal factors that range from the military through the ideological to the bureaucratic.[38] The most common counterargument (for example, Cohen 1973) is that the Great Powers accumulated colonies for the purpose of military security, as part of broader attempts to amass power.

A second, related issue is whether imperialism was spurred by domestic or international developments. Domestic arguments, of which Lenin-Hobson is one variant, are based on the idea that something intrinsic about the industrial societies changed after the mid-1800s to drive them toward the acquisition of colonies. Noneconomic but nonetheless domestic explanations emphasize the "atavistic" groups discussed by Schumpeter (1951), imperial ideologies, or other metropolitan forces. A similar approach is that of Jack Snyder (1991), who argues that "cartelized" systems in which influence was concentrated in powerful logrolling groups had a strong tendency toward expansionist goals. Internationally driven explanations focus on global roots of imperialism. Most emphasize the struggle for military power and the displacement of intra-European conflicts to the periphery; some look at the rise of new military or other technologies in allowing Europe to dominate other societies.

The third major debate is over the role of peripheral societies themselves in the race for colonies. The "metrocentric" view that imperialism grew out of characteristics of the metropolitan powers was challenged by Gallagher and Robinson (1953), at least in the case of Great Britain. They argued that colonialism was only one of several means to Britain's aim of free trade and that it was pursued only reluctantly, where conditions in the periphery made it necessary. This places the roots of colonialism in the colonized regions rather than the metropolitan countries: Where peripheral collaborators for British free-trade imperialists were available, colonialism was superfluous (Robinson 1972).

---

[36] The phrase is misleading. An economic theory typically argues for relationships between variables, such as economic growth and income distribution; in the literature, however, it has taken on the meaning of a simple assertion that economic factors are important in explaining imperialism.

[37] Apart from the obvious (Lenin 1939), two useful discussions are Cain 1985 and Stokes 1969. More recent presentations or evaluations of the argument that the principal goals of imperialism were economic include Cain and Hopkins 1993a, 1993b; Davis and Huttenback 1986; and Lipson 1985. For a survey of the British case, see Cain 1980.

[38] Krasner 1978 is a parallel evaluation of contending views of American motivations in "neoimperialist" intervention in the developing world, which favors one that regards endur-

Despite the longevity of the controversy and outstanding historical research on the topic, little progress has been made in resolving the principal explanatory issues. At least some of this lack of progress can, in my view, be ascribed to the analytically faulty way that the discussion has been organized and conducted.

The debates are about two related issues in which preferences play a central part. The first is the relative importance to explaining imperialism of the preferences of the imperial powers and of the strategic setting. One set of scholars believes that if the strategic setting had been different—with changed European power balances or local conditions—the metropolitan countries would not have embarked on colonialism or would have done so in fundamentally different ways. Another set sees colonialism as the natural and direct outgrowth of the preferences of the metropolitan countries, with the strategic setting at best affecting the relative fortunes of different contenders for colonies. The second issue, closely related to the first, is precisely what the preferences of the major powers were. One group sees them as inherently economic, the others as noneconomic.

The debate is rife with the problems discussed here. The intermingling of preferences and the strategic setting confounds much of the literature. For example, two commonly presented positions are that of Lenin and what might be called a "power politics" perspective. Both views include an argument about preferences folded together with one about the strategic setting. They differ only with regard to preferences. The "Leninist" view sees metropolitan preferences as the maximization of returns to finance capital, whereas the latter sees state preferences as noneconomic, typically geostrategic. But both emphasize the impact of the competitive environment prevailing among colonial powers in the late 1800s. The disagreement is not, in fact, about the role of interstate competition but rather about the definition of state goals.

So, too, do many of the statements of contending perspectives confound preferences and the environment. The debate is often structured to imply that concern for interstate competition is in contradiction with concern for economic goals, and vice versa. But even the most economically motivated of states faces a strategic environment within which it tries to achieve the best possible outcome. A government primarily—even solely—motivated by the search for financial gain might engage in colonial expansion if, and only if, the strategic setting led it to believe that the acquisition or preservation of wealth depended on using colonialism to secure it. If the expansion of other countries threatened, immediately or prospectively, to reduce available economic opportunities, a wealth-maximizing country might well act strategically to preempt. The two

ing ideological features of the American political economy and the American state as the principal motive for the use of force by the United States to protect its overseas investments.

concerns—a preference for wealth maximization and a strategic setting that requires concern for power balances—are not in contradiction, and, indeed, one might flow from another. The same logic might work in reverse: A military strength-maximizing country might pursue colonialism to accumulate wealth that could be used for military spending

Fruitful analysis requires a clear separation between preferences and the setting, and a clear sense of how the two interact. If current lines of demarcation were to be retained, the power politics school would need to specify precisely which features of the strategic setting drove all metropolitan countries, regardless of preferences, toward colonialism, and how these features led to a lack of colonialism in some regions and time periods. Proponents of preference-based explanations would, for their part, have to explain exactly what the preferences were that made colonialism so common in particular time periods and regions and why the environment was not a major constraint on the pursuit of these preferences.

One might hope, however, that a clearer statement of the problem would lead scholars to generate less heat and more light, perhaps to agree that the *interaction* of preferences and the setting determined outcomes. In this context they could endeavor to design research to help determine the character of this interaction in general and in particular historical instances.

Scholars need to state clearly their assumptions or assertions about the actors' preferences and about the strategic setting. They need to provide an analytical backdrop to conceptual experiments, for example, in which preferences are held constant and the strategic setting is altered. The number of observations is large: There is a wide variety of experiences including many different metropolitan nations and a large number of underdeveloped regions, from a long period of time in the the nineteenth century. Scholars might specify how features of the strategic setting, for example, are expected to affect national behavior given constant preferences. Comparisons could then be made among different environments to see if a country's behavior varied as expected. Indeed, one of the great attractions of the "imperialism of free trade" approach, exemplified by Gallagher and Robinson (1953), was its insistence that British free-trade preferences were stable while *peripheral* conditions determined colonial *strategies*, which made the argument eminently subject to empirical evaluation.

But empirical evaluation of the interaction of preferences and the strategic setting requires some prior notion of national preferences, which brings us to the second big issue in the imperialism debate. Here, the two principal positions are relatively clear: One sees economic goals as paramount; the other, noneconomic goals.

However, the controversy over national preferences—the "economic theory of imperialism"—is dominated by attempts to do the impossible. It is largely oriented toward trying to observe preferences directly, to see what countries and groups wanted on the basis of what they did. Much of the debate has thus taken the form of proponents of the "economic theory" finding cases in which colonialism was profitable, and opponents finding cases in which colonialism was unprofitable. These findings are taken as evidence that the governments in question were imperialist for, respectively, economic and noneconomic motives. But because preferences cannot be observed independently of strategies, empirical investigation simply cannot resolve the issue without a clear separation of actors' preferences from the setting. All we can observe is the outcome—a region colonized, for example—from which the causal mix of preferences and the strategic setting cannot be inferred.

Whether a colony ended up being profitable does nothing to resolve the question of the colonial power's goals. A government interested in engaging in colonialism for "economic" reasons (i.e., to increase private fortunes) might well have faced an environment in which unprofitable colonies were more desirable than no colonies at all (perhaps to deny them to competitors). Alternately, a government with no colonial economic motives might have found itself with profitable colonies as a by-product of its attempts to pursue other goals (perhaps, again, to deny profits to competitors).

To compound the problem, while preferences play so central a role to all aspects of the debate, there are few theoretically sound derivations of colonial preferences. In addition to a clear analytical separation between preferences and the environment, another way to move forward would be to focus on the development of theories of colonial preferences.[39] On the basis of these theories of preferences, we could formulate expectations about differences among national policies in similar settings or some other form of analogous conceptual experiment.

The debate over colonial imperialism in the forty years before World War I is an important one, both historically and theoretically. Yet, the current state of the debate does not lend itself to the generation of comparative statics, even less of testable propositions or observable implications of these comparative statics. And the argument can only move in this direction on the basis of a clear delineation of preferences and strategic environments, of their effects, and of the origin of colonial preferences.

CONCLUSIONS

Insistence on close attention to the origin and influence of preferences is of more than pedagogical interest. Much of international relations is

---

[39] For my own tentative efforts to contribute to a theory of colonial preferences, see Frieden 1994b.

consumed in battles between views whose analytical positions are never carefully stated. Neorealists, neoliberals, intergovernmentalists, neofunctionalists, and other such coreligionists typically argue about principles rather than explanations. Often such arguments are inflamed and exacerbated by the lack of enough common language to evaluate contending explanations.

Many differences among students of international relations have to do with the character of the preferences of nation-states, groups, and individuals. Many other debates have to do with the relative explanatory importance of preferences and of the strategic setting. Of course, there is no unambiguous set of preferences that all might adopt, and, of course, both preferences and the environment matter for outcomes. However, the true nature of the disagreements is often masked by careless or inconsistent definitions and applications. And agreement on preferences, or on the impact of preferences and the environment, is impossible without explicit attention to them.

Indeed, these issues are rarely raised explicitly. The goal of improved analyses of international politics would be better served if they were—if preferences were defined more carefully, if they were derived more methodically, and if their implications for outcomes were stated and evaluated more systematically. More care toward these would, I believe, raise both the quality of debate and the quality of scholarly explanations.

Establishing the preferences of the units deemed important to international politics is, to be sure, but a first step in a complex endeavor. It is every bit as important, in general, to understand the constraints and opportunities within which the units labor, whether these constraints and opportunities are technological, informational, geostrategic, or otherwise. And the beliefs and perceptions of individual policy makers can also be of significance in explaining strategies and outcomes. The other essays in this volume examine these factors in some detail.

Nonetheless, no analysis of relations among actors—whether the actors are individuals, firms, groups, or nation-states—can be undertaken without a notion of the actors' preferences. Just as preferences alone give only a partial view of the world, so, too, is the strategic setting only part of the story. Insufficient, or insufficiently careful, attention to the role of preferences in international politics has been responsible for many fruitless debates and much poorly designed research.

Scholarship in international relations needs to pay closer and more careful attention to the explanatory role of preferences. This means working hard to differentiate preferences from the strategies to which they give rise and to provide convincing arguments and accounts of how we can know what these preferences are. Only on this basis can progress be made in the social-scientific analysis of international politics.

CHAPTER THREE

The Strategic Setting of Choices:
Signaling, Commitment, and Negotiation
in International Politics

JAMES D. MORROW

THE STRATEGIC setting together with preferences determine choices. The previous chapter discussed preferences; this chapter examines how strategic settings affect choices. The choices of many actors determine outcomes in international politics. The international system is defined by actors and by the actions of those actors that compose it. An actor cannot simply choose a course of action that produces its preferred outcome because the choices of others also affect the final result. They choose a course of action both for its direct effect on the outcome and its indirect effect on the actions of others. The strategic-choice approach draws on game theory to understand the complexities of strategic interaction.

In this chapter I do not simply review the principles of game theory and list maxims drawn from those principles. Rather, I discuss in detail three different strategic problems—signaling, commitment, and bargaining—that recur in international politics. Individual cases reflect several of these strategic problems and others, so the three problems discussed here do not fully explain any particular case. We can understand the strategic dimensions of many cases by understanding these strategic problems in the abstract because they recur in many cases. By presenting these abstract problems rather than strategic maxims, I hope the reader will get a better sense of what game theory tells us about strategic interaction. I conclude with a review of what we have learned from our understanding of the three abstract strategic problems about two general problems in international politics—alliances and crisis bargaining.

This chapter directly complements the preceding one on preferences. Together, they present the two elements of the strategic-choice approach—actors' preferences and the strategic setting—and how these two factors produce choices.

I would like to thank all the participants at the conferences in preparation of this volume and single out Jim Fearon, David Lake, and Bob Powell for exceptional praise for their comments and consultations during the writing of this essay.

THE SECURITY DILEMMA AND THREE STRATEGIC PROBLEMS

The security dilemma is built on a paradox. If states are purely interested in their own security, there should not be a dilemma. The security dilemma contends that states must always be wary of one another because the growth in one's power makes another less secure. According to Waltz's version of neorealist theory, all states are interested in security (Waltz 1979, 118, 126). If all states were interested solely in such preservation and their sole interest in security was known to all, no state would pose a threat to any other; all can maintain their position by upholding the status quo. Because all are interested only in security and all know that, no state need fear that another will attempt to overturn the status quo.

Nevertheless, states are concerned about one another's power and policies. Even if all states are only concerned with maintaining their own positions, they cannot be certain that others will limit their designs to maintain their positions or even to moderate revisions of the status quo. Consider the archetype of this problem—Great Britain and France facing Nazi Germany during the 1930s. Clearly Hitler's government sought changes in the status quo established at Versailles and Locarno. The British and French governments had to judge the range of such demands when responding to German demands. Had they known Hitler sought continental hegemony from the moment he took power, they would have taken stronger steps sooner. Had the Sudetenland been Hitler's last territorial demand and had Britain and France known that, the crisis that led to the Munich agreement could have been avoided. But because they did not know the extent of Hitler's ambitions, they had to make judgments about the relative risks of an aggressive versus a conciliatory policy. The uncertainty of Britain and France about Hitler's future actions defined the strategic setting they faced in the 1930s.

Uncertain motivations also create problems for the side whose motive is unknown. Consider the problem facing a hypothetical Germany seeking moderate revisions in the status quo during the 1930s—a Germany seeking to bring all Germans together in a Greater Germany, but nothing more than that. Such a Germany would have to be concerned with how to achieve its demands without provoking a strong response from Great Britain, France, and the Soviet Union. Because a demand to unify all Germans in one state went beyond the status quo before World War I, the other major powers might see such a demand as the beginning of a German quest for continental domination. How could the moderate revisionist Germany convince them that it did not seek continental domination? It would have to take actions that a Germany seeking such domination—that is, the real Nazi Germany—would not take. Other states could then conclude that they were facing a Germany with limited demands. For example, the moderate revisionist Germany could disarm its military while demanding a "Greater Germany." Of course, disarmament would also undermine the credibility of the threat of war implicit in its demand to revise the status quo. Part of the bargaining leverage of the moderate revisionist Germany arises from other states' fear of war; the actions that reassure others that German demands are limited also undermine their fear of war, and thus Germany's bargaining leverage.

If concessions such as the annexation of the Sudetenland are made, another problem arises. Great Britain and France make such concessions in the hope that the new status quo can be maintained. They would like to make commitments to each other and to other minor powers threatened by further German expansion. These commitments would have to be credible to others, namely, Germany and the parties receiving them. Because honoring those commitments is costly, others have reason to doubt them. If the commitment deters further threats, it is successful at little cost. Simple promises may not be sufficient; the British commitment to Poland in 1939 proved to be hollow. However, there may be other ways for a state to commit itself to future actions in the face of others' uncertainty about its willingness to carry out those actions. The positioning of British troops in Poland, for instance, probably would have convinced Hitler that the British would fight for Poland.

The renegotiation of the status quo gives rise to a third strategic problem. Any concessions to Germany are negotiated among the parties. In bargaining, everyone wants the best deal possible but not at the expense of failing to get any deal. In our hypothetical 1930s Europe, Germany would like to unify as many Germans as it can without triggering war. The British and French would like to make as few changes to the status quo as are needed to satisfy the Germans and keep the peace. Because neither side knows exactly what deals the other side will accept in lieu of war, both must negotiate with an eye to judging the other side's motivation as well as its current offer. Differences among the states negotiating with Germany complicate this problem further. Some, such as the Soviet Union, may be less willing to make concessions; others, such as France, may be willing to make far-reaching concessions to avoid war.

Uncertainty about the motivations of others raises at least three strategic problems in politics. First, can parties signal one another about their motivations? In other words, is it in an actor's interest to disclose to another what its precise goals are, and for the latter to believe that disclosure? Second, can the parties commit themselves in ways that are credible to others who do not know their precise motivations? What mechanisms make such commitment possible, and what limits do such mechanisms place on actors? Third, how can the parties negotiate differences when they are uncertain about what deals the other will find acceptable? These three strategic problems are the focus of this chapter.

Although I address only these three problems at length, uncertainty gives rise to a host of political problems that are common both in security and political economy and across systemic, state, and lower levels of analysis in international politics. Some of these other strategic problems are principal-agent relations (Bueno de Mesquita and Siverson 1995), coordination (Morrow 1994b; Stein 1990, chap. 2), collective action, moral hazard (Downs and Rocke 1995, chap. 3), and repetition and conditional punishments (Downs and Rocke 1990, 1995). Like the three problems I discuss here, credibility and uncertainty are at the heart of these other strategic problems. Noncooperative game theory, developed in economics over the last twenty years, provides a tool for the formal analysis of all these strategic problems. Credibility and uncertainty are central strategic issues that noncooperative game theory seeks to address. Concern with these issues has grown over the last fifteen years; the techniques of noncooperative game theory have entered the field because they provide a way to analyze these issues.

GAME THEORY AND INTERNATIONAL POLITICS

All three of these problems are strategic; an actor must consider other actors' likely choices when making its own decisions. Game theory is the best-developed formal tool we have to date for the analysis of strategic interaction. International-relations theorists have been interested in applying game theory since its advent in the 1940s. Schelling (1960) is the best-known early proponent of using game theory to illuminate problems in international politics, although both Ellsberg (1960) and Kaplan (1957) were also early proponents. Interest dimmed after the initial bloom in the late 1950s until the 1970s. That decade saw a return of interest in using games to model strategic interaction in crises, most notably Snyder and Diesing (1977) and Jervis (1978). These models relied on "two-by-two games," the familiar matrix games where each player has two strategies and there are four possible outcomes. Among the complete set of two-by-two games are Prisoner's Dilemma and Chicken (Figure 3.1). Each player has two strategies in each game, labeled C and D for Cooperate and Defect. The four possible combinations of strategies define the outcomes of each game. The players' preferences over those outcomes are given by the numbers in parentheses in each box, with Player 1's preference given before Player 2's, with higher numbers denoting more preferred outcomes. The players' preferences across the four possible outcomes completely describe the game. In Prisoner's Dilemma, for example,

Prisoner's Dilemma

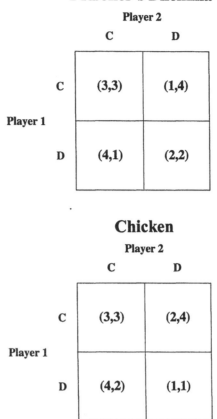

Figure 3.1. Illustrated here are two "two-by-two games"—Prisoner's Dilemma and Chicken—where each player has two strategies and there are four possible outcomes.

if one player defects and the other cooperates, the outcome is the best possible for the defecting player and the worst possible for the cooperating player. Informal arguments, rather than formal solutions, were used to explain what strategies each player would play in these games. Variation in preferences accounts for the differences in actions chosen, and thus behavior. Such games require only a specification of preferences, as detailed in chapter 2.

This application of game theory to international politics has important limitations (Wagner 1983). Two-by-two games assume that the actors only have two choices and that they move in ignorance of each other's moves. Most situations in international politics present a wider range of choices than just two; how to cooperate is often as big a problem as whether to cooperate. Further, strategic problems in international politics typically are dynamic; each actor knows the moves the other actor has made so far. The applications of two-by-two games dealt with these issues with informal arguments about how the players would choose their strategies. For example, Snyder and Diesing (1977, 88–106) conclude that crises with Prisoner's Dilemma preferences can end peacefully, in direct contradiction to the strategic logic of that game.[1] However, Snyder and Diesing's informal argument has the actors making and responding to multiple offers; that is, they give the actors more than two strategies and allow them to bargain with knowledge of each other's earlier offers. A better representation for such sequential bargaining is a game tree with multiple moves. A two-by-two game cannot represent the strategic setting in Snyder and Diesing's argument because it requires the players to move simultaneously.

Dynamic interaction raises the question of credibility. Although an actor may promise to take certain actions in the future, will those actions be in its interest if the time comes to live up to its promise? If those actions may prove to be contrary to its interest, other actors doubt the credibility of the promise. Game theory deals with the question of credibility through the concept of perfection. Strategies are perfect if every move is in the moving player's interest when he or she must make the move, given all future moves in the game. If a promise satisfies the test of perfection, then the promise is credible.

Iterated games provide one way to think about dynamic interaction. Axelrod (1984) brought the iterated Prisoner's Dilemma and the efficacy of reciprocal strategies like Tit-for-Tat to the attention of international-relations scholars. Reciprocal strategies select current actions, in part, on past behavior. Actors then can enforce an agreement among themselves by using reciprocal threats to punish deviations from the agreement. Oye (1986a) applied the logic of reciprocal threats in iterated Prisoner's Dilemma to a variety of problems in international politics. However, sequence matters in situations that are not repeated, and thus where reciprocal threats are not feasible. These applications of iterated games also assumed that a simple two-by-two game was repeated.

International-relations theorists were also concerned about actors' uncertainty regarding the motivations of other actors. Two-by-two games cannot address uncertainty in motivation; the game is known to all by definition. Some (Stein 1982 is the best effort) tried to analyze situations where the players did not know what game they were playing. These ef-

---

[1] Both players have a dominant strategy to defect in Prisoner's Dilemma, so they are always better off playing "Defect" rather than "Cooperate" no matter which strategy the other player chooses.

forts did not specify exactly what the players knew and did not know about each other's motivations. Without such a specification, you cannot always know what moves are in a player's interest.

Games of incomplete information specify those uncertainties. In such a game, at least one player possesses private information—it knows something about the game that the other players do not. A player's payoffs, for example, could be its private information, matching the argument that actors are uncertain about one another's motivations. A player's private information determines its *type*. The other players know the set of possible types of that player and know the chance of each type. They may be able to infer the player's type from its actions, but they do not know its type. Games of incomplete information, then, provide a way to think about uncertainty in a game.

An illustration may clarify the concept of types. Let us return to the example of Europe during the 1930s. The motivation of Germany determines its type. There are two types of Germanys: one seeks continental domination, the other only modest revisions in the status quo. Only Germany knows which of these types it actually is. Great Britain and France know only that Germany could be either type and how likely each type is; they do not *know* whether Germany seeks continental domination or modest changes in the status quo. They can try to infer the extent of German demands from its actions. Those inferences must consider what each type of Germany would do in the current situation precisely because Great Britain and France do not know which type of Germany they face. Such inferences are important to Great Britain and France because knowledge of Germany's type would help them predict future German actions and respond appropriately.

Noncooperative game theory links perfection arguments with incomplete information.[2] This combination is useful for problems in international-relations theory because it provides a way to analyze credibility in the face of uncertainty. Consider the problem of the security dilemma presented earlier in this chapter. The security dilemma occurs because of uncertainty confounded with a problem of credibility. Each side worries about whether the other will attack because it is uncertain about the other's motivations; if a state knew the other had only peaceful ambitions, it would be certain the other would not attack. Further, statements about intentions may not be reliable. Neither side can eliminate its freedom in the future to attack the other. Each must be concerned about the credibility of any promise the other makes not to attack. It may not be in the interest of the other state to live up to such a promise. Noncooperative

---

[2] I modesty recommend Morrow 1994a for an introduction to noncooperative game theory and its application in political science.

game theory provides us with a way to consider in detail the strategic logic of problems like the security dilemma.

Credibility is a central issue in noncooperative game theory. Actors cannot fix future choices in advance; instead, we must ask what choices will be in their interest when they must make them. In the 1930s example, Germany may say that the Sudetenland is its last territorial demand, but its decisions whether to make further demands in the future are the test of that statement. Germany cannot choose to forego the possibility of further demands by merely claiming that it has no further demands. Noncooperative game theory models credibility issues in the sequence of moves in a game. An extensive-form game specifies the players' moves, their sequence, and how those moves lead to outcomes. A player must consider other players' future moves when deciding to make a move. Credibility issues arise when a player's choice hinges on a later choice of another player: The other player has an incentive to induce the first player to make a particular move now, but the first player has reason to doubt that what the latter says now is a reliable guide to its future behavior. The credibility of the other player's statements resides in the head of the first player in this situation; what does the first player think the other player will do in the future?

Uncertainty is also central to noncooperative game theory. Actors cannot know one another's motivation; instead, they make judgments about those motivations. Sometimes they can judge others' motivations from their actions. Noncooperative game theory requires that we describe what information the players know at each of their moves. We assume that unknown information, such as motivations, takes on one of a possible set of values. In the 1930s example, Great Britain and France know that Germany is one of two types: a state seeking only moderate revisions to the status quo or a state seeking continental domination; they do not know, however, which type of Germany they face. Their beliefs about Germany's goals are described by probabilities that each type is correct; the more probable a type, the greater the probability Britain and France believe that Germany's goals are consistent with that type. Beliefs affect actions because the actions Britain and France would like to take depend on which type of Germany they think they are facing. British and French beliefs about Germany's type can also affect German credibility. Inability to precommit one's future actions and uncertainty about types of other players are two of the three central ideas in noncooperative game theory.[3]

Credibility in a game is a product of the sequence of the game, the players' preferences, and their uncertainty about one another's types. If a

---

[3] The other central idea in noncooperative game theory is Nash equilibrium. When the Nobel Prize in economics was awarded for game theory in 1994, it was shared by John

player knows another player's type—that is, its preferences—the former can predict the latter's moves in the future. The sequence of moves may create a situation where it will not be in the latter's interest to carry out its promises when the time comes to do so. The former then has reason to doubt the credibility of those promises. If the former does not know the latter's type, the latter's promises may lack credibility if one possible type will not live up to its promise. In this case, the latter's credibility depends on the former's beliefs about which type of the latter it faces; if the former thinks there is a sufficient chance it is facing the type that will violate the promise, then the promise lacks credibility. Credibility, then, is not a simple matter of whether the actor making the promise intends to carry it out.

This chapter builds on the previous chapter by exploring how strategic logic affects the means actors choose to pursue their preferences. The previous chapter addressed actors' preferences and how they can be examined systematically. However, preferences alone do not dictate action. As in the opening example, both the Germany with limited ends and the Germany seeking continental domination—that is, Germanys with different preferences—take the same actions within their strategic environment. At the same time, choices are generally not dictated by a player's situation. Choices depend on both preferences and the strategic environment. Actors select their moves to produce preferred outcomes, and outcomes depend on all the moves made in the game. As the prior chapter laid out how preferences can be studied systematically, this chapter asks how strategic choices, given preferences, can be studied systematically. Both are necessary for understanding political decisions.

The application of these techniques to international politics has gone both from international-relations theory to developments in game theory, and back again. The inability of two-by-two game models to capture the arguments of international-relations theorists led formal modelers to seek new tools. The tools were found in economics, but their application to international politics required careful thinking about that subject. The strategic problems in our field have common elements with those in certain areas of economics, so the tools can be useful. However, the two sets of strategic problems are not identical. The questions go in both directions: How can models capture arguments about international politics, and what do those models then tell us about international-relations theory? When the modeling process works, it illuminates and advances our understanding of arguments about international politics.

Nash, for Nash equilibrium; Reinhart Selten, for perfection; and John Harsanyi, for games of incomplete information—the three central ideas of noncooperative game theory.

Another advantage of the use of noncooperative game theory is its concurrent application to the study of domestic politics, particularly American politics. Formal models of elections, legislatures, and bureaucracies have been published over the last fifteen years that use noncooperative game theory. These studies find the same strategic problems that occur in international politics, albeit in different forms. States worry about how they can commit to carrying out military threats that are costly; presidents worry about how they can commit to vetoing bills that contain small provisions they find objectionable. The parallel structure of strategic problems makes the integration of domestic politics and international politics easier. They no longer seem like two disparate realms of politics.

Here, the discussion proceeds with an examination of the three strategic problems of signaling, commitment, and bargaining. An examination of how formal models have changed our understanding of alliances and crisis bargaining follows. I conclude by laying out directions for future research.

SIGNALING

Signaling can occur when one actor knows something of relevance to another actor's decisions. If the decision of the uninformed party affects the informed actor, the latter may wish to signal its information to the former. In international politics, signaling is a way to consider the problem of unknown motivation. We think of an actor's motivation as its type. An actor makes its choices based, in part, on what other actors are likely to do in the future. Knowing other actors' motivations can help the former judge what its best responses are. Let us again return to our example of 1930s Europe. Whether German aspirations are limited or unlimited is central to the decision Great Britain and France face concerning how to respond to German demands for specific changes in the status quo. However, the German government may not wish to make its precise aspirations clear to Britain and France. The strategic logic of signaling addresses the conditions under which Britain and France can infer Germany's type from its actions.

The history of the late 1930s offers a concrete example of signaling. The British and French governments had difficulty determining whether Hitler's demands were limited to the creation of a Greater Germany that unified all ethnic Germans in one state or whether Hitler sought domination of the European continent. Their proper response to his demand for the Sudetenland in the Munich crisis hung on this point. The action that convinced most, but not all, outside Germany that Hitler's demands were not limited was the German occupation of the rump of Czechoslovakia.

A Germany that sought only to unify ethnic Germans in one state would not have occupied the non-German parts of Czechoslovakia. The signal embedded in Hitler's occupation of Czechoslovakia was that his aims were not limited to a Greater Germany alone.

The strategic logic of signaling depends on the *separation* of types. If discrete types take different actions, then observers can infer the actor's type from its actions. The actions each type would take, however, depends on its own motivations and the strategic setting. It may be that some types deliberately imitate other types in order to prevent others from ascertaining their precise motivations. Hitler deliberately acted early on as if he sought limited revisions in the status quo to conceal his true long-term objectives. If he had made it clear in 1933 that he sought to overturn the European status quo, then Britain and France would have taken a stronger stand against him at that time. Hitler's ultimate goals were served by imitating a less belligerent type. When types take the same action, they are said to *pool*, and others can learn nothing new about their type from that action. What might lead types to separate as opposed to pool?

After the Yom Kippur War of 1973, negotiations between Israel and the Arab states were difficult to initiate in spite of the apparent common interest in a negotiated settlement of territorial issues. A signaling problem loomed here. Israel could make territorial concessions now in the hope of Arab recognition and willingness to live in peace together later. But territorial concessions made Israel more vulnerable to later attacks. Further, Arab leaders seeking the destruction of Israel would be willing to make statements indicating otherwise if those statements could lead to territorial concessions that would facilitate their ultimate goal. How could an Arab leader convince the Israelis that he was the type with whom they could live in peace?

Sadat demonstrated his willingness to live in peace by going to Jerusalem, addressing the Knesset, and declaring "no more war." This action was extremely costly for Sadat; his foreign minister resigned, Egypt was expelled from the Arab League, and eventually Sadat was assassinated by extremists upset at the peace deal with Israel. It was precisely these costs that made Sadat's declaration of peace a credible signal of his intentions. That action declared to a variety of audiences, international and domestic, what Sadat's intentions were. He could not deny that he was offering peace to Israel. Sadat would bear the costs outraged Arabs would bring to bear even if Israel did not reciprocate with territorial concessions (and, as it turned out, he would pay with his life even after Israel returned the Sinai Peninsula to Egypt). Around the same time, other Arab leaders, such as King Hussein, were meeting in secret with Israeli leaders. But their offers of peace did not carry the same credibility as Sadat's signal precisely because they were private. King Hussein bore no costs from his offers as long as the negotiations stayed private.

Sadat's signal was credible because it separated him from the other types of leader he could have been. Think about Israel's problem of trying to infer Sadat's type from his actions. He might be sincere or he might be using negotiations to seek a military advantage to attack after regaining the Sinai Peninsula. But which type would be willing to bear the costs of the unilateral public declaration of peace? The sincere type might be willing to do so, but the insincere type would be unlikely to accept that cost given that the Israelis were under no obligation to reciprocate the gesture. Indeed, the return of the Sinai to Egypt took long and hard negotiations before it was completed. There was no guarantee of tangible rewards to counter the outrage of many Egyptians, inside and out of Sadat's government. Because the sincere type might make a public statement and the insincere type would not, Israel could infer that Sadat's offer was sincere and that he intended to live in peace with Israel if the Sinai were returned.[4]

Separation of types is central to successful signaling. One type has to do something another type is unlikely to do. Then the observer can conclude it is facing the former and not the latter. If all types take the same actions, then others gain no new information about what type they are facing. One way to separate types is by costs. A type can signal its intentions by taking actions that inflict costs it is willing to bear but other types are not. *Costly signaling* is the common term for the idea that costs can separate types.

In international politics, creating such costs for separation can be difficult because the costs must be created endogenously among actors; they cannot be imposed by a higher body. In the 1930s example, consider the problem facing an opportunistic Germany that does not seek continental domination. Although it does not seek war with Great Britain and France, it is happy to absorb any territory, say Poland, that Britain and France will not fight to defend. Because Britain and France want to preserve the independence of the Eastern European states, they make promises to defend those countries against a German attack. Are those promises credible? The only way Germany can test British and French resolve to defend

---

[4] Maoz and Felsenthal (1987) describe Sadat's declaration as a self-binding commitment. In their definition, a self-binding commitment exists when a party offers compensation to be held by a third party and which is awarded to the aggrieved party if the former violates its commitment to the latter. However, this case does not fit that definition. Sadat paid the cost of his public declaration regardless of what he did later. A self-binding commitment here would be if Sadat offered to let the Israelis assassinate him if he broke his pledge or some other costly sanction that would be imposed on him only if he violated his commitment. I have drawn on Maoz and Felsenthal's description of the case for relevant facts in my discussion.

Poland is by attacking Poland. Lesser threats short of war are not sufficient to discourage irresolute types of Britain and France that wish to
deter German aggrandizement without being willing to pay the price to
defend Poland. However, if an attack on Poland reveals that Britain and
France are committed to its defense, then Germany does not want to attack Poland. Germany is in the difficult position of being unable to impose
the costs necessary to separate the possible types of Britain and France
short of war. This problem is common in international conflict because
often the prospect of war is the source of possible costs that could create
separation. But if one side can convince the other that it is willing to fight,
the other will back down. However, if such a threat always deters the
latter, then any type of the former—even the type that does not want to
fight under any circumstances—would like to make that deterrent threat.
If there is no chance of war, there is no cost for making the threat in this
situation (Fearon 1995, 390–401).

The Sadat example is different. In that case, outside audiences, the other
members of the Arab League and domestic groups in Egypt, impose the
costs on President Sadat. Sadat's act of going to Jerusalem is designed
precisely to produce those costs from those outside actors. Israel benefits
from these costs because they allow Sadat to demonstrate that he is sin-
cerely interested in a lasting peace. *Audience costs* are one way actors can
separate their type and convince others of their motivations (Fearon 1990,
1994a). These audiences could be domestic or foreign; the key point is
that they are not the intended recipients of the signal.[5] The costs are not
purely derived from the actions of the side the sender is trying to inform.

Sometimes types separate even without costly signals (Morrow 1994b).
Costless signals can help actors coordinate their actions. Coordination is
a problem when multiple acceptable courses of action are available, and
it is important that all agree on what will be done. Actors can use costless
signals to decide which course of action to adopt. United Nations resolutions may be an example of such costless signals in action. The act of
voting on such resolutions does not impose costs; of course, a vote may
prove to be costly because of the actions that follow the resolution. After
Iraq's invasion of Kuwait in 1990, the first United Nations resolution
expressed common outrage at the invasion, and all members of the Security Council, even Cuba, voted in favor of Resolution 660. Once Iraq
failed to comply, the problem of coordination loomed. Courses of action
ranged from moral condemnation of the invasion to the use of military
force to eject Iraqi forces from Kuwait. International coordination would
make any course of action more effective. The Bush administration used

---

[5] Fearon (1994a) uses the term *audience costs* to refer only to the costs imposed by domestic audiences on their own leaders.

further Security Council resolutions to steer the international response to the Iraqi invasion, first through economic sanctions and then Operation Desert Storm. Voting on these resolutions provided a way for states to signal costlessly their support (or lack thereof) for the course of action the United States advocated. The strongest resolution received the weakest support; China abstained, and Cuba and Yemen voted against Resolution 678, which authorized the use of military force after January 15, 1991, if Iraq did not withdraw from Kuwait.[6] The resolutions did not prevent states from taking actions they felt were justified. The Bush administration could have launched Operation Desert Storm even without Resolution 678. Nevertheless, that resolution did reflect the willingness of most nations to accept the American position on how to get Iraq out of Kuwait. The resolutions had both international and domestic value to the Bush administration. Seeking those resolutions was a signal within the international community of the solution the United States preferred. Voting on them provided a way for other nations to express their support or opposition. Saddam Hussein, on the other hand, held out for a costly signal of American intentions, but he had more at stake in Kuwait than any other actor (see Freedman and Karsh 1993 on the Gulf crisis).

The strategic logic of signaling requires different types to take different actions. Other actors do not know an actor's type, so they must infer its type from its actions. If all types take the same action, other actors cannot draw any inferences from its actions. Costs for taking certain actions are often, but not always, necessary for types to separate. In most political situations though, the actors typically impose these costs on one another.

This observation has two important implications. First, partial separation of types rather than complete separation is likely to be the rule. Think of extended deterrence when the threatening state has incentive to doubt the resolve of the state making the deterrent threat. The latter may be the type that will carry out its threat or it may be the type that is bluffing. The threatening state wants to press its threat only if the deterring state is bluffing. Complete separation of these two types requires an action that the resolute type is willing to take while the bluffing type is not. After observing this action, the threatening state can conclude that it is facing the resolute type and so back down from its threat. The action that separates the types would be a perfect deterrent threat—it would never be challenged. However, the bluffers would also like to take that action because it will always succeed with no risk of war. That incentive undermines the logic of separation; the threatening state can no longer conclude that it is facing a resolute defender after observing the action. Partial sepa-

---

[6] Because Cuba and Yemen were temporary members of the Security Council, their "no" votes could not veto the resolution.

ration resolves this paradox. All the resolute states and some of the bluffers make the deterrent threat. After observing the deterrent threat, the threatener challenges some of the time, but not always. The chance that the threat must be carried out imposes a cost, and the chance that the threatener may back down in the face of the deterrent threat provides a benefit.

Second, we should expect that all events exhibit a selection bias when uncertainty is present in a conflict (Morrow 1989; Fearon 1994b). An actor chooses a course of action based on both observable factors, such as military capabilities, and unobservable factors, such as its motivation. Together both determine its ability to prevail in a conflict. The other actor also chooses using the observable factors and its own unobservables. If the former is strong on the observable variables, the latter is less likely to challenge it because it is weaker overall. But if the latter does challenge the former when the former is strong on the observable factors, we know the latter's unobservable factors must be very favorable to it. When the weak challenge the strong, they must have unseen advantages to compensate for their weakness. Those unseen advantages make them more likely to win than the observable factors alone would indicate. The cases we observe are selected on the basis of the unusually favorable private information of actors. This effect may account for the paradox of power, that is, that the powerful do not always prevail (e.g., Mack 1975). It also implies that ex post measures of resolve, such as actions taken in a crisis, must be better predictors of success than ex ante measures. The latter are the observable factors that drive the selection bias.

COMMITMENT

Commitment is a problem because actors often want to make promises that others doubt the actors will be willing to carry out later. If the latter could believe the promises of the former, then both would be better off. When signaling is a central strategic problem, an actor's type determines its future actions. Other actors can infer its future actions from its signal. Commitment, on the other hand, is a dynamic issue. Even if actors know one another's motivations, they have reason to doubt that any of them will carry out actions that are in their interest now. In our earlier 1930s example, Germany knows what types Great Britain and France are. It is in the latter's interest to promise to defend Poland after Hitler occupies the rump of Czechoslovakia. All can avoid costly war if Germany believes that Britain and France are committed to the defense of Poland. But will it be in the interest of Britain and France to fight when Germany threatens war against Poland later or are the costs of war so high that they will back down rather than fight? Or, in the terms used at the time, who is willing to "Die for Danzig?"

Commitment is a problem when actors' incentives change over time. Consider the position of a debtor nation's leader negotiating with the International Monetary Fund (IMF) over loan renegotiation. At the moment, securing new loans is the paramount problem. As the terms of the new loans, the IMF is likely to demand substantial changes in the debtor nation's fiscal and monetary policies. These concessions help restore the debtor nation's economic health, increasing its ability to pay off the new loans. If it reduces its budget deficit over the long run, the interest rate on its debt may drop, making it easier to service both the old and new debt. These arrangements may also increase economic growth in the country. Both are better off if the promise is kept: The country's economy improves, and the IMF's loans are paid off.

These changes are also likely to be painful politically because they will cause a substantial drop in the real incomes of important sectors of society. The leader may very well agree that these changes in policy are necessary to restore economic health to his or her country and agree to make those changes with the full intention of carrying them out. But when elections arrive two years later, the political costs of the new policies are likely to include the government losing reelection. Then both the leader and the IMF might prefer undoing the reforms at that time to the alternative of seeing a party come to power that is opposed to those reforms as a matter of policy. If the debt market anticipates such reneging on the earlier promises (and markets always seem to), the beneficial effects of the initial reforms will not materialize.

This is a commitment problem in that the government would like to commit to the new policies, but others understand that the government's interest in those policies is likely to change over time. If the government could carve those policies in stone, it would. But it cannot, and so others must judge the government's motivations to violate its promises in the future. A problem of commitment also differs from signaling in that others know the type of the actor with the commitment problem. Signaling does not raise a problem of commitment because an actor's actions follow from its type.

Giving other actors power is a common way to make a credible commitment to them. Countries in a balance-of-payments crisis face pressure to tighten capital controls and increase trade protection; both these actions improve a country's balance of payments by reducing capital outflow and decreasing imports. However, those same actions convince the nation's creditors that investing additional funds in the nation will put those funds at risk. States finance trade deficits with capital inflows; a crisis occurs when investors doubt that their funds are safe within a state, and so are unwilling to provide additional funds to meet the trade deficit. Capital controls and trade protection place further investment in the country at risk, exacerbating the crisis. Under the right economic conditions, a better response is to open up capital markets within the country. Investors have confidence, then, that they can get their money out of the country if necessary and so are willing to put more money into the country. By giving investors the power to get their money out, the government has made a commitment to them that increases their willingness to invest further (Haggard and Maxfield 1996). If one actor is worried that another will not honor a commitment, giving the first some power over the outcome can be sufficient to assure that actor of commitment. No one else holds an actor's interest so closely as the actor itself does. Ceding power to an actor gives it the capability to limit its damage if policy changes and thus increases the actor's confidence in acting on behalf of the policy.

Further, capital mobility can be a self-enforcing commitment. Increasing economic openness benefits segments of society with international ties and makes developing international economic ties attractive to firms and individuals that do not have them. Foreign firms have an increased interest in lobbying the government to maintain open capital markets as their involvement in a country increases. All these effects increase the political pressure to continue openness as a policy, making the commitment self-enforcing (Haggard and Maxfield 1996).[7] Some commitments lead to changes that raise the costs for reneging or boost the benefits of continuing the commitment. Both these changes make living up to the commitment more attractive than when it was made. If such costs or benefits are large enough, the commitment can be self-enforcing in that all actors wish to honor it.

Domestic institutions can create ways for leaders to commit themselves internationally. Institutions can share power across many actors, making it difficult for a leader to renege on commitments. The other actors can use their power to make reneging more painful for the leader than carrying out the commitment. Again, Europe in the late 1930s provides an example of such commitment. The German occupation of Czechoslovakia convinced most observers that Hitler could only be stopped by war. Consequently, Britain and France offered guarantees of protection to sev-

[7] Haggard and Maxfield describe this problem as signaling rather than commitment. Clearly there are issues in signaling here because investors try to judge future government policy and pull their funds out in advance of new controls. The commitment problem exists because investors know that the government has the incentive to freeze their capital in the country and fear that the government will do so to meet the crisis, regardless of the government's strength to free movement of capital. This case is an example of how actual problems often contain several strategic problems. Viewing these strategic problems separately helps us to understand the particular strategic logic of each problem.

eral Eastern European nations that were possible future targets of Nazi
Germany, especially Poland. But carrying out those commitments meant
war, and war was a heavy burden to bear. After Germany invaded Poland
on September 1, 1939, Neville Chamberlain and Lord Halifax spent most
of the next two days trying to work out a compromise agreement that
would avoid war between Britain and Germany. The cabinet and the
House of Commons blocked their attempts to wriggle out of their government's commitment to Poland. Had Chamberlain not presented the ulti-
matum to Germany on September 3, his government would have fallen
and a new government would have been formed that would honor the
British commitment to Poland (Watt 1989).

Because political institutions can create credible commitments, the
study of institutions is central to the strategic-choice approach. The next
two chapters address institutions. Chapter 4, by Ronald Rogowski, analyzes how institutions shape strategic choices, and chapter 5, by Peter
Gourevitch, discusses how actors choose among different possible institutions. The points I am about to make are directly relevant and often paral-
leled in the next two chapters, both of which extend and deepen the issues
I raise here.

The precise form of domestic institutions affects the credibility of commitments (Cowhey 1993). First, because leaders wish to hold power, electoral systems in democracies produce different incentives to honor
agreements. Systems, like the British parliamentary system, that focus on
national issues and reward parties for providing collective goods are more
likely to honor commitments that provide such collective goods to their
electorate. Other systems, like the Japanese system, that focus on local
pork barreling and negotiation inside the government are less likely to
support commitments that produce broad-based benefits. The American
system is a combination of the two, a nationally elected president and a
locally elected Congress. Second, transparent procedures increase other
states' confidence that they will be able to determine when commitments
will be violated, and thus protect themselves from the violation. Open
procedures also allow outsiders to judge the strength of the commitment
when it is offered. Because others can judge the strength of a commitment,
the uncertainty about a government's future actions is reduced, allowing
others to take actions in the interest of both without fear of unpredictable
changes in government policy.

Third, divided powers make the establishment and the violation of
commitments more difficult than concentrated power, as in a parliamentary system. The very difficulty of making a commitment can make that
commitment credible. In a parliamentary system, a government can take
on commitments of which the opposition does not approve. An electoral
shift in power can lead the new government to renege on the commitment.

The Constitution of the United States requires a two-thirds vote of the Senate to ratify an international treaty. The required supermajority allows minorities of the Senate to block the ratification of a treaty that the president has negotiated. The president could choose to sign an Executive Agreement instead of negotiating a treaty as an international agreement. Because domestic rules for concluding such an agreement are less stringent, it is easier to get it approved. On the other hand, the treaty has greater credibility precisely because ratification is more difficult. A ratified treaty requires a broad coalition of support in American politics, and so other states can be confident that the treaty commitment is unlikely to be reversed unless the political complexion of the Senate changes dramatically. The commitment is credible precisely because only commitments shared broadly across the spectrum of American politics can be ratified as formal treaties (Martin 1997).[8]

Force may be an attractive option for an actor when other parties are unable to commit themselves to protect its interests. Frieden (1994b) argues that colonialism may be a consequence of an inability to commit. Foreign investors fear expropriation by host governments or other local authorities. So how can host governments commit themselves to protect foreign investments? Not all investments are equally vulnerable to expropriation. Primary production for export, such as oil wells, mines, and plantations, are quite vulnerable. Such operations are tied to their location and can be operated after being seized. Their products can be sold on world markets. Local subsidiaries of transnational corporations are generally not vulnerable to expropriation. Those firms require expertise and connections to branches of the corporation in other countries to produce their goods. Removing the firms from those connections greatly reduces its value. Expropriation of firms producing primary goods, then, is a difficult commitment problem. One solution is for the home country of the investor to establish political control over the host country of the investment—that is, make the host country a colony. Investors receive the same protections they would in their home country. I am not saying that the production of primary goods causes colonialism. Whether primary production leads colonialism or colonial control invites investment in primary production is unclear and irrelevant for the argument here. Colonial control solves the commitment problem for investment in resource extraction and cash-crop agriculture. We should expect greater investment in

---

[8] To be careful, this third argument is screening rather than commitment. Screening is related to signaling. In signaling, the informed party takes an action that signals its type to the uninformed party, which then acts. In screening, the uninformed party offers a series of deals to the informed party, which then accepts one of those deals based on its type. Here the two types of agreements, treaties and executive agreements, screen out the United States based on its inherent political commitment to an international agreement on that issue.

these areas in colonies than in noncolonies, and Frieden (1994b) provides evidence that this is so.[9]

In review, commitment is a problem when an actor wants to make a promise that others doubt. The promise, if honored, leads others to take actions in both parties' interest. However, the promising actor's incentives may change over time, making it unwilling to live up to its promise at a later date. The change in incentives can be anticipated and is the source of others' doubts about the promise. Otherwise, others would treat the promise as fully credible and take the actions in the interest of both. Such predictability does not imply that all promises will be broken, but rather that there is reason to doubt whether promises will be honored. Some commitments prove to be self-enforcing. Those commitments create rewards for honoring the commitment or penalties for reneging on it. Giving power to the party receiving the promise can also make a commitment credible. That power allows the receiver to protect itself from the damage it would suffer if the promise is broken. Domestic institutions can also make international commitments credible. Other domestic actors check a leader's power to renege on his or her promises by opposing such attempts. Ratification procedures restrict leaders to making promises that will be supported by broad domestic coalitions. Such coalitions are less likely to abandon their commitments.

BARGAINING

Actors bargain when many solutions are available and they do not agree on the ranking of those solutions. The question is not only "Should we reach an agreement?" but also "Which agreement should we reach?" Even if all parties prefer a set of possible agreements to the absence of an agreement, they may differ over which possible agreement each likes best. In our example of 1930s Europe, the creation of a joint front against Hitler required not only the agreement to do so but also a specific agreement of what steps would be taken against Nazi threats (Morrow 1993). Even though the Western Allies and the Soviet Union shared a common desire to deter further German expansion in 1939, they could not agree on common measures against the Nazi threat. Stalin sought passage for the Red Army through Poland and Romania; Britain and France were reluctant to ask those countries to grant such passage out of fear the request would force them into the arms of Germany.

---

[9] Frieden's argument is both more subtle and complex than my crude summary. Space prevents me from reiterating his complete argument. None of this argument should be read to imply that either Frieden or I believe that colonialism is just. The argument is merely that

This example identifies a problem of applying the familiar public goods problem to international politics, such as buck passing in the case above. The public goods argument asks whether a public good will be provided but does not ask at what level, in what form, or through what means of taxation. But providing a public good requires answers to the last three questions as well as the first. This is not to say that the problem of individual incentives to avoid contributing to a public good is unimportant or irrelevant. Rather, the provision of public goods may also be frustrated by negotiations over the exact form and level of provision. Different actors may desire different levels and be unable to reach a final agreement. Cooperation theory (Axelrod 1984; Oye 1986a) suffers from the same problem. Prisoner's Dilemma as a model focuses our attention on whether actors cooperate but away from how they choose to cooperate (Krasner 1991; Morrow 1994b).

As an example of negotiations in general, we can use the analogy of bargaining that occurs between a buyer and a seller over an object. The buyer would like a higher price; the seller would like a lower price. Both have a reservation level—a price at which each is indifferent between making the deal and not. The seller's reservation level gives the minimal price he will accept in exchange for the object. The buyer's reservation level gives the maximal price she will pay to gain the object. An actor's reservation level depends on how it views the breakdown of negotiations against the possible settlements. If the seller's reservation level is higher than the buyer's, then there is no price at which both would be willing to make the deal. Otherwise, there is a zone of agreement—a range of prices at which both are willing to make the deal. But within the zone of agreement, the seller wants a higher price, the buyer a lower price.

Reservation levels depend on outside options—each side's alternative to a negotiated agreement. In our hypothetical sale, the seller has an outside option to keep the object, the buyer an outside option to walk away and perhaps seek another seller of a similar object. In a crisis, war is the outside option for both sides. Reservation levels are the agreement a side sees as equivalent to its outside option. In negotiations over a trade regime, the outside option is trade under the current regime with the possibility of one or both sides invoking sanctions.

Outside options reflect the importance of power in negotiations. Because an actor can always choose its outside option rather than negotiate, it can use that power to secure a deal at least as attractive as its outside option. Krasner's (1991) review of the politics of global communications leads him to conclude that power plays a central role. What is power in

---

home countries of investors can solve the commitment problem inherent in some international investments through colonialism.

global communications? When satellite communications became possible in the early 1960s, the United States and leading Western European states created an organization to manage international communications via satellite. The United States held 61 percent of the votes in the organization; Western Europe held 30.5 percent; and Australia, Canada, and Japan shared the remainder. The United States was able to secure such a favorable position because it controlled the technology and could always walk out if it was unhappy with the organizational arrangements. The Europeans, on the other hand, could block access to their national telecommunications networks, reducing the value of any satellite system. This outside option provided the leverage they needed to secure some rights in the organization. Both sides' outside options restrict the range of bargains that were feasible.

What makes the problem of finding an agreeable price difficult is that neither knows the other's reservation level (Chatterjee and Samuelson 1987). When making offers, each must weigh the benefits of asking for a more favorable deal for itself against the risks that the other will reject that offer as unacceptable. Because neither knows the other's reservation level, neither knows what deals the other sees as acceptable. Similarly, each has to think about what a counteroffer is likely to produce when deciding to accept or reject any offer. Negotiations, then, can fail for two reasons: when there is no zone of agreement or when one side breaks off negotiations because it concludes a deal cannot be reached.

Signaling, then, is a critical part of bargaining. An actor's reservation level determines its type. Offers and responses to offers are signals about an actor's reservation level. Effective signals typically require some costs to separate types. Delay in reaching an agreement is a source of costs that allow separation in negotiations. In economics, future consumption is discounted; a dollar today is better than one tomorrow. If we measure the gains of a deal in dollars, a deal today is better than the same deal tomorrow. A buyer who places a higher value on the object may be willing to make higher offers than a buyer who places a lower value on the object simply to get the object sooner. Actors can differ in how they value the present versus the future, what we could call patience. Actors with more patience can secure better bargains than those with less patience (Rubinstein 1982).

In politics, bargains typically cannot be denominated in dollars (and when they can, the dollar amounts rarely indicate the value of each possible bargain to the participants). Political systems can provide actors with powerful reasons to prefer a deal now over the same deal later. The electoral cycle in the United States appears to have been central to progress in arms-control negotiations between the United States and the Soviet

Union during the cold war (Morrow 1991b). Presidents have a strong motivation to deliver results before rather than after an election. They can claim credit for such achievements while running for reelection. But this incentive does not imply that arms-control treaties are signed only during election years. Accomplishments are substitutes, with a strong economy being the best accomplishment an incumbent president can claim. The anticipation of the coming election and the possibility that the sitting president may seek a treaty to enhance his electoral chances influences both sides' negotiating stances. Good economic conditions lead the American administration to believe its electoral chances are better, reducing the need for a treaty, and the reverse is true when economic conditions are poor.

Political systems can also structure bargaining to one actor's advantage over another within the same system. Take-it-or-leave-it offers can provide great bargaining leverage. The side that can make such a final offer can extract the best possible deal from the other side if it knows the latter's reservation level. If it does not know its opponent's reservation level, it must judge the risk of a breakdown against the benefits of receiving a better deal when it makes a take-it-or-leave-it offer. Such offers, then, are not an unalloyed boon. They do, however, eliminate the problem of delay in negotiations. They also reduce the threat of bargaining breakdown if the side making the final offer has a firm idea of what the other side will accept.

Why might actors agree to bind themselves by granting one side the power to make a take-it-or-leave-it offer? The United States Congress has repeatedly voted "fast-track" procedures that allow the president to negotiate trade treaties and then submit them for an up-or-down vote. It appears that Congress is giving the executive branch the power to make the Congress a take-it-or-leave-it offer in the area of trade policy. The president, elected by a national constituency, seeks different deals on international trade than does Congress, composed of many locally elected members. This structural advantage in the negotiations between the president and Congress has helped Presidents Bush and Clinton negotiate the North American Free Trade Agreement (NAFTA) and the General Agreement on Tariffs and Trade (GATT) without direct congressional interference and then submit the final treaties for the approval of both houses of Congress.

Given their different preferences over trade policy and the power of a take-it-or-leave-it offer, why would Congress submit themselves to such an offer? First, Congress renews fast-track authority only for a limited time, although it does so repeatedly. The approval typically lays out ground rules for the negotiations, so that central congressional interests will be protected. Fast-track procedures also provide a way for Congress to oversee the negotiations with another country (O'Halloran 1994). Second, fast-track procedures make negotiations between the president and Congress more predictable. Ratification of treaties requires two-thirds of the Senate according to the U.S. Constitution. The fast-track procedure requires majority votes of both chambers, seemingly introducing the House into the business of international treaties. The House always had indirect power over a trade agreement because it could affect barriers and other measures that influence international trade. Including the House in the procedure directly reduces its motivation to seek remedies outside the negotiations. Such measures make it easier for the president to head off congressional pressure against a final treaty by including the concerns of Congress in the international negotiations. The president gains greater confidence in getting a treaty approved, and Congress gains greater control over the substance of the treaty. Throughout history, Congress has found a variety of institutional innovations that allow it to influence ongoing international trade negotiations (Goldstein 1988). The question of choice among institutions is the topic of chapter 5 of this volume.

Bargaining among the members of Congress themselves provides a third reason for adopting fast-track procedures. Many members have some local interest that each would like to protect from foreign competition. In total, trade protection is a negative-sum proposition; although some may benefit, others lose more in aggregate through higher prices. Members of Congress then wish to logroll—that is, combine a large package of protective measures into one large bill that benefits its supporters and harms all others. The majority benefits at the expense of the minority. Some districts have to be excluded from the deal because each individual protective measure is a losing proposition; if all districts received protection, then all would be net losers. Their small losses on measures to protect other districts would cancel out their large gain on the protection of their own interest. The strategic logic of this multilateral bargaining can lead to inefficient logrolls, bills where a total net loss occurs (Baron and Ferejohn 1989; Baron 1991). The problem resembles the child's game of musical chairs. Those included in the bill are moderate losers, those excluded are big losers, and the member who proposes the bill is the big winner. A member votes for a bill where his or her district is protected to avoid the possibility of being excluded in the replacement bill if the current bill fails. Better to grab one of the chairs than be left out totally. This dynamic of multilateral bargaining within Congress can lead to inefficient protection.

Fast-track procedures provide a way around this problem by placing the power of proposal in the hands of the president. The president has a national constituency, so he is more sensitive to the total costs and benefits of trade protection. He is likely to propose protection only for districts where he needs the political support, either to pass the bill or to help his party (Lohmann and O'Halloran 1994). The third reason for fast-track procedures is to reduce the logrolling of protective interests in Congress. Fast-track procedures serve as a commitment device for Congress among its members against the incentive to engage such district-specific protection.

Multilateral bargaining presents other strategic problems as well (Kahler 1992; Martin 1992a). The more parties in the negotiations, the less likely a zone of agreement for all parties exists. Further, the more parties in the negotiations, the greater the negotiations are delayed simply because more positions must be exchanged. A possible solution to this problem is to reduce the number of parties needed to reach an agreement. Recalcitrant parties can be dropped from the negotiations and excluded from the final deal. Small groups of powerful parties can create minilateral negotiations and then present their agreement to the full body for approval. Such minilateral negotiations could occur either by delegation from the entire body or by presumption of the minilateral negotiators. Removing recalcitrant groups or permitting minilateral negotiations, both of which reduce the number of negotiators, have the same strategic effects: First, they increase the chance that a zone of agreement exists among the active parties; second, they reduce the time needed to reach a final agreement. Other parties might agree to minilateral negotiations in order to secure a less favorable deal sooner than they would through full multilateral negotiations.

Bargaining can be over multiple issues as well as among multiple actors. Linkage across issues can create a zone of agreement when none exists on one issue alone (Tollison and Willett 1979; Stein 1980). Linkage is possible when the parties do not perfectly agree on the relative importance of the issues; it need not be that they disagree about which issue is more important.[10] But often parties do not explore linking issues when linkage might solve a crisis (Morrow 1992). For instance, China did not offer linkage to India before their 1962 border war, even though two different areas of the border were in dispute. A trade of concessions in each area seemed obvious. However, the Chinese believed that the Indians would view a linkage offer as a signal of Chinese weakness. They did not offer linkage and instead tried to persuade the Indians of Chinese military superiority. That attempt failed, the crisis escalated, and China humiliated India in a brief border war.

Persuasion can be crucial to bargaining. Negotiations on environmental issues often center on the use of policy positions to convince other actors

---

[10] Like international trade, linkage depends on comparative, not absolute, advantage.

of the magnitude of the problem. For example, the United States adopted a strong position on restricting the production of chlorofluorocarbons (CFCs) in 1986 (Haas 1992, 206–11). This position advocated controls that the then current understanding of the problem of ozone depletion did not say were necessary. This strong stance was adopted, in part, as a negotiating ploy to ask for more than the U.S. negotiators were willing to settle on. Nevertheless, it also dramatized the issue and created room for the scientific community to agree on appropriate policies and convince their governments to adopt these policies. Persuasion is possible when actors are uncertain about their own reservation levels (Morrow 1994b). The alternative to a negotiated deal is often unclear. In the ozone case, scientific uncertainty about the consequences of CFCs for the atmosphere made the value of the status quo unclear. The economic and political costs of restricting the production and use of CFCs were clear to governments, but how bad the problem was in the absence of controls on CFCs was not apparent. A more complete understanding of the problem, primarily through dramatic new evidence, helped convince recalcitrant states to sign the agreement to restrict CFCs.

Finally, commitment problems can make bargaining fruitless. There is little point in negotiating an agreement to which one side cannot commit. Consider the problem of an ethnic minority negotiating with the majority group over the constitution of their country (Fearon 1993). A zone of agreement exists in the sense that both sides would prefer a range of settlements to warfare. But if the majority is large enough and the institutions such that the minority cannot block institutional change or influence future policy, the majority cannot commit to a settlement. They can always use their superior numbers to undo the agreed-on institutions and policies. The minority group will get nothing in the future, so even a dismal prospect in war is better than any agreement. The inability of the majority to commit themselves to uphold the agreement eliminates any need to negotiate. The commitment problem must be solved before bargaining can begin.

In summary, bargaining occurs because reservation levels and often the existence of a zone of agreement are not common knowledge. An actor's reservation level is the deal it sees as equivalent to its outside option, its alternative to a negotiated agreement. Signaling and commitment are central to bargaining. Negotiating stances operate, in part, as signals of reservation levels. Delay can create the costs needed for types to separate. Inability to solve commitment problems can render bargaining pointless. Political institutions can give special powers, such as the ability to make a take-it-or-leave-it offer, to one or more parties in bargaining. Linkage can create a zone of agreement where one does not exist on each issue individually. Multilateral bargaining is typically more difficult because the presence of more actors reduce the likelihood that a zone of agreement exists. However, the threat of exclusion can make multilateral bargaining easier than bilateral bargaining. If actors are uncertain about their own reservation levels, then other actors can persuade them through negotiations.

WHAT HAVE WE LEARNED FROM THE STRATEGIC-CHOICE APPROACH?

How do these three strategic problems change the way we think about central issues in international politics? This section discusses two issues in international politics, alliances and crisis bargaining, where the strategic approach has led to a fundamental rethinking. These two illustrations are not the only examples; rather, they are a sample of how the strategic approach has changed the field. The last three sections examined how three strategic problems were common across many issues in international politics; this section asks how strategic interaction has changed our understanding of two issues in international politics. Just as signaling, commitment, and bargaining are not the complete set of strategic problems possible in international politics, alliances and crisis bargaining are not a complete survey of all the issues where the strategic approach is changing how we think.

Alliances

Alliances are typically thought of as a way to "balance," that is, amass capabilities against a common threat (e.g., Walt 1987). This idea led to a pair of questions: What constitutes a threat, and what factors might lead states to fail to balance when they should? The distinction between balancing power (Waltz 1979) versus balancing threat (Walt 1987) addressed the first question. Empirically, the explanation of an alliance revolved around the determination of whether a common threat existed to both parties.

In answer to the second question, states might fail to balance in order to "pass the buck." This argument draws on the theory of public goods. Defeating a potential dominant state provides a security benefit for all states. However, war is costly for the states that fight the aspiring hegemon. A nation might not join in the common effort against an aggressive state in the hope that others will have to pay the cost of defeating the threatening power. Further, perceptions about the offense-defense balance could strengthen these incentives to "free ride" (Christensen and Snyder

1990). Because the security calculation solely addresses international concerns, domestic politics can only be an impediment to wise policy in the typical approach.

The public goods analogy to alliances faces at least two problems. First, two nations fighting together against a common threat have a greater chance of winning than either does alone. Security, then, is not a pure public good because the level of the good increases with the number of nations contributing. Second, winning a war provides selective benefits to the victors; they can alter the status quo as they wish. For example, the Soviet Union had gone a long way to defeating Nazi Germany on land by May 1944. If the public goods argument was correct, then the United States and Great Britain need not have launched the D-Day invasion of Western Europe. The success of that invasion sealed Hitler's military fate, increasing the chance that the United Nations would win, and gave control of Western Europe to the Western Allies, a selective benefit for them. Both these problems suggest that the public goods analogy is inappropriate for the question of intervention in war.

A straightforward cost-benefit calculation is more appropriate (cf. Altfeld and Bueno de Mesquita 1979). Do the benefits of intervention—a greater chance of victory for the side you favor and a share of the spoils for yourself—exceed the costs of intervention for the state considering whether to enter the conflict? A state might decline to intervene because its costs of war exceed the benefits it receives from its intervention even when the total benefits produced by its intervention—including the added chance of victory to other states on its side—exceed its costs. However, this explanation differs from a free-riding story about public goods.

There is a deeper problem to the conventional approach to alliances. *It does not explain why states need formal agreements in advance to come to one another's aid.* A state is free to intervene on behalf of another that has been attacked even if they lack an alliance. Alliances are not a precondition for intervention. Further, alliances cannot bind parties to intervene in each other's behalf. A state can fail to come to the aid of its ally if it deems that the cost exceeds the benefit of its intervention when war breaks out. Alliances are formal commitments to coordinate policies, typically codified in a treaty. Because actions can be coordinated without such a formal agreement, the key question about alliances is why write it down.

Presumably it is costly to form alliances; otherwise, states would form alliances freely. Alliances might provide a benefit that would always be attractive were there no cost in forming an alliance. Why would a state make a costly commitment if the commitment is not necessary for intervention? This is the question the strategic-choice approach asks about alliances.

Alliances could deter threatening powers or increase the allies' chance of winning a war through prewar coordination (Morrow 1994c). The possibility of an alliance deterring a threatening power requires the latter to be uncertain about the credibility of the allies' commitment to one another. A threatening power may be uncertain about the strength of the allies' interest in one another. It might suspect that the cost of intervention for one ally exceeds its benefit of coming to the other ally's aid. An alliance could deter the threatening power if it lessened the threatener's uncertainty sufficiently.

Even if an alliance does not deter a threat, it could have value if it raises the allies' ability to fight together. Wartime coordination of military effort is difficult. Prewar coordination through an alliance could lessen that difficulty. The militaries of the allied nations could arrive at joint war plans and coordinate the structure of their forces. Even if deterrence of a threat is impossible, an alliance could still be useful.

Deterrence could be accomplished if an alliance convinced the threatening state that the allies would, in fact, come to one another's aid if it attacks one of them. Alliances could deter if they signal the intention to intervene or if they raise the costs of failing to intervene (Fearon 1997; Morrow 1991a, 1994c; Smith 1995). A decision to intervene in a war on behalf of another nation involves a comparison of the costs and benefits of such intervention. The threatening power may be uncertain about the degree of shared interests between the prospective allies—the benefits of intervention—and about how the prospective intervening state views the likely costs of war. An alliance could deter the threatening power if the formation of the alliance convinced that power that the allies would come to one another's aid.

A costly signal could convince the threatening state that the allies will come to one another's aid if it attacks one of them. A state that was unwilling to come to the aid of its ally might not be willing to pay the cost of forming the alliance. Alliances could impose such costs by forcing the allies to reconcile conflicting interests (Morrow 1993) or by restricting a state's autonomy (Altfeld 1985). In the former case, domestic groups would be unhappy that their leader has compromised on foreign-policy goals which they view as important. In the latter case, the coordination of policy in an alliance could restrict a nation's foreign policy in the future.

An alliance could be credible because it changes the basic calculation for intervention. Military coordination could raise the allies' ability to fight together, raising the benefit of intervention (Morrow 1994c). Domestic or international audiences could punish leaders that fail to honor their alliance commitments (Smith 1995). Both these effects could make an alliance a self-enforcing commitment. Once made, each ally wishes to live up to its commitment; the consequences of backing down are worse than the costs of honoring the commitment.

At an extreme, the credibility problem could be dealt with by forming a stronger form of security relationship, such as a protectorate (Lake 1996). If the threatening power still doubts the credibility of a security guarantee made through an alliance, it may be in both parties' interest to seek a closer, tighter relationship. For instance, Churchill offered French leaders a formal union between their states as France was falling in June of 1940, in an attempt to convince them to continue to fight against Nazi Germany. Protectorates can form when the parties are quite different in capabilities; the stronger gains a greater degree of political control over the weaker than would be possible under an alliance, and the weaker gains greater security against external and internal threats (Morrow 1991a discusses asymmetric alliances that have similar motivations). The typical approach to alliances had difficulty recognizing such arrangements as anything but alliances among equals. That approach cannot explain why the parties seek a tighter institutional form than a simple alliance.

All the arguments above require alliances to be costly; what are these costs? First, allies align their foreign policies to enhance the credibility of their mutual commitment. These shifts require the allies to abandon some of their own policies that they like and adopt some of their ally's policies which they would not adopt in the absence of the alliance. These changes in foreign policy are costly to the allies. Second, some alliances lead to the coordination of the allies' military forces so their joint forces will fight more effectively. Such specialization makes each ally's forces less effective if they have to fight without their ally. Military coordination in itself can also be costly.

The strategic-choice approach suggests that alliances are signals or commitment devices. They might operate as signals of mutual interest among the allies, deterring threatening powers. The threatening power's uncertainty about the allies' willingness to come to one another's aid is reduced by an alliance precisely because forming an alliance is costly. Alliances might serve as commitment devices so that leaders will live up to their commitment if push comes to shove. National leaders intervene on behalf of their allies because they will be punished if they do not intervene.

All these arguments differ from the typical approach to alliances. Domestic politics, which are simply a hindrance to wise policy in the typical approach, become central to an understanding of alliances. Domestic audiences impose costs on leaders who form alliances. These costs could occur in peacetime, making the alliance a signal, or, if the alliance is abrogated, creating a commitment mechanism. In the extreme case of a protectorate, the protector limits the autonomy of the protected nation's domestic politics and foreign policy. The arguments drawn from the strategic-choice approach address the question of why nations choose to write down their agreements. The typical understanding cannot answer that question.

Crisis Bargaining

What determines which side prevails in a crisis? Before the strategic-choice approach, the typical answer was a demonstrable advantage in capabilities or resolve. Crises, in this view, were competitions in risk taking. As Jervis (1979, 292) put it, "each side decides whether to stand firm by examining its payoffs and estimating the likelihood that the other will retreat." The risk of war arises because of the chance that neither side backs down. A state's resolve (or capabilities, depending on the specific version of the argument) determined its payoff, and thus its willingness to hold firm. The state with lesser resolve would back down first, and so the state with greater resolve would win. I will call this argument "the received view."

This position led to two arguments about why some crises ended in war, misperception, or miscalculation, on the one hand, and an incorrect distribution of capabilities, on the other. According to the first argument, war occurred when the side that should back down failed to realize its inferiority. It knew its own resolve but misperceived its opponent's resolve, and thus the likelihood that the other side would back down. The latter argument addresses whether the balance of capabilities led to war or peace. There were opposing views here. Some contended that an even distribution of capabilities led to peace; others argued the opposite, that a preponderance of capabilities prevented war.

These arguments were examined empirically through case studies and statistical tests. The results of the statistical tests were mixed. Huth and Russett (1984), for example, tested whether advantages in resolve and capabilities led to greater success in crises of extended deterrence. Some measures did predict success, others did not, but the argument did not predict any variation in which measures should fit. Extensive research was done on the relationship between the distribution of capabilities and the occurrence of war. Again, the results were mixed (cf. Siverson and Sullivan 1983). Some found that equal distributions of capabilities led to peace; others found that a preponderance led to the peaceful resolution of crises.

Both the accepted theory and the empirical work based on it raised questions. According to the received view, the balance of resolve (or capabilities) determined which side prevailed in a crisis. If so, why would the side with less resolve even enter, much less escalate, a crisis? If it knew that it would lose in a crisis, then it should submit immediately. The side with less resolve would enter and escalate a crisis only if it did not know that it was less resolved than its opponent. Arguments about the psychological origins of misperception tried to fill this gap (e.g., Jervis 1976). On the empirical side, why did the measures of resolve often fail to predict the outcome of crises? If the more resolute state prevailed, then simple measures of resolve should be correlated with success, and the positive correlation should hold across different measures.

The answer is that a state's resolve is its private information, and such private information generates uncertainty that has critical effects on bargaining (Morrow 1989; Fearon 1995). States cannot know each other's resolve and so must make judgments about the other's future actions when deciding what to do. Such judgments are based on what a state believes regarding its opponent's intentions before the crisis and what it can learn about them from that opponent's actions during the crisis. Actions in a crisis operate as signals of a state's resolve. Each side in a crisis can try to convince the other that it is willing to fight for the stakes, and so the latter should back down rather than risk war.

As we saw in the section on signaling, costs are needed to separate types. If escalation is cost-free, then even the least resolute type of state wants to escalate. Consequently, the other state can learn nothing about the former's resolve from its escalation of the crisis. If escalation is costly, then less resolute types may prefer surrendering the stakes to escalating in an effort to prevail. Escalation signals greater resolve.

At first blush, the risk of war could be the cost that makes escalation a signal. However, war occurs because one side decides that war is better than continuing bargaining.[11] If a state prefers bargaining to war at the beginning of a crisis, why might it change its mind later in the crisis? It cannot simply be that it now believes the other is unwilling to offer an acceptable deal because it assumes the answer to the problem. A state's leader requires information to change his or her judgment about the other side's likely future actions. Such information requires separation of types—the other state's less resolute types must back down—and separation requires costs for continuing.

Crises are public actions, and those not directly involved can learn from them as well as the involved parties. Outside actors can be the source of costs that allow leaders to signal their resolve. Domestic actors may choose to punish leaders who lose a crisis or war (Bueno de Mesquita and Siverson 1995; Smith 1996); such costs are called "audience costs" (Fearon 1994a). Leaders of other states could draw inferences about the lack of resolve of a state that backs down, and then take advantage of it in the future; call these "reputation costs" (Nalebuff 1991). In either case, a state leader could reach a point where these audience or reputation costs were so high that he or she preferred war to backing down. These costs

---

[11] In the interest of space, I avoid discussing the contention that war can arise purely from events exogenous to the decision makers. Obviously such exogenous chances of war can create costs that could separate types (e.g., Powell 1987). The real question is whether such exogenous chances of war exist, and, if so, why leaders tolerate them.

build during a crisis, explaining why a state that went to war began by bargaining and only later decided that war was preferable to continued negotiations (Fearon 1994a). Because these costs increase over the lifetime of a crisis, less resolved types want to back down sooner than more resolute types. Although all types prefer prevailing to backing down, the less resolved types are more likely to back down the longer the crisis continues. At some moment, accepting the costs of backing down is better than continuing the crisis because the chance of eventually getting the other side to back down does not outweigh the cost of continuing the conflict.

This argument is complex, so let us review it briefly before following its implications. Outside actors impose costs on a state's leader if he or she backs down in a crisis. These costs build over the life of the crisis. These costs allow the possible types of the leader to separate; more resolute types are willing to continue the crisis longer and bear larger audience costs if he or she must back down in the end. At some point these costs are so great that the leader prefers war to further negotiations. The process of separation is necessary because only a leader knows his or her resolve in the crisis. The opposing leader must judge that resolve from the leader's actions and what he or she knows before the crisis. The willingness of a leader to suffer costs convinces the opposing leader of the former's resolve to accept costs. The greater the audience (or reputation) cost, the more convincing the signal. In crises, then, the state with the greater ability to generate audience costs, not the state with the greater resolve, has the advantage. The state with greater resolve cannot convince the other side of its resolve if it lacks the ability to generate substantial audience costs for backing down. The only way a state can demonstrate its resolve is to place itself in a position where backing down in the face of war is extremely costly. This demonstration works precisely because an irresolute state—one that would like to back down at the brink of war—would not place itself in that position.

This view clarifies and modifies the received view substantially. Let us return to the quote from Jervis: "Each side decides whether to stand firm by examining its payoffs and estimating the likelihood that the other will retreat." The payoffs of the other determine the likelihood it will retreat. Bargaining tactics in the received view attempt to change the other side's payoffs (cf. Snyder and Diesing 1977). What exactly does "changing the other side's payoffs" mean? Each side presumably knows its own value for the stakes and its willingness to fight.[12] In the new view, informa-

---

[12] Some models assume that states do not know their value for war because they are uncertain about each other's capabilities (Morrow 1989, Bueno de Mesquita, Morrow and Zorick 1997). The difference is not important for the argument here.

tion about the other side's payoffs changes, and so judgments about its likely future actions, and consequently a state's own judgment about what it should do now, change with that information. Further, actions that a resolute type would take, but an irresolute type would not, transmit information. The received view lacked this insight and so tried to determine empirically which bargaining tactics were effective. However, the actions that generate costs for a nation in one crisis do not necessarily generate costs for another nation in a different crisis.

Misperception and miscalculation are central to the received view. War occurs because a state misjudges what the other side will do. The new view places uncertainty about the other side's private information as central. When knowledge is not available and both sides have incentives to misrepresent their private information, misperception must be endemic. Indeed, perceptions during a crisis that prove to be correct after the crisis are exceptionally unlikely in the face of such uncertainty. The new view stresses the difficulty of separating types and eventual "lock-in" from growing audience costs as triggering war. As a crisis continues, both sides become increasingly convinced of the other side's resolve. Meanwhile, the costs for backing down are growing. At some point the costs of backing down and a state's belief that the other side will not back down grow sufficiently that even a costly war is better than continuing to negotiate. In a sense, both sides have misperceived in such a situation. Both would have preferred backing down at the beginning of the crisis if they knew it would end in war. However, they could not know that the other side would not back down at the beginning and so were willing to enter the crisis.

The new view is more pessimistic than the received view. In the latter, psychological causes are the source of misperceptions, and thus war could be eliminated if those psychological biases could be overcome. The new view stresses that uncertainty, and thus misperception, is essential to the process. Actors cannot know what each other's resolve is, and both have incentives that make honest revelation of their resolve incredible and so impossible. Even if actors could overcome their psychological barriers (as they do in a game-theoretic model), they still could not know each other's private information and so could not guarantee that their perceptions were accurate. The strategic logic of a crisis requires and maintains such uncertainty.

How does the new view address the empirical problems presented by the received view? Consider the problem of the inconsistency of measures of resolve as predictors of which side prevails in a crisis. A side's resolve in a crisis depends on both observable factors, such as the size of its military and its commitments before the crisis, and unobservable factors, such as its willingness to accept the costs of war and its precise value for the stakes of the crisis. The latter factors are a state's private information—

what it tries to signal during a crisis precisely because the other side cannot know them. However, the other side does know the observable factors before the crisis begins and can use them to form its judgments when it decides whether to enter a crisis. Those observables that increase a state's resolve are likely to convince the other side to stay out of a crisis. If the other side is willing to start a crisis in the face of such observable advantages for the other side, it must hold unobservable advantages to compensate for its observable disadvantage (Bueno de Mesquita, Morrow, and Zorick 1997; Fearon 1994a). For example, Kugler (1984) has observed that nonnuclear powers often successfully challenge nuclear powers in contradiction of the idea that states with superior capabilities should prevail. Fearon (1994b) points out that nonnuclear powers only challenge nuclear powers over interests that are peripheral to the nuclear power, as Vietnam was for the United States. The nonnuclear power has good reason to doubt the resolve of the nuclear power in such a situation.

This logic produces a selection bias in observed crises. When a state has an observable advantage before the crisis, a crisis only occurs if the other side has unobservable advantages to compensate. Such advantages make it more likely that the side that appears weaker before the crisis will prevail than the observable advantages suggest. This selection effect washes out the significance of measures of resolve that are observable before the crisis (Morrow 1989; Fearon 1994b). Measures of resolve that include behavior during the crisis should and do predict the outcome better. Such measures include both the observable and the unobservable facets of resolve. They also reflect the costs each side was willing to accept during the crisis and thus its actual resolve. This pattern—that ex post measures of resolve perform better than ex ante measures of resolve—is generally true in the empirical literature (e.g., Maoz 1983; Huth 1988).

The other empirical puzzle from the received view concerns the distribution of capabilities and the likelihood of war. Although different arguments based on the received view concluded that roughly equal capabilities made war more or less likely, neither position was consistently supported by empirical studies. The new view contends that there should be no relationship between the distribution of capabilities and war, and so we should not expect to find consistent results across empirical studies. First, war occurs if the parties fail to find a settlement that both prefer to war (Wittman 1979; Morrow 1985). Both demand more than the other is willing to grant. A state's resolve, both the observable and unobservable parts, determines its bargaining position. The balance of capabilities is one of the observable components of resolve. The range of settlements considered should reflect the balance of capabilities; weak states expect a less favorable outcome than strong states do. However, the unobservable part of resolve and the difficulty in signaling that private information clearly determine when they fail to find an agreement acceptable to both. There is no reason to expect that the unobservable dimensions of resolve, such as the willingness to suffer the costs of war, should be systematically related to the observables. If they were, the parties would use the observable part of resolve to reach judgments about the unobservable part of their opponent's resolve.

Second, a state initiates a crisis when it is dissatisfied with the status quo; it believes it can gain through a crisis (Powell 1996a, 1996b). The status quo results from the outcome of earlier disputes, where the balance of capabilities determined the resolution of issues. The status quo, then, incorporates the distribution of capabilities. Dissatisfaction should not be related to the balance. If the balance has changed, the state that has gained should demand more and the state that has lost should be willing to grant a change in the status quo. The success of these negotiations does not depend on the balance because both sides include the balance in the observable part of their resolve. Both these arguments lead to the conclusion that the balance is unrelated to the likelihood of war, the general pattern found in the literature.

The new view of crisis bargaining drawn from the strategic-choice approach changes our understanding of crises. Audience (or reputation) costs allow a state to demonstrate its resolve and convince the other side to back down. Crises are contests in risk taking in the sense that both sides are running the dual risks of war and backing down, while raising the cost of the latter risk and thus making the former one more likely. As with alliances, domestic politics is necessary to explain international politics. Further, states select themselves into crises based on the observable portion of their opponent's resolve. We should expect that ex ante measures of resolve should, at best, be weakly correlated with success in crises. In particular, there should be no systematic relationship between the distribution of capabilities and war.

CONCLUSION: WHERE DO WE GO FROM HERE?

Strategy is fundamental to the study of international politics at all levels of analysis. This paper focused on three strategic problems—signaling, commitment, and bargaining—that are central to the strategic-choice approach. Uncertainty and sequence shape strategic choices. Actors choose their moves to produce preferred outcomes, with outcomes resulting from all the moves made in the game. A player would like to anticipate other players' future moves when it must make a move. Uncertainty about other players' types may make such anticipations difficult. Signaling is a problem of uncertainty and sequence; the sender of the signal is trying to inform the receiver whose later move affects the sender. Commitment depends on sequence; what an actor does now depends on what another will do later, and the former has good reason to doubt the latter's promises about that future move. Bargaining has uncertainty and sequence, signaling and commitment.

Although I have separated the three strategic problems in this paper, international politics presents bundles of strategic problems. The combinations of strategic problems I discussed in the examples of alliances and crisis bargaining are typical. Pure examples of each strategic problem are rare. The examples I have used to illustrate the three strategic problems in this paper should not be considered complete discussions of those cases. The strategic-choice approach directs us to focus on parts of the issues we analyze, rather than all facets of those issues. So we study the signaling problem in alliances separately from the commitment problem. This separation helps to clarify the analysis by eliminating possible confounding effects from other problems. This point implies that we should not expect single explanations drawn from the strategic-choice approach to explain the entirety of a case. Precisely because there are multiple strategic problems in every case, we should not expect any one explanation to account for all the events of a particular case. Rather, the proper tests of these arguments are the variations in behavior that the argument predicts.

Strategic logic requires that we, as analysts, know both actors' preferences and their strategic environment. Both affect choices. In theory, the strategic-choice approach does not give either preferences or the strategic setting priority. Actors select actions to obtain preferred outcomes. Outcomes are the result of the strategic interaction, so the strategic setting determines what outcomes could result. Still, an actor's evaluation of the outcomes—its preferences—determines which outcomes it would like to realize. Action then depends both on preferences and the strategic setting.

Consequently, one cannot directly infer preferences from actions. Signaling highlights the problem of inferring intentions from actions. If all types take the same action, then observers can learn nothing new about the actor's preferences from that action. However, types do not always pool. They often separate, allowing us to make judgments about an actor's motivations from its actions. Only a strategic understanding of the situation allows us to determine whether actions reveal motivations, that is, whether the types pool or separate.

In what directions does the strategic-choice approach point the field? First, the three strategic problems in this chapter often invoke the importance of domestic politics for international politics. Domestic institutions serve as a source of the costs that make signals credible; these institutions can allow states to make credible commitments. Further, domestic institutions face the same strategic problems. It is time to unpack the unitary actor.

A complete understanding of states' strategic settings requires attention to their domestic politics and how those politics affect their foreign policy.

The strategic-choice approach is particularly apt for this unpacking. Because the same strategic problems occur in both international and domestic politics, a general understanding of these problems carries across both levels. This is not to say that the two types of politics are identical. Rather, the same problems recur in different forms in both types of politics. States worry about commitments to one another; domestic groups worry about their ability to commit to one another when domestic institutions that reinforce such commitments are lacking.

Two-level games provide a way to study domestic politics (Putnam 1988). State leaders in such games must consider both the international and domestic audiences for their policies. They choose policy to satisfy both domestic and international conditions. The negotiation of treaties under the pressure of ratification is the common example of a two-level game. Negotiators must consider what treaties can be ratified when they negotiate. They do not have complete freedom to pursue their nation's interest as they define it. Instead, they must keep an eye over their shoulder for what domestic groups will accept.

Principal-agent models provide another way to unpack domestic politics (Bueno de Mesquita and Siverson 1995; Morrow 1991b). Leaders have a large degree of autonomy to set national policy, but they face the possibility of being removed from office if that policy produces bad results. A national leader must consider who has the power to replace him or her and what their interests are. Domestic politics defines who has the power to make and break leaders and under what conditions.

Second, the strategic-choice approach seems ripe for further application in international political economy. Although I have discussed some examples from political economy, most work based on noncooperative game theory has addressed security issues. However, the same strategic problems occur in international political economy. Further, political institutions have been the means to alleviate these strategic problems in both international and domestic politics. The role and scope of institutions is much greater in international political economy than in international security. Institutions shape how actors respond to these strategic problems. Understanding issues in political economy through the strategic-choice approach should help us understand these institutions.

At the same time, there is still much work to be done with the strategic-choice approach on security issues, assuming unitary actors. Central questions about alliances versus arming as sources of security, the roles of military strategy and political bargaining during wars, and foreign policy on security issues in a noncrisis setting remain open. One of the strengths of the strategic-choice approach is its applicability to many different theories of international politics.

CHAPTER FOUR.

Institutions as Constraints on Strategic Choice

RONALD ROGOWSKI

THE PROBLEM

Do domestic political institutions affect the formulation of foreign policy and hence the strategies that actors choose? In the process of aggregating the preferences of various individuals and groups, do institutions exert an independent effect on policy outcomes? More strictly, can we take institutions as exogenous when we analyze strategic choice?

Except in the short run, realism insists, domestic institutions are endogenous, determined wholly by more fundamental variables. Just as the organizational structure of firms is determined by exigencies of the market and of available technologies of production (Williamson 1985), domestic political institutions are shaped by the merciless competition of the anarchic international environment and prevailing military technologies (Hintze 1906; White 1962, chap. 2). Like maladapted firms, maladapted states or alliances[1]—whose organization consistently yields less than optimal policies—must reform or perish. Hence at any given time, most actors face similar institutions and a similar strategic environment.[2]

Non-realists, including a Nobel laureate economic historian (North 1990), observe that competition in the international arena is (surprisingly) often less fierce than in the domestic economy; hence even manifestly suboptimal institutions (the Ottoman and Hapsburg Empires, the former Soviet Union) survive for decades or centuries. Thus most histori-

---

[1] I discuss in this essay the "domestic" institutions of all international actors, including not only conventional post-Westphalian states but alliances (e.g., NATO), confederations (e.g., the European Union), supranational organizations (e.g., the International Monetary Fund), and some nongovernmental organizations (NGOs, e.g., Greenpeace or the Roman Catholic Church). See the fuller discussion below, p. 119 ff.

[2] Two exceptions may be noted. First, sometimes two or more kinds of institutions are equally well adapted to the same environment, somewhat like "factor-intensity reversals" in economics. Charles Tilly (1990) argues, for example, that in the early modern era "coercion-intensive" and "capital-intensive" regimes performed almost equally well. Second, just as in the market, not all actors face identical circumstances; for example, naturally isolated countries, such as Switzerland and, in earlier times, the United States, face fewer external threats.

cal periods display a variety of institutions, and these must be regarded, for practical purposes, as exogenous. And realists concede that we can analyze short-run institutional failure and change only if we understand precisely how domestic arrangements conduce to effective or ineffective policies.

Ultimately the question is empirical, and empirical research to date compels us to regard domestic institutions as exogenous over more than the short run. Institutions vary, and they independently affect the contestation, formulation, and execution of foreign policy in at least five fundamental respects: *policy bias*; *credibility of commitments*; *coherence and stability of policy*; *mobilization and projection of power*; and, not least, *strategic environment of domestic actors*. As selected examples below also make clear, international institutions, such as the European Union or the United Nations, differ in similar ways with similar effects.

Policy Bias

In the felicitous phrase of the late William Riker (1980, 445), institutions are "congealed preferences"; that is, in a world where collective decisions by any nondictatorial mechanism are likely to be unstable and arbitrary (Arrow 1951; McKelvey 1976), institutions "induce equilibrium" (McCubbins, Noll, and Weingast 1987, 1989), indeed inevitably privilege particular equilibria. By defining inter alia whose preferences matter (the franchise), how those preferences will be counted (the electoral system), and how directly representatives must account to constituents (term length, removability),[3] institutions powerfully affect how the "national interest" is defined and what goals foreign policy will pursue. As Peter Gourevitch notes in the next chapter of this volume, that is chiefly why institutional changes are so bitterly contested.

Three kinds of policy bias have attracted particular interest: toward pacifism or aggression; toward protectionism or free trade; and, especially in recent years,[4] toward particular monetary or redistributive policies (stable or inflationary currency, fixed or flexible exchange rates, egalitarian or inegalitarian outcomes).

---

[3] A fuller taxonomy of regime features, extendable to nondemocratic systems and non-state international actors, is presented in the second section of this essay.

[4] Keohane and Nye (1989, 156–58) evidently erred in believing in the 1970s that monetary issues, being "more technical than trade questions," would excite less political controversy.

Credibility of Commitments

Historians, economists, and political scientists have, in recent years, analyzed fruitfully and extensively rulers' problems of time inconsistency and credibility vis-à-vis domestic actors: Governments that can credibly commit *not* to renege on their promises—to respect property, pay debts, keep taxes and inflation low—gain enormously, not least in their ability to mobilize credit (North and Weingast 1989); but how can a sovereign power (by definition unconstrained) credibly constrain its own future actions? In Hilton Root's (1989) memorable query, how does one go about "tying the King's hands"? Parliaments, independent courts, and, most recently, independent central banks—generically, strategies of "delegation"—have all proved part of the answer.

Only recently, however, have students of international politics made the obvious extension of this argument: If the ability to commit oneself credibly matters in domestic politics, it should matter all the more in the anarchic international realm, where treaties that conflict with *raison d'état* have routinely been regarded as "scraps of paper."[5] Putnam (1988), Cowhey (1993), Martin (1995), and Milner (1997, esp. chap. 4) have argued cogently, if at this point still speculatively, that such domestic institutions as ratification procedures, separation of powers, and party discipline strongly affect the credibility of states' international promises. But the precise role of delegation, particularly in multi- or supranational contexts (e.g., the European Union), remains underexplored.

Coherence and Stability of Policy

Even without reneging on commitments, some governments and alliances act less consistently, over time and across policy domains, than others. Fourth Republican France, Italy through much of its modern history, the United States in the 1920s and again since Viet Nam, and the League of Nations of the interwar period have been thought exceptionally mercurial in their foreign-policy orientations and preferences, with domestic agencies working at cross-purposes and overall policy lurching unpredictably. At the opposite extreme, Fifth Republican France, Finland, Switzerland, Federal Germany, and the International Monetary Fund have been seen

---

[5] Not least by the United States, as Robert Keohane (1996) notes. Throughout the nineteenth century, the U.S. government basically kept treaties only with states powerful enough to enforce them; it cavalierly ignored treaty commitments not only to Native American peoples but to China and to Latin American states. Even since 1945, the United States has repeatedly violated its most solemn obligations in the area of international trade, most re-

as relative paragons of consistency. Presumably these differences are, in part, a result of the extent to which domestic institutions successfully "congeal" group and individual preferences (see above).

Mobilization and Projection of Power

Regimes vary in their ability to tax and, when necessary, to fight. Somewhat surprisingly, it turns out that quasi-democratic Britain[6] performed far better in this regard than authoritarian Germany during the run-up to World War I (Ferguson 1994; D'Lugo and Rogowski 1993). Lake (1992) generalizes the point: Democracies have proved far superior in war over the last two centuries (winning roughly 80 percent of their conflicts with autocracies [Lake 1992, 31]) chiefly because of their greater abilities to encourage investment and to mobilize social resources. At a much earlier point, absolutist states enjoyed a similar advantage over late-feudal "estate" regimes (Anderson 1974); but, as Tilly (1990) has argued, the "coercion-intensive" absolutist governments were not clearly superior to the more participatory "capital-intensive" ones of the early trading states. However nebulous the concept, *legitimate* regimes—ones regarded by the great majority of their subjects as entitled to rule, and as representative of society's interests—seem better able to extract resources and to project power abroad.

Strategic Environment

The first four aspects affect how preferences of domestic actors are translated into foreign policy. In addition, institutions constrain those domestic actors' choice of strategies. Strategies that optimize chances of success in a monarchy may negate them utterly in a democracy; what works politically in an American-style system of separated powers can be singularly inept, or criminal, in a Westminster-style cabinet regime.

If these five broad categories are the dependent variables of our story, what are the independent ones? What aspects of institutions influence foreign policy, and how precisely do they work? While students of international relations have advanced perceptive (if, usually, case-specific) hypotheses over generations, the most impressive recent work on institutions has come from analysts of legislatures (chiefly the U.S. Congress),

---

cently by passage of the Helms-Burton Act. See also Morrow's discussion of treaties in chapter 3 of this volume.

[6] Recall that in pre-1918 Britain only about two-thirds of adult males, and no females, could vote.

of regulation, and of delegation. Undergirding this whole stream of analysis is *principal-agent theory* (usefully summarized in Eggertsson 1990, 40–45, and part 2, passim). In this essay I shall rely on this body of work to suggest a research agenda, an analytic scheme, and (by extension from domestic to foreign policy) some hypotheses worth pursuing. The next section lays out the analytic scheme; the third section suggests research topics and hypotheses; and the final section offers conclusions.

ANALYTIC SCHEME

For any given international actor,[7] we posit some set of *principals* with preferences over foreign-policy alternatives.[8] Within a country, this group may consist of the whole population or any proper subset: only adults, only adult males, only adult males of particular races or religions or wealth, only hereditary aristocrats, only the leading members of a ruling party or of an officer corps. Within an alliance or a supranational agency, the set will typically comprise delegates of the constituent states; in a nongovernmental organization (NGO), it will comprise all (or particularly influential) members. Whether restrictive or open, this is the group whose preferences "count" in any meaningful sense, and this group's extent—the outer limit of the informal "franchise"—is the most basic aspect of domestic institutions.

We assume that the group of principals is too numerous to decide policy directly (e.g., by voting) with the requisite dispatch. Rather, policy decisions are delegated to agents, whom, for convenience, we shall call *representatives*;[9] the makeup and mode of selection of these representatives constitute the second chief aspect worth knowing about a country's institutions. We observe at once that issues of agency faithfulness or "slack," of effective monitoring, and of incentive-compatibility (to name only the most prominent), extensively addressed in the principal-agent ("P-A") literature, arise inevitably in any such arrangement.

Finally, we need to know the *decision rules* that bind the agents themselves: When, and in what circumstances, can they commit the larger organization to a particular course of action?

---

[7] Typically, in the post-Westphalia era, a state; but sometimes a supranational agency, a nongovernmental organization, or an alliance.

[8] For what I am calling principals, Bueno de Mesquita and Siverson (1995, 844 ff.) use the term *stakeholders*. Roeder (1993, 24–27) and Shirk (1993, 71–72) refer to the set of principals as the selectorate.

[9] Agents may be chosen through "layers" of delegation, as when U.S. senators were chosen by state legislatures (or, nominally, presidents are still chosen by the Electoral College). So long as these intermediate layers are not themselves engaged in day-to-day formulation or supervision of policy, they are not counted here as agents.

As we shall see momentarily, all the following points about each of these three major aspects likely affect our dependent variables in important ways.

Franchise

Who formally exerts influence, and with what formal weight?[10] Within states, are rural areas, property owners, aristocrats, "peak" interest groups, or particular regions or units (states, provinces, cantons) more powerfully represented?[11] Within alliances or supranational organizations, are all constituent states represented equally or in proportion to wealth of population or (as in the UN Security Council) by status as major victor in a previous war?

Representation

Is there one, or are there few or many, representatives?[12] If more than one, are they members of a single body or of several? What degree of independence do particular kinds of representatives enjoy (are terms fixed or variable; short or long; revocable or guaranteed)?[13] Are representatives chosen by large constituencies (at the extreme, the entire membership or citizenry voting together) or small ones (e.g., geographically defined, single-member districts)? Is the method of choice for a particular body calcu-

[10] Note that some principals, as defined immediately above, may be excluded from the formal franchise, typically by some doctrine of "virtual" representation. Women in the pre-1920 United States had no vote, as is true today for Catholic bishops who are not Cardinals; however, women of that time were supposedly "represented" by the voters (husbands, brothers) whom they could influence, as Catholic bishops today are thought to be "represented" by fellow bishops of princely rank.

[11] In some pre–World War I European states, the wealthy and educated were explicitly granted more votes; typically the greatest landowners were represented in a separate "house" of parliament.

[12] In some of de Gaulle's grander interpretations, the Fifth Republican presidency was sole representative of the nation, all else being embellishment and detail. That extreme to one side, parliaments with strict party discipline may be viewed for most purposes as having only as many representatives as there are party leaders. (One Weimar theorist actually proposed to save time and money by making the Reichstag a small committee of heads of party lists, each armed with a bloc of votes equivalent to the seats his party received under the prevailing system of proportional representation.)

[13] Because principals' contracts with representatives are almost inevitably incomplete, and, moreover, in or among sovereign states are normally unenforceable by independent authority, P-A theory suggests that election and revocation will normally prevail as appropriately incentive-compatible mechanisms of enforcement (cf. Williamson 1985, chap. 12).

lated to insure that representatives replicate the median[14] and/or the variance of their (weighted) electorate? How accurately, and with what lag, do representatives reflect shifts by their median voters, and what penalties attach to "faithless" representation?[15]

Decision Rules

If representative(s) constitute a single body, does that body act by majority or supermajority?[16] If there is more than one body, does any have (limited or absolute) veto?[17] Does the veto bar only passage or also consideration;[18] and how many total "veto points" (Tsebelis 1995) are there? Who initiates proposals, and who sets the agenda for their consideration? Are specific issue areas (e.g., monetary or agricultural policy, education, adjudication) reserved to specialized bodies (states or provinces, commissions, boards, parliamentary committees, courts) or is authority centralized for most purposes in a single body (e.g., a politburo or national cabinet)?[19] Overarching all these considerations, and perhaps most important: Are the decision rules clear and generally respected or are they hazy or frequently violated?

Drawing together the discussion thus far, Table 4.1 presents the independent (institutional) variables vertically and the dependent (foreign policy) variables horizontally. The individual cells will later contain specific hypotheses linking the two.

[14] In a multidimensional policy space, read, in place of "median," "center of gravity."

[15] Long, nonrenewable terms are often designed to insulate representatives from median voter shifts, and plurality systems cost faithless parties (i.e., ones that fail to reflect the median voter) more seats than do systems of proportional representation (think of the Canadian Progressive Conservatives).

[16] Coalition cabinets, for example, normally require for important decisions unanimity of all participating parties; for ratification of treaties, a two-thirds vote of the United States Senate is required (U.S. Constitution, Art. II, Sec. 2, § 2); in the European Union, virtually all legislation requires a "qualified majority" (in practice, a majority of votes and of states) in the Council, while some legislation (and all amendments of the fundamental treaties of Rome and Maastricht) requires unanimity.

[17] Constitutional courts may be considered as having absolute veto, particularly where they enforce provisions that (as in the German Basic Law, Art. 79, § 3) are designated as unamendable.

[18] "If in the course of legislative procedure, it shall appear that a private member's bill or an amendment is outside the domain of legislation [as defined by the Constitution] or is counter to a delegation of authority [previously voted by Parliament], the Government may declare it out of order" (Constitution of the French Fifth Republic, Art. 41).

[19] A familiar example of issue-area fragmentation is the "iron triangles," namely, legislative committee, bureaucracy, and pressure group, that characterized particular policy areas (agriculture, education) under the French Fourth Republic and the long Democratic hegemony in the U.S. Congress (Williams 1966; Mayhew 1974; Lowi 1979).

TABLE 4-1
Domestic Institutions and Foreign Policy:
The Independent and Dependent Variables

Institutional Features (independent variables)	Foreign-Policy Characteristics (dependent variables)				
	Bias	Credibility	Coherence	Mobilization	Strategy
Franchise					
Representational Mechanisms					
Decision Rules					

RESEARCH: FINDINGS AND QUESTIONS

What Biases Outcomes?

THE FRANCHISE

Almost self-evidently, a franchise that overweights a specific group privileges that group's preferences. If only landowners can vote, and if agriculture is threatened by imports, agricultural protection becomes a near certainty. On the other hand, landowner privilege in a country of booming agro-exports ought to undergird free trade. More generally, Garrett and Lange (1994) have argued that a more democratic franchise is conducive to more rapid adjustment to changed comparative advantage.

Perhaps because it seems so self-evident, surprisingly little research has been done on this hypothesis. Imports threatened agriculture throughout Europe in the later nineteenth century, but did countries' resultant protectionism vary (controlling for size of agricultural sector) consistently with the restrictiveness of their franchise?[20]

Much less obviously, but by now famously, a democratic franchise may bias a society toward a more pacific foreign policy, either in general or toward other democracies (Doyle 1983, 1986a; Lake 1992; cf. literature surveys in Lake 1992, 28; and Mansfield and Snyder 1995, n. 1).[21] Supposedly it does so by enfranchising those whom war is least likely to benefit or whose ingrained taste for it is far less pronounced.[22] Analogously

---

[20] However, Hallerberg (1996) demonstrates that within the states of the post-1871 German Empire, taxation of land varied inversely with landowner dominance of the franchise.

[21] A less sweeping hypothesis is that democratic states are likely only to initiate wars they are confident of winning (Bueno de Mesquita and Siverson 1995, 852; Reiter and Stam 1998).

[22] Mansfield and Snyder (1995), however, advance equally strong evidence that democratizing societies—ones in the transition from authoritarian to more open rule—are particularly prone to war.

Schumpeter (1951, 73–74, 122–23) had argued that political overweighting of a warrior aristocracy increased the probability of expansionism and war, and (as today we too easily forget) female suffrage was originally supposed to strengthen the constituency for peace.

At the supranational level, equal weighting of poor and rich states (e.g., in the Council of the European Union or in the projected European Central Bank) predictably yields a more redistributive and inflationary policy than a system that allocates votes by wealth.

Parsing more finely, some have hypothesized that overweighting of *immobile* (i.e., nonredeployable) factors—aristocrats' estates and military skills, guild members' crafts, narrowly based trade unions—favors protectionism, while grants of privileged access to highly *mobile*, and particularly to internationally invested, interests (banks, multinationals) advantages free trade (Milner 1988; Frieden and Rogowski 1996; Mansfield and Snyder 1995, esp. 25). Plausibly, if still quite speculatively, Mansfield and Snyder (1995, 25, 28) suggest that states dominated by nonredeployable elites may also be more prone to imperialism and war.[23]

In the realm of monetary policy, Frieden (1991) has argued, overweighting of tradables producers biases policy toward a depreciated currency; overweighting of nontradables producers biases it toward appreciation. A strong voice for finance capital (as under the Republican hegemony after 1896 or the long dominance of the City in British politics) creates a tilt toward fixed exchange rates.

Perhaps the most intriguing idea in this area is the possibility that rational principals might choose to bias outcomes toward a position different from their own. In a justly renowned paper, Rogoff (1985) showed that to demonstrate adequate commitment to a noninflationary policy a rational voter would delegate power to a central banker markedly less inflationary than the voter herself. Similarly, a society that needs to convince others of its commitment to some policy (peace, fixed exchange rates) might choose to bias its franchise even more than the median principal would (in isolation) desire.

MECHANISMS OF REPRESENTATION

Here, the most convincing argument is that large constituencies—at the extreme, a single voting unit that comprises the entire citizenry or membership—attune representatives to the general welfare, whereas small ones encourage particularism and logrolls. (In the United States, the more national orientation of the president, and the more particularistic one of

---

[23] Lurking behind such speculations is an implicit theory about how mobility of assets affects preference formation—a topic Frieden addresses more fully in chapter 2 of this volume.

Congress, has frequently been noted; for a particularly lucid summary, see Lohmann and O'Halloran 1994, 598–99.) Since, according to standard economic theory, free trade almost always improves aggregate welfare but harms particular groups, it might be expected that large-district representation would be more conducive to free trade, small districts more to protectionism; research so far mostly bears out this expectation (Rogowski 1987; Mansfield and Busch 1995; cf. Schattschneider 1935).[24]

Almost as well established, at least in domestic politics, is that representatives who are insecure in office—with short or revocable terms and with low probability of reelection—discount the future heavily and incline toward short-term opportunism. In the domestic fiscal arena, this takes the form of budget deficits and debasement of the currency (Grilli, Masciandaro, and Tabellini 1991). In foreign policy, anecdotal evidence suggests, insecurity in office may mean servility toward stronger powers (avoid war in the short run, no matter the long-term costs) and aggression toward much smaller ones (quick and cheap victories bring short-term popularity).[25] The foreign-policy implications, however, need to be worked out more systematically.

Long and secure terms, by contrast, privilege the status quo and encourage a longer-term perspective. James Rauch (1995) has shown that civil-service reform in U.S. cities, by assuring to key decision makers a more secure tenure, produced higher investment and lower current consumption. Presumably the more prominent and powerful role of career civil servants in European policy making biases the states of that continent toward a longer-term perspective. Within the governance structure of the European Union, the tenure and insulation of the Commission, and even more of the Brussels-based "Eurocrats," are intended precisely to give them a more "European" and less opportunistic point of view.

DECISION RULES

In this arena, obvious disputable points produce results that are not so obvious. Plainly multiple bodies and veto points, or requirements for supermajorities, bias results toward the status quo and entrench minority power (cf. Tsebelis 1995), whereas authority over the agenda ("gatekeeper" power) advantages holders of that authority. Much less intuitively obvious are some by now widely accepted concrete implications of this logic, for example, that multiple-veto systems bias policy toward

---

[24] Relatedly, Garrett and Lange (1994) reason that proportional representation should be more favorable to rapid adjustment; but Mansfield and Busch (1995) fail to validate this conjecture empirically.

[25] This I take to be the conventional understanding of Italy, the French Third and Fourth Republics, and Weimar Germany, all characterized by the rapid turnover of cabinets.

inflation (Roubini and Sachs 1989), away from fixed exchange rates (Eichengreen 1992; Simmons 1994), and toward slow and inadequate response to exogenous shocks (Poterba 1994; Spolaore 1997, chap. 1). Briefly the argument is that these devices—division of power among executive, legislature, and courts; multiparty coalition governments; and, in federal systems, powerful representation of subunits at the national level—delay response and discourage sacrifice, thus encouraging "easy" policy responses (deficits, inflation, devaluation).

Decision rules may augment biases already present: The grant of extensive agenda-setting power to the Bundesrat of Imperial Germany or the Commission of the European Union creates a yet more marked bias—in the former case, toward the narrower franchise of the member states (Prussia, Saxony, Bavaria, etc.); in the latter, toward the "European" perspective already noted.

What Makes Commitments Credible?

THE FRANCHISE

Tilly (1990), North and Weingast (1989), and others have contended that a wider franchise lends greater credibility to commitments, precisely by making both their creation and abrogation more difficult. This claim contrasts strongly with traditional realism, which held democracies to be more fickle and mercurial, and with the "strong-state" literature on investment and growth, which focuses most strongly on the cases of the "Asian tigers" (Amsden 1985, 1989; Wade 1990).[26] In the latter body of work it is argued that powerful, insulated bureaucracies can commit more reliably. Finally, some suggest that "corporatist" bargains, struck by especially powerful peak associations that can commit their followers, are more credible (Gourevitch 1986; Hall 1986; Katzenstein 1985; Olson 1982).

One kind of empirical test is easy but still partial and likely to be less than conclusive, namely, states' *creditworthiness*, as measured by risk premiums in bond markets; another would be confidence in, and use of, official money (as measured inventively by Clague et al. 1995).

MECHANISMS OF REPRESENTATION

The literature on delegation (particularly on central bank independence), and inadvertently some on the franchise, suggests strongly that not

---

[26] Raising, of course, the possibility that the link could be spurious: Wealthy countries are both more creditworthy and likelier to be democratic.

democracy, but insulation from short-term democratic opinion, lends credibility. Thus courts, central bank boards, and many regulatory commissions are granted long terms, and—in the strongest cases—barred from reappointment and hence from the temptation to please the majorities that can reappoint.[27] In foreign policy, similar arguments could be advanced for the superior credibility of career diplomats, for a foreign-policy "establishment" well insulated from democratic opinion and for powerful parliamentary foreign-affairs committees staffed by respected senior members with great experience and prospects of long tenure.[28] In supranational bodies, it is routinely understood that the appointment of an expert and independent secretariat, or even more of judicial or quasi-judicial bodies (ranging from NAFTA Dispute Panels to the European Court of Justice), sharply shifts power away from member states and toward the supranational level.

DECISION RULES

It is standardly argued that credibility is enhanced by specialized and irrevocable delegation: Interpretation of laws and contracts devolves to courts; formulation of monetary policy, to an independent central bank. As Frieden (1996, 113) observes, such agencies are typically pressured mainly by specialized groups (in the case of central banks, the financial community), whereas more general representatives (e.g., members of Congress) must balance diverse issues and groups.[29] Further, specialized agencies quickly acquire some of the characteristics of an "epistemic community" (Haas et al. 1992) or indeed of a priesthood, whose body of doctrine guarantees both continuity and (toward "lay" outsiders) impenetrability. In extreme cases, outsiders are actually barred from attempting to influence the decision makers, except in particularly formalized and transparent ways (e.g., the prohibition on ex parte communications with judges).

---

[27] U.S. Federal Reserve governors are appointed for fourteen years, most judges in most countries for life. An instructive exception is the German Constitutional Court, some of whose judges were formerly appointed for life, some (to provide continual renewal) for renewable eight-year terms. When it appeared that judges in the latter category were "trimming" their opinions as reappointment time drew near, a sensible reform was agreed to: nonrenewable, twelve-year terms for all judges of the Court. See Law on the Constitutional Court (BVerfGG) of February 3, 1971, § 4.

[28] Perhaps paradoxically, such committees were a remarkable feature even of the otherwise highly unstable French Fourth Republic (Williams 1966).

[29] Perhaps a better way to say this is that specialized agencies face unidimensional policy spaces, while generalized representatives must deal with multidimensional (and hence less stable) arenas.

Particularly interesting is the strategy of *supranational* delegation, in which states or other international actors devolve power over some class of decisions to an agency that is domiciled in no state and often, at least indirectly, represents several, for example, the European Court of Human Rights, the International Monetary Fund, the European Court of Justice, and the European Central Bank. Here, other international actors, rather than (or in addition to) the "epistemic community," serve as watchdogs against violation of commitments. Yet, neither domestic nor supranational delegation can reliably guarantee against strongly motivated violation of commitments: A government may repeal laws, amend or violate its constitution, withdraw from international communities, no matter how solemnly it had pledged never to do so.

Weingast (1995), Cowhey (1993, 315), and others have therefore contended—in contradiction to the previous arguments—that credibility is best enhanced by *multiple-veto* systems. Here, allegedly, commitments are harder to make but also harder to break. Thus the very difficulty of treaty ratification in the United States, relative, for example, to parliamentary systems, implies both a fullness of consideration and a degree of consensus that inspire greater confidence in the commitments made (cf. Martin 1995).[30]

Whether credibility is best guaranteed by delegation (and thus insulation from potential veto players) or by a multiple-veto system presumably depends on whether it is action or inaction whose credibility is to be guaranteed. If positive action will be required to maintain an announced policy (e.g., austerity to maintain a fixed exchange rate, war to keep treaty commitments), delegation is superior. If inaction suffices (e.g., to prevent abrogation of the legal arrangements guaranteed by a treaty and perhaps embodied in property law), a multiple-veto arrangement enhances credibility. Even so, any gains in credibility from multiple-veto points may well be offset by losses in coherence and stability (see below).

In this area, perhaps above all, *clarity* of decision rules matters. In strongly "constitutional" regimes, the allocation of authority is precise enough, the rules of ratification and abrogation sufficiently specific, that both domestic and foreign actors can calculate probabilities and understand results. Where the rules change frequently or are ignored—as in many developing countries, present-day Russia, or Fourth Republic France—commitments are even more malleable.

---

[30] The argument would be more convincing if treaties stood above ordinary laws, but in U.S. jurisprudence they do not. Many of the most flagrant breaches of U.S. treaty obligations have arisen when a subsequent Congress simply passed a law that violated the treaty, and the incumbent president either yielded cravenly or saw his veto overridden. The Burton-Helms Act is only the most recent example, if one of the baldest.

What Assures Coherence and Stability of Outcomes?

THE FRANCHISE

Formal theory and comparative political observation agree that an important guarantee of stable outcomes is an agreed *single dimension* of policy on which all individuals hold "single-peaked" (i.e., transitive) preferences. As early as the 1950s Duncan Black showed that this condition was sufficient for a stable voting outcome; in the 1970s, McKelvey (1976) (to the surprise of many) showed it ordinarily to be necessary.[31] When voters divide independently over more than one dimension (e.g., over both left-right redistributional issues *and* religion), a majority can often be mustered against any particular outcome and results can wander unpredictably throughout the entire policy space.

Empirical work had run ahead of this. Many students of unstable democratic regimes, most notably Philip Williams (1966) on the French Fourth Republic, had noted the practical link between "cross-cutting cleavages" and regime and cabinet instability.[32], [33] Cross-nationally and historically, Lipset and Rokkan (1967) had observed that the most stable regimes were ones that had expanded the suffrage gradually enough to embrace a new dimension of conflict (e.g., class) only after a previous one (typically religion or region) had already been resolved.

For foreign-policy purposes, the same general point holds: Entities that divide internally on multiple independent[34] issues (e.g., class and religion) will be less stable in their choices than ones whose conflicts essentially array on a single dimension (typically nowadays class). From this standpoint the United States, where not only class but race and religion matter, should be less consistent than Britain, where class remains overwhelm-

---

[31] More recent work has identified some exceptions.

[32] In France, for example, there was both a clerical and a secular Left and Right: The MRP represented the clerical Left, the CNIP the clerical Right; on the secular side, the Communists represented the Left, the Socialists the center, and the misnamed Radicals the Right. If a particular government was united on the social issues (e.g., bridged clerical and secular Right), its opponents were sure to bring religious conflicts into play. If it was united on religious questions, opponents would mobilize social conflicts.

[33] Ironically, some leading comparative theorists of the period, largely divorced from empirical observation, had argued that cross-cutting cleavages were conducive to stability. The most notable of these was David Truman (1951).

[34] The modifier is crucial. If two issues are almost perfectly correlated—for example, in post-1918 Austria, almost all workers were secular, almost all nonworkers Catholic—then these amount really to only one dimension. (In Austria, unfortunately, a third dimension—the question of an Anschluß with Germany—was orthogonal to the others.)

ingly dominant.[35] By the same logic, alliances of states similar in wealth, culture, and internal governance will cohere more successfully—a point admitted in practice by Europeans' hesitation to admit Turkey, or even Eastern Europe, to their Union.

MECHANISMS OF REPRESENTATION

A similar logic suggests that fewer bodies, or a clear hierarchy among multiple bodies, are conducive to greater coherence and stability. Independent power for the president, Congress, and the courts subjects U.S. foreign policy to greater instability than the clear dominance of a powerful cabinet (subject only to ultimate parliamentary oversight) in a Westminster-style system. Similarly, strong party discipline within bodies, by reducing the effective number of actors (cf. above, n. 12) better guarantees stability and coherence (Milner 1997, 41 ff.).

Even within a single body, multiple small constituencies present the risk of "accidental" majorities, in which a minority of votes in a particular election is translated into a majority of seats either by an unintentional gerrymander or by a split in the majority.[36] Independent of those possibilities, election by plurality or majority (in contrast to systems of proportional representation, or PR) magnifies the electoral effect of even small swings in voters' sentiments, thus increasing the likelihood of instability.[37] Some forms of federalism, in which member states cast blocs of votes (Germany's Bundesrat, the Council of the European Union), magnify this

[35] Most non-Americans find it incomprehensible that an increase in IMF funding or a payment of back dues to the UN can be held hostage, in the U.S. Congress, to arcane fights over abortion and contraception. To an American (and, possibly, to Israelis), nothing is more obvious.

[36] Suppose 10 million voters are to fill one hundred parliamentary seats. Each constituency consists of precisely one hundred thousand voters. Conservatives win 4.2 million votes, liberals 5.8 million. In the first case, suppose exactly seventy thousand conservatives happen to be located in each of sixty constituencies; the other forty constituencies are entirely liberal, so that 4 million liberals are in "packed" districts and 1.8 million are in majority-conservative ones (60 x 30,000). Then the 42 percent conservative vote elects a 60 percent conservative parliament. In the second case, each district is "fair," but liberals split into two factions: "A" liberals capture 3.8 million votes, "B" liberals 2 million; obviously the conservatives can win an overwhelming majority of seats. Cf. Garrett and Lange 1994.

[37] Where proportional representation, by design, creates a votes-seats elasticity of 1— that is, a 1 percent shift in popular vote effects a 1 percent shift in seats—majority and plurality election in single-member districts yields an average elasticity of about 2.5: Winning 52 percent of the votes will bring a party about 55 percent of the seats; 54 percent will yield a 60 percent majority; and so on (Tufte 1973; cf. Taagepera and Shugart 1989, esp. chap. 14). Recent results in the U.S. House of Representatives and the French National Assembly have demonstrated this effect with remarkable precision.

danger: A change of political direction in a few states can reverse federationwide majorities (on the danger in the European Union, see Rogowski 1997).[38]

Under proportional representation, the median representative is far likelier, on average, to reflect the policy preferences of the median voter; but instability can arise from the endless machinations and shifting alliances of many small parties (it suffices to think of the Israeli case). Majoritarian electoral systems have at least the virtue of keeping the number of parties low (Duverger 1959).

On the link of electoral system to policy stability generally, let alone to foreign-policy stability in particular, virtually no research (so far as I know) has been done. A working hypothesis, however, would be as follows: greatest stability in PR-parliamentary systems with high thresholds of representation (and thus, as in Germany, few parties); next greatest in low-threshold PR systems and under Westminster-style majoritarian parliamentary rule; less in bloc-vote federal systems;[39] and least in separation-of-powers governments, like the United States (cf. Garrett and Lange 1994).

DECISION RULES

The two clearest results are that decisions are stabilized and made consistent by (a) centralization of authority in a single body (nonfragmentation); and (b) grants to that body of extensive agenda-setting power, including the right to bar consideration of particularly destabilizing proposals.

The authors of *The Federalist*, arguing for a strong presidency, emphasized the malign foreign-policy effects of divided authority.[40] Where power is fragmented, for example, among many legislative committees or independent commissions, contradictory actions and "turf battles" become all but inevitable. A budget committee seeks to impose restraint even

[38] In the model developed by Bueno de Mesquita and Siverson (1995, 844), the median stakeholder would move with much greater volatility in majority-parliamentary or bloc-vote systems.

[39] Note, however, that Germany's Bundesrat is, by comparison to cabinet, Bundestag, and Constitutional Court, a weak body; hence the potentially destabilizing effect is attenuated.

[40] "That unity is conducive to energy will not be disputed. Decision, activity, secrecy, and dispatch will generally characterize the proceedings of one man, in a much more eminent degree, than the proceedings of any greater number; and in proportion as the number is increased, these qualities will be diminished. . . . In the conduct of war, in which the energy of the executive is the bulwark of national security, every thing would be to be apprehended from its plurality" (Hamilton, Madison, and Jay 1787–88, 356, 358; Hamilton, *The Federalist*, no. 70).

as committees on education, armed services, or welfare approve greater outlays in their areas; a free-trading foreign ministry is undercut by a protectionist agricultural committee. Even a single, centralized authority (typically a cabinet) may face interest-group challenges in the form of irresistibly popular backbench amendments.

France, which in the Fourth Republic suffered one of the most severe cases of the disease,[41] has in the Fifth adopted the most radical cures: the "package vote" (in which the cabinet may insist on a vote on its original proposal, with only such amendments as it accepts) and the referendum (in which the cabinet and president have unlimited power to frame the proposal submitted).[42] In the United States, presidential "fast-track" authority in the ratification of trade agreements, committing the Congress to vote on the original proposal without amendment, served a similar crucial purpose (Destler 1980, 1986; Ikenberry 1989). And the agenda-setting prerogative of the Commission of the European Union, while yet weaker, is nonetheless one of its most important weapons against the member governments represented in the council—hence, as in the Maastricht changes in legislative procedure, one of those governments' most tempting targets (Garrett and Tsebelis 1996).

By easy extension of the point raised earlier about multiple bodies (above, pp. 129–130), it may be argued generally that multiple-veto systems produce less consistent policy.[43] If proof were needed, the experience of the United Nations force in Bosnia would amply provide it.

Vague allocations of authority, finally, seem to compromise consistency as much as they do credibility.[44] Where power shifts among cabinet, politburo, and armed forces, between president and prime minister, or between secretary-general and security council, the divergent preferences of these officials and agencies lead to confused and inconsistent policy.

---

[41] As Williams (1966) notes, Fourth Republican cabinets not infrequently wound up opposing proposals on the floor that they had initiated but that had been amended out of recognition in one or more of the specialized parliamentary committees. On the cure, see Williams and Harrison 1973.

[42] Constitution of the Fifth Republic, Articles 44 and 11, respectively.

[43] Tsebelis (1995) observes accurately that a greater number of veto players biases outcomes toward the status quo, that is, toward inaction. Consistency in foreign policy, however, requires clarity of purpose and intent. When a U.S. president, backed unanimously by the Republican leadership of the Congress, assures all concerned that the United States will back a financial "bailout" of Mexico, only to renege days later in the face of back-bench Republican opposition, U.S. policy is not consistent.

[44] On the other hand, some features that seemed to enhance commitment (specialized, and therefore fragmented, authority; multiple vetoes) appear to undermine consistency. This paradoxical result probably flows from the fact that many policy areas cannot easily be compartmentalized.

What Facilitates Mobilization and Projection of Power?

THE FRANCHISE

As noted at the outset, it has become almost a commonplace that democratic regimes mobilize resources more effectively and, when pushed, fight
better than their authoritarian counterparts (see again Lake 1992; also
Stam 1996, 176 ff.). Indeed, Ginsberg (1982, chap. 1) argues that many
expansions of the franchise have been motivated precisely by the need to
mobilize more effectively; Stein (1978) notes that other kinds of participation appear to have been expanded by the exigencies of war. A lesson of
earlier broad-franchise regimes (the ancient Greek democracies, the post-
Secession Roman Republic) might be that a suffrage linked directly to
military service, or weighting soldiers' votes more heavily, will elicit even
greater sacrifice.

MECHANISMS OF REPRESENTATION

A similar logic would suggest that "more democratic" regimes—ones in
which the link between principals and agents is made more direct by
shorter terms, easier recall, fewer layers, more severe punishment of faithless representation, and so on—will attract greater support; Ferguson
(1994, esp. 156–63) and D'Lugo and Rogowski (1993), generalizing from
the pre-1914 Anglo-German comparison, argue essentially this position.[45]

DECISION RULES

Multiple-veto systems, by encouraging disagreement about level and allocation of sacrifice, impede mobilization and projection of power—another lesson of the pre-1914 German experience.[46] Indeed, U.S. history
suggests that strong agenda-setting powers for the central executive are
almost a prerequisite of successful mobilization. Again, these assertions
have at this point more the character of conjectures than of findings;
more, and more comparative, research is required.

---

[45] "Germany and its ally [Austria-Hungary] were thus fiscally constrained—above all, by
their federal structures. By contrast, the powers of the Triple Entente were, albeit to varying
extents, centralized states with no more than two tiers of government" (Ferguson 1994,
161).

[46] The democratic Reichstag actually wanted higher military outlays but insisted on financing them by less regressive taxation. The conservatives, powerful in the state governments and the national executive, as always put private greed ahead of national welfare and
preferred lower military outlays to any curtailment of their own budgets for horses, spas,
and jewelry (cf. Ferguson 1994).

How Are Domestic Actors' Strategies Affected?

THE FRANCHISE

Clearly variations in the franchise affect domestic principals' strategies of influence: Demagoguery works best where the *demos* has some influence, cabals where lines of authority are genuinely obscure, the *cuartelazo* where those who inhabit the eponymous barracks exert outsized influence. Research remains largely anecdotal or inductive, for example, historical accounts of Gladstone's then shockingly innovative exploitation of the "Bulgarian horrors" to drive Disraeli from office (Magnus 1954). More intriguing is the possibility that a change in franchise alters strategies in ways that bias outcomes: Thus Mansfield and Snyder (1995; cf. above, n. 22) suggest that democratization initially makes war likelier, as traditional elites find a bellicose foreign policy their best strategy to retain power.

MECHANISMS OF REPRESENTATION

Where power is centralized within a single body, foreign policy can be influenced only through domination or intimidation of that body. In Westminster systems of majoritarian cabinet governance, for example, one must either control the cabinet or form so powerful a faction within the majority party as to threaten the cabinet. Peel's conversion to free trade in 1846, or the Liberal government's decision for war in 1914, was an example of the former; the efforts of anti-appeasement Tories in the 1930s or Euroskeptic Tories under John Major exemplify the latter.

Where power is more dispersed, for example, in a multiparty coalition or under separated powers, multicameralism, or federalism, strategies of influence can be more varied and intricate.[47] From the 1950s until reunification, for example, export-oriented West German interests found massive financial support for the Erhard faction of the Christian Democratic Union (CDU) and the pivotal centrist Free Democratic Party (FDP) the surest guarantee of favorable policy (Heidenheimer 1957, 383–94; cf. Heidenheimer 1964, 37–39); the leftist Social Democrats (SPD), understanding this calculus, probably drove Erhard from power and entered the Grand Coalition (1966–69; SPD and CDU, excluding FDP) in part to attract some of that support (Heidenheimer and Langdon 1968, 72, 85–87). In the United States, capture of a crucial committee rather than a party or faction is usually the key; or particularly skilled legislators can attach "riders" to financial bills that force significant policy change, for

---

[47] On strategies under multicameralism, see Tsebelis and Money 1995.

example, the Jackson-Vanek Amendment that pressured the Soviet Union to permit emigration to Israel. Where representatives are elected from small districts, as in France or the United States, interests often do best by putting massive effort into a few crucial constituencies: Sen. Joseph McCarthy for example acquired enormous influence over U.S. foreign policy by demonstrating his (and his supporters') ability to decide crucial Senate races.

The intricacy of these "games" arises from the role that threat and counterthreat play in them. The greater the number of veto points, the easier it becomes to hold some other group's preferred policy hostage to one's own: If you do not give me what I want, you will be deprived of what you expect. In such situations, as is by now well understood, reputation and "signaling" (see the comprehensive discussion in Kreps 1990b, chap. 17) play a crucial part. Actors may gain by cultivating a reputation for "toughness," implacability, even a degree of craziness (cf. the pioneering insights of Schelling 1960).

On the other hand, a powerful and popularly elected executive, as in France, the United States, and Russia, channels domestic pressures on foreign policy into the contest for influence on, and election to, this central post. Strategy turns to mobilizing particularly effective groups of contributors and voters: In the United States, in particular, this means "swing" groups in the larger states that cast big blocs of Electoral College votes.

DECISION RULES

Here, *delegation* is a particularly important determinant, and object, of strategizing. Where courts have significant powers of judicial review, as in Germany, the United States, and the European Union, astute minorities often seek influence by honing their constitutional arguments rather than maximizing their votes or contributions. In West Germany, conservatives petitioned the Constitutional Court to block ratification of the treaties of *rapprochement* with Poland, the USSR, and East Germany; liberals, to bar deployment of German troops in Somalia and Bosnia; Euroskeptics, to limit the effects of the Maastricht Treaty.[48] In the early years of the United States and the European Union, their highest courts—respectively, the U.S. Supreme Court and the European Court of Justice—were used by actors *within* existing units to expand federal authority in ways that could never have won legislative approval.

---

[48] U.S. courts, while more deferential to executive prerogative in foreign affairs, have decided cases (e.g., on unitary taxation and the interpretation of treaties) that opened the door to jurisprudential determination of foreign policy.

TABLE 4-2

Hypothesized Links between Domestic Institutions and Foreign Policy

Institutional Features (independent variables)	Foreign-Policy Characteristics (dependent variables)				
	Bias	Credibility	Coherence	Mobilization	Strategies
Franchise	Female Suffrage → pacific policy.	Strong bureaucracy → credible commitment.	Cross-cutting cleavages → unstable policy.	Democracy → greater extractive capacity	Democracy → demagoguery as influence on policy
Representational mechanisms	Larger constituency → free trade	Longer, more secure term of office → greater credibility	Single-member districts → chance of "accidental" majorities	Short terms, easy recall → low slack and more extractive capacity	Multiple bodies → more bargaining, bluff, signaling
Decision rules	More veto points → status quo	More veto points → greater credibility	More veto points → instability, incoherence	More veto points → less extractive capacity	Delegation → more specialized access, advocacy

Note: Cell entries are illustrative, but of course not exhaustive, of specific hypotheses.

CONCLUSION

Table 4.2, drawing on the discussion of the previous section, indicates how research in this area is beginning (here, literally) to "fill in the blanks" of the broad schema indicated earlier. Four central points deserve further emphasis.

Institutions vary, and their variations matter. The classical realist position, according to which domestic institutions quickly and automatically evolve toward a single "best adapted" form, finds little support in the research to date. Countries differ greatly in their institutional forms— extent and effectiveness of franchise, methods of election, decision rules— and there is good evidence that these differences profoundly affect the style and relative success of their foreign policy.

Research and theorizing on this topic are in their infancy. Scholars have barely begun to incorporate in their work, or to consider the implications of, the important and insightful studies of recent decades on economic and legislative institutions, particularly from the principal-agent perspective. This is an "import" that can vastly improve scholarly welfare, and its introduction is an immediate and crucial scholarly task.

A strategic-choice approach, even at this stage, yields important new insights. One could hardly begin to think clearly about the effects of representational mechanisms and decision rules on foreign policy without recognizing (1) that both principals and their representative agents are characterized by "self-interest seeking with guile" (Williamson 1985, 30); and (2) that all players endeavor to take into account others' strategies and actions. To take but one example: Delegation, understood as deliberate limitation of one's own freedom of action, often makes sense precisely as a strategy that will elicit greater cooperation from others.

Microfoundations remain weakly explicated. The most head-turning results in international relations have been statistical—for example, that democratic states almost never fight each other, that they win the great majority of wars they enter—and have usually posed rather than answered theoretical questions. An instructive example is Mansfield and Snyder (1995, esp. 20): The statistical results are compelling, the proffered explanation a confessedly shaky conjecture built on very few cases. This sin is hardly original to political scientists or to students of international relations. The early work of Coase and Williamson on economic effects of institutions was largely devoid of microfoundations (supplied only recently in pioneering efforts by Tirole), and the often brilliant insights of legislative scholars who "soaked and poked" in the data (Fenno 1978) remained disconnected from individual motivations and processes. Those histories, however, only underline the point: Vast gains occur precisely through the coherent explication of microfoundations. The impressive recent blossoming of scholarship on legislative and regulatory questions, the startling breakthroughs on economic organization, have proceeded from logically consistent modeling of individual-level processes. Beginnings of the kind of work that needs to be done in this area of international relations are provided by Lake (1992, 25–28), Cowhey (1993), Lohmann and O'Halloran (1994), Bueno de Mesquita and Siverson (1995), Stam (1996), and Milner and Rosendorff (Milner 1997, chap. 3).

This is an area in which both research possibilities and policy implications are unusually exciting and in which the work of the last few years is of extraordinarily high quality. It invites, indeed virtually compels, work by the best and most ambitious students of the field.

CHAPTER FIVE.

The Governance Problem in International Relations

PETER ALEXIS GOUREVITCH

WHAT HAPPENS when everything is "in play," when nothing is constant? In analyzing strategic interaction, it is helpful to begin with assumptions either about preferences or about institutions. If we hold institutions constant, we can show how changing the preferences produces different outputs. Conversely, if we hold preferences constant, we can show how changing the institutions produces different outputs. Each of these conceptual experiments is powerful, and it is that power which led the editors of this volume to obtain chapters that do each of these. Frieden (chapter 2) examines preferences, which shape the strategies of actors within a well-defined strategic setting. Morrow (chapter 3) explores the strategic setting itself, which is often heavily influenced by institutions. Rogowski (chapter 4) continues by showing the importance of institutions directly; these influence the outcome of strategic interaction by structuring the way preferences aggregate.

If institutions are so important, they may themselves become the objects of struggle. People understand that institutions influence the outcome of strategic interaction, and therefore people challenge the institutions themselves. If the outcome can be altered by changing institutions, then people will try to change them. Anything important is likely to become a target of political action. When institutions are fluid, they become part of the game itself and are not able themselves to structure the outcome of a political process. Indeed, fluidity of institutions, by changing options available to actors, may induce reevaluation of strategy.

Institutional change poses specific challenges for the analysis of strategic interaction. The effort to hold one thing constant, either institutions or preferences, becomes more difficult. Both may be in play. This is the governance problem in international relations: the politics of contested institutions.

Actors in politics, at all levels, from the smallest local governments to the most global international level, from formalized government settings to the least institutionalized arrangements far from the shadow of the state, understand that rules and procedures shape outcomes. When actors are not satisfied with an outcome, we should expect them to consider changing the procedures that produce it.

And they do. Congress wants to increase the chances of reaching free-trade agreements with other countries and so changes its internal procedures by adopting a fast-track rule. Europeans wish to deepen economic integration, and so they alter the voting rules within the community executive and authorize monetary union; they wish to strengthen political support for community, so they adopt direct election of deputies to the European Parliament; they seek the benefits of a single currency, so they adopt the European Monetary Union. Nations wish to strengthen cooperation around free trade so they create a new institution replacing GATT with the World Trade Organization (WTO). After World War II, the Allies wanted to build new institutions of international cooperation that would be more effective than the League of Nations, so they wrote different rules for the United Nations. The inhabitants of Yugoslavia rejected the orientation of the Serbian leadership and so the federation broke up, leading to civil war. Inhabitants of the Soviet Union rejected communist leadership in Moscow, and the USSR disintegrated into fifteen new countries. Franco rejected the authority of the Spanish Republic and so civil war broke out, drawing in foreign intervention.

These examples deal with conflicts over the institutions of governance, the rules and procedures which make up the structures that shape the interaction of units within a system, be it domestic or international. That governance disputes matter is by no means universally accepted among international-relations theorists. To realists, governance disputes are not particularly interesting because for them institutions are not of primary importance. International institutions, for realists, have no capacity to enforce compliance among their members. Since they cannot sanction, they lack authority. Since they lack authority, they have no power. They exist only to the extent countries choose to delegate authority to them. Should countries dislike what the institution does, the delegation can be revoked. Governance institutions are thus epiphenomena of other elements of power relationships, and disputes about them are best analyzed from the standpoint of these other elements.

The institutionalist response to this criticism disputes the test given for the importance of institutions. The power of an institution arises not just, or even principally, from its capacity to use physical force. Rather, it emerges from the benefits members derive from participation in them. Institutions do things for members that they cannot obtain without them. Members acquire incentives to preserve institutions. The test of the power of an institution is thus its utility, not its coercive force. Institutions serve a purpose for their members. To withhold compliance, thus to weaken them, means losing something valuable. Members have an incentive to care about institutional preservation and, as a result, institutions have force.

Seen this way, the fight between institutionalists and realists is generally misstated. The issue is not whether one or the other has correctly interpreted all international relations, but rather, under which conditions does one or the other model best characterize reality (Mearsheimer 1994–95; Keohane and Martin 1995)? When is it that institutions are able to provide benefits sufficient to obtain support for their preservation? When is it that institutions cannot obtain that kind of support and are thus weak? Each position is accurate depending on empirical conditions. The task is to specify which these might be.

To the extent institutions matter, then, governance disputes are important and require examination. Working this out requires some discussion of why institutions exist, why they are formed, what makes them strong or weak, why they have the form that they do, why they are contested, and how these conflicts are resolved. The discussion may be sketched out in the following way: To explore why quarrels occur about the governance of institutions and how they are resolved, we begin with an exploration of why institutions are formed in the first place. This allows us to examine what political actors seek from institutions and what kind of institutions they want. Since actors want institutions to provide them benefits, and the type of institution influences who gets those benefits, it then follows that the governance of institutions will be contested: Actors fight when the stakes are important. As institutions are formed or altered, actors seek the best possible institution from their point of view.

Having established why governance conflicts occur, it is then possible to examine how they are resolved. The outcome of a governance dispute turns on several key variables. First, it matters whether the disputes occur in a context of strong or weak institutions. Disputes occurring within a strong institution will be resolved by the rules of those institutions, whereas disputes in a context of weak institutions will be resolved by the power resources of each actor and the bargaining process of their unmediated interaction.

A second important variable influencing governance quarrels has to do with collective-action problems. Institutional design is influenced by problems of monitoring, delegation, and incentives to provide the public good of institutional provision. The concept of "joint product" can solve some of these problems.

A third set of issues has to do with information costs and knowledge. Relaxing assumptions about perfect and costless information provides an important role in governance disputes for ideas about institutions—political philosophies, or encoded shorthands of calculation about future effects of institutional arrangements on actors in shaping the outcome of a conflict. In these instances, actors' preferences over alternative institutions may themselves be unclear. It is difficult to anticipate one's specific desires over some policy outcome in the distant future or under unknown contingencies. As a result, actors fall back on broad philosophical beliefs or positions in selecting institutions. In these domains, some of the convergence and differences among constructivists and methodological individualists, as well as realists and institutionalists, can be explored.

The discussion below deliberately makes use of examples from both international and domestic politics in order to emphasize that there is no difference analytically between these two levels. They differ along continua, in the values of the parameters in each, but not in the analytic issues. In both domains we can find areas of high or low stability of governance institutions, high or low contestation of the rules. In both, we can find cases where preferences and rules are in play at the same time. In both, we need to understand how the governance disputes are resolved. What differs between them is the extent to which we find higher or lower levels of institutionalization, not whether institutions exist solely in one domain or the other.

WHY ARE INSTITUTIONS FORMED?

A crucial entry point into an evaluation of governance disputes lies, then, with an understanding of why institutions are formed in the first place. A utilitarian approach dating back to Hobbes, Locke, Madison, and Mill sees institutions as deliberate human inventions, constructed more or less self-consciously to provide solutions to problems. Without institutions, chaos reigns. In chaos, cooperation is difficult, thus its rewards go unattained. Strategic interaction leads to the formation of institutions because it provides benefits to the actors that they cannot realize without them. Institutions create order and stability out of chaos and provide information to their members that is vital for cooperation.

Without fixed rules, preference aggregation leads to multiple and unstable equilibria (Vaubel and Willet 1991; McKelvey 1976). With two or more dimensions of policy on the table, the pursuit of any set of preferences can produce "cycling" between multiple outcomes, where no preference dominates. Because cycling is possible, political actors challenge everything. They have no incentive to moderate their demands, as there is no way of being sure that any agreement will stick. Without a method of forcing equilibrium, order cannot develop. Institutions end the chaos by structuring preference aggregation so that cycling is eliminated (Shepsle 1979; Shepsle and Weingast 1982; Krehbiel 1987). With clear procedures, preferences lead to fixed outcomes. The strategic interaction is now stable, and thus cooperation is more likely.

Institutions further aid cooperation by providing information, lowering transaction costs, and reducing the risks of opportunism. Strategic interaction poses risks of free riding and cheating. Institutions help monitor agreements by providing information on compliance, rules, policies, and outcomes. This reassures the partners of a bargain, increasing the chances of cooperation (Keohane 1984).

Since institutions are such powerful instruments, actors have strong incentives to create them. In their well-known article on law merchants in the Middle Ages, Milgrom, North, and Weingast (1990) show that highly motivated individuals can form an institution even without the shadow of the state—without coercive authority—as members find the role of a mediator so valuable that they accept his judgment voluntarily (see also Grief, Milgrom, Weingast 1994). Robert Ellickson (1991) demonstrates the power of informal institutions in the mechanisms farmers and ranchers in the California Sierras have developed to work out disputes over cattle trespassing without any state intervention at all. In another article, North and Weingast (1989) show that by subjecting the executive (the Crown) to monitoring by the legislature (Parliament), England reduced the arbitrariness of the executive in the eyes of investors and was thus able to borrow money at lower rates than their absolutist counterparts.

This institutionalist mode of reasoning turned a set of arguments about state power on its head (Krasner 1978; Katzenstein 1978). Britain and the United States were usually classified as weak states because their bureaucracy was less fully developed and the executive subject to legislative supervision. But Britain was able over several centuries to project power in international relations for colonization and war with the great European powers, as well as develop her economy. The institutionalists explain this as an expression of the strength of the British system. Parliamentary power, and bureaucratic weakness, gave to the English state greater credibility of commitment. In contrast, the absolutist states of the continent were weakened by their bureaucratic system because it came at the expense of less engagement by the population, hence lesser credibility for the monarch (Brewer 1989). The supposedly weaker English state proved more effective in mobilizing resources for international engagement than its supposedly stronger absolutist rivals. Recently Weingast (1997) applied this reasoning to a range of issues including civil war termination and social pacts in Latin America.

Commitment to an institution requires a belief that it will bring benefits that outweigh the costs of membership. Senator Lodge opposed the League, not, as is often argued, because he was an isolationist opposed to American engagement abroad, but because he was critical of constraints on American freedom of action in world affairs that membership in the League as constituted would entail. Lodge believed in the value of U.S. involvement in international matters—he was thus an internationalist—but was concerned about binding constraints—thus he was a "unilateralist" like de Gaulle and Thatcher, rather than a multilateralist. Membership incurred obligation, he thought, in which the decision-making system of the League could not provide protection of U.S. interests (Lake 1999). Institutions will fail to be generated if members do not believe that the benefits outweigh the commitment.

Institutions can solve problems. If everyone agrees to the institutions, they manage affairs in a self-enforcing manner. So long as each actor sees that the institution provides advantages, the incentives to cooperate are powerful, and actors will act so as to preserve the institution. Obedience derives not from coercion, but rather the capacity to coerce derives from the interest each actor has in preserving the institution. If enough actors want to preserve an institution, it will be able to coerce the recalcitrant. The dissidents to any action will face a choice: Comply with the majority, or leave. If they wish to retain the larger benefits of the institution, they will then have to give in on the specific point of dispute. The institution allows members to obtain goals they cannot achieve without it. To sustain the institution, members must alter their behavior: They cannot behave unilaterally in ways that provoke others to disband the organization. The incentive to obtain the benefits of an institution thus provides it with a powerful lever to obtain compliance. This form of coercion is not like a gun; nonetheless it can be quite powerful.

The discussion so far has provided an instrumentalist account of institutions, a contemporary version of the approach taken by Hobbes, Locke, and Bentham. It marks one of the differences between a strategic-choice account of international relations and other types of approach, such as culturalist or historicist, though there may be more crossover than is initially apparent. Edmund Burke, along with Tocqueville, thought institutions evolved organically, over time, by custom, habit, tradition; he rejected the mechanical metaphors of the utilitarians, and their self-consciousness, voluntarism, deliberate intentionality. Institutional "design" seemed absurd to him, since public institutions grow like an oak from an acorn, organically, unconsciously. Deliberate change was likely to produce "perverse effects," the opposite of what was intended (Hirschman 1991b). Yet, in thinking about what institutions did, in exploring their "function," Burke was also an instrumentalist. Institutions resolve disputes, solve collective-action problems, manage public affairs; they are, in short, useful. When features of institutions no longer work, they should be altered: "A constitution without the means of changing itself is a constitution without the means of preservation," is the famous phrase attributed to Burke. Change must occur, but gradually. Burke hated "revolution."

Like Burke, modern constructivists stress the importance of meaning, discourse, rhetoric, conversation, and culture in defining and sustaining the actual practice of institutions, and yet, like Burke, many of them agree that institutions are social constructs that play a specific role. Like Burke, they do not think that the utilitarian approach provides a full account of the role of ceremony, affect, and tradition in the way institutions actually operate.

Nonetheless the utilitarian argument does provide a coherent account of the creation of institutions. Cooperation is assumed to provide advantages, raising the level of outcomes to a superior equilibrium by overcoming a variety of problems posed by collective action. In order to have cooperation, institutions are needed. Following the utilitarian logic, the next step in the discussion turns to the question of conflict over institutional arrangements.

WHY DO GOVERNANCE DISPUTES OCCUR?

Institutions, while powerful, are nonetheless challenged. Why do nations fight about international rules in organizations such as the World Trade Organization? Why do interest groups, politicians, and bureaucrats fight about procedures within countries? Why does Congress demand that the president report on human rights in other countries? Why do congressional representatives fight over the rules that govern trade negotiations? A rationalist answer to these questions focuses on costs and benefits. Institutions are challenged if actors think a change will bring them benefits, and if these benefits outweigh the costs of the challenge: They compare the costs of change verses the expected benefits from it (the realized benefits of change times the probability the change will occur). The more specific assets invested in any given institution, the less likely actors will see the benefits of change outweighing the costs.

This may seem quite straightforward: In a rationalist world, actors, of course, do not do things when the costs of action outweigh the benefits. Understanding the costs and benefits of changing institutions is not quite so obvious, however, as rather strong analytic disputes exist on these points. For realists, as was noted above, institutions provide few benefits. Challenging them is rather costless, and, because it is cheap, challenges will occur often. Institutions are changed frequently when it suits actors' interests to do so, and governance disputes are of little interest. This attitude toward institutions makes sense if the institutions are weak.

If institutions are strong, however, challenges to their structure are considerably more important. Institutions are strong if their members see them as providing substantial benefits. Beneficiaries of any given structure will not wish to see it weakened nor will they accept changes that may preserve the institution but weaken their power within it. Conversely, those who see benefit from change will fight for it.

Since institutions are important, actors care about institutions' internal arrangements. Political actors develop investments, "specific assets," in a particular arrangement—relationships, expectations, privileges, knowledge of procedures, all tied to the institutions at work. Where investments in the specific assets of an institution are high, actors will find the cost of any institutional change that endangers these assets to be quite high; indeed, actors in this situation may be reluctant to run risks of any change at all. Where such investments are low, the costs of change are low. With little at stake, risks are more likely to be run. Investments in institutions include not only direct involvement in a specific institution (a job in Congress or in the civil service); there are also investments premised on institutions creating particular political outcomes. Trade groups invest in fast track if they want free trade, but oppose it if they do not (see discussion below).

It is where investments are high that institutions matter. If the costs of change are high because actors enjoy the benefits of the specific institutional arrangement, the institution itself will have a substantial impact on the outcome of any quarrel to change the rules. If the costs of change are low, actors will be tempted to be opportunistic about change, and the institution will have a low impact on the outcome. Realists focus on those situations in the world where institutions are weak, easy to change, and thus epiphenomenal to a conflict. Neoliberal institutionalists focus on those situations where institutions are stronger, harder to change, and thus able to influence the outcome. Realists are likely to see investments in institutions as covering a narrow range of issues, with little interaction or linkage; institutionalists are likely to see investments in institutions as having a broad scope, with extensive interaction and linkage. From the standpoint of strategic interaction theory, either situation is possible; from that approach, the importance of governance quarrels is not a constant, but a variable, one that changes with the strength of the institutional context within which the quarrel occurs.

A famous example of specific asset investment concerns driving: As a coordination problem, it does not matter much whether cars ride on the left or right side of the road, but once the convention is established, the investment is so great that change becomes costly; as a result, once achieved, the convention proves highly durable. Airline agreements, postal conventions, telecommunications systems, bank-settlement systems, currency-exchange procedures, diplomatic conventions, and count-less other issue areas show how entrenched a set of arrangements can become, even without deeply institutionalized machinery; the concept "regime" was developed to express just this set of arrangements. The same kind of investment can be found in security arrangements, where weapons procurement and specialization take place within the armed forces of each country, and then similar specialization occurs among the various national militaries in an alliance (Lake 1999).

Investment of specific assets helps to explain institutional persistence. As actors in each society invest in a particular institutional arrangement, they have incentives to protect their investment by opposing change. If the institution achieves its goals, there may even be an effort to find new ones in order to preserve the institution. The pioneering conceptualization of this concept in the social sciences dealt with the March of Dimes: Once the discovery of the Salk and Sabine vaccines ended the threat of polio, the organization shifted its attention to new diseases rather than go out of business. The same logic may be at work in extending the life and functions of NATO.

Challenge to institutional arrangements, or any other dispute, is influenced by the "reversion point"—the outcome that prevails if no agreement is reached. In 1995 the Republican Congress assumed that if it failed to pass a budget, it would benefit from the reversion point, namely, shutting the government down, which GOP leaders assumed would politically be blamed on President Clinton. Instead, the public blamed Congress for the costs of the reversion point. In the budget negotiations of 1997, Congress sought to redefine the reversion point at a level just below current funding, thereby creating less spending without a shutdown. Disputes over airline agreements or telecommunications or the trade regime in general all share this particular characteristic: The bargaining power of the various parties is affected by their evaluation of the reversion point, that is, their assessment of what happens if the discussion collapses and the status quo is preserved (Richards 1997).

Even failed institutions can influence an outcome by force of example. Planners at work designing the United Nations were well aware of the League's failures. Authors of the U.S. Constitution reflected on the weaknesses of the Articles of Confederation. In writing the WTO treaty, negotiators examined the weakness of GATT.

Governance disputes occur, then, because they matter. Institutions, even comparatively weak ones, can have importance to political actors because they are able to influence the strategic action that takes place among them. The next step in our discussion requires, therefore, that we seek an account of how struggles among competing institutional arrangements are resolved. Once actors begin fighting over institutional design, how will this conflict be resolved? The answer turns substantially on the degree of institutionalization of the conflict itself, to which we now turn.

WHAT KINDS OF INSTITUTION ARE SOUGHT?

Institutions influence power. We should therefore expect political actors to seek the institutional arrangement that best suits their goals. Political actors know that each arrangement produces different results. They fight to get the one that benefits them the most.

The general argument that institutions arise to solve collective-action problems does not explain which among several efficient institutions is actually selected. The motive of efficiency predicts a drive to Pareto optimality but does not explain which particular set of institutions among a set of equally efficient ones will be chosen. Institutions may also be sought to benefit some groups at the expense of others, such as a cartel that benefits its members but exploits the "consumer" public. Choice reasoning can model the Pareto optimal institution but can also be used to explain the quest for and success in seeking institutional arrangements that skew the benefits away from the optimal (Vaubel and Willet 1991).

Institutional differences produce variance in policy output—the theme of Rogowski's essay in chapter 4 of this volume. Unanimity rules mean decisions are harder to reach: the librum veto in the Polish parliament of the eighteenth century is a frequently cited reason for Poland's failure to develop the military capacity to resist Russia, Prussia, and Austria; conversely, the autocratic rules of these three empires are argued to have enabled them to build stronger military machines able to deploy force in international affairs (Gourevitch 1978a, 1978b). Against the absolutist bureaucratic model, Brewer and Weingast argue the superiority of the British parliamentary model: Legislative oversight of the executive reassured investors and domestic constituents that the monarchy would be restrained; this increased the ability of the British state to extract resources allowing it, in turn, to deploy the force that led to the world's greatest empire (North and Weingast 1989; Brewer 1989).

This argument currently figures in debates about democracy in foreign affairs. Because democratic leaders pay high audience costs, their commitments are held to be more credible and they are therefore more able to engage in durable alliances.[1] Democracies are also held to be more peaceful in that they appear less likely to go to war with one another than are other political forms. In the field of trade and other political economy

---

[1] See the literature summarized by Morrow in chapter 3 of this volume.

activities, research has extensively explored the impact of institutions on the influence of different groups and therefore on policy outcomes.

Since institutions influence policy outcomes, we should expect political actors to demand institutions that increase their leverage. An effort to create or amend institutions is likely, therefore, to bring about conflict over which institutions shall be established. The next step in our discussion requires that we seek an account of how struggles among competing institutional arrangements are resolved.

HOW ARE GOVERNANCE DISPUTES RESOLVED?

Once a quarrel over institutions begins, how is it resolved? The answer depends on several issues: the strength or weakness of the institutional context within which the quarrel takes place, the collective-action issues that underlie institutional change, and issues concerning information costs.

A quarrel over changing institutions, once launched, will be shaped by the preexisting arrangement of institutions, if these are strong to begin with. Conversely, if the institutions are weak, other factors will be more important. Debates in the U.S. Congress over fast-track authority—changing the rules whereby Congress examines trade treaties negotiated by the president—are examples of the former. These are governance disputes within a highly developed set of arrangements for resolving a change of the rules. The formation of the League of Nations and its application, the creation of GATT and the IMF, and many international security treaties are examples of the latter.

When institutions are contested in a strong institutional framework, we have fairly clear models of how to analyze the outcome. When institutions are contested in a weak institutional framework, then other variables, external to the institutions themselves, come into play in working out the result.

The Case of Strong Institutions

Some governance disputes take place within a highly ordered institutional framework. Political actors demand changes in the rules but accept the existing rules as the proper procedure for considering the change and for resolving any disputes that may arise from it. In this setting, the processes work along the lines Rogowski analyzes in chapter 4 of this volume. The outcome of the governance dispute will turn on the way any given set of institutions refracts the preference/interest aggregation.

A typical example may be drawn from the case of trade legislation in the United States. Fights over trade policy correlate with fights over rules. In the 1930s Congress delegated some authority to the president to engage in reciprocal trade negotiations. In 1974 Congress gave the president "fast-track authority." In the 1990s Congress, on several occasions, has failed to reauthorize fast track. How are we to understand the connection between institutional innovation (the delegation of authority to the president) and the content of policy and policy preferences (toward freer trade)? It seems clear enough that members of Congress support or oppose this kind of institutional creation as a function of their preferences for or against the substance of the trade issues. The reasoning is as follows: Some members of Congress want free trade. They know that if Congress can amend the treaties, the temptation of each member to seek exemptions for the special products of his or her district may prove irresistible and a logroll takes over, leading to a protectionist outcome (Schattschneider 1935). They know further that procedures can be set up to prevent this process: the president negotiates a treaty that is accepted or rejected by Congress without amendments; since the president has a broader constituency, he will negotiate for open trade, and the particularistic interests cannot make side deals to stop it. A self-denying ordinance of no amendments increases the probability of getting free trade.

Since members of Congress understand the implications of a fast-track procedure, a vote for that procedure or institution is, by proxy, a vote for free trade, and vice versa. When both the congressional Democratic majority of 1994 and the new Republican majority of 1995 refused to authorize a renewal of fast track, this was clearly a sign of rising protectionist sentiment in both parties.[2]

The change in procedures was motivated by a change in policy preferences. How was the dispute over changing procedures resolved? The procedures for changing procedure were quite clear, namely, the structures of the U.S. Constitution and the rules of Congress. The outcome of the governance quarrel can thus be understood with the analytic tools of institutional analysis: preferences plus political resources refracted by institutions equals policy outputs. The quarrel over the institutions is in this case a proxy for the quarrel over substance. Notice that this differs from arguments that trace the shift in policy to a shift in institutions, a shift that is independent of the trade preference itself: for example, that the U.S. presidency grew in power because of the growth of economic activity

---

[2] For contrasting views of trade bargaining, institutional delegation, and preferences over trade policy, see Lohmann and O'Halloran 1994; Haggard 1988; Lake 1988; and Milner 1988.

and foreign policy involvement and that this growth in power then made possible the construction of a free-trade coalition of support.

The trade case shows the way rules of procedure for the treatment of policy (trade treaties) are processed by a highly structured political system within a formalized constitution. Although many constitutions have formal procedures for revision, some element of how the text actually works turns on usage. Justice Marshall made rather more out of judicial review than many authors of the original U.S. Constitution had expected. Had Congress actually turned Andrew Johnson out of office, the meaning of impeachment would have changed drastically, and the U.S. presidency could have become subordinate to the shifting political tides of Congress.

The Case of Weak Institutions

The case of trade legislation in the U.S. Congress is clearly one in which the institutional rules are powerful enough to shape the treatment of the dispute. Many governance disputes occur where institutions are much weaker or nearly nonexistent. In trade, many regimes are like this. OPEC is a classic cartel. It works only so long as its members feel the compulsion to make it work, only so long as they want to cooperate. Collective-action theory expects that some members will find the temptation to cheat irresistible. Choice theorists expect cartels with many members to break down, and, in fact, they usually do.

Many security arrangements have this character. After World War I, France pledged support for its allies in Eastern Europe in order to balance Germany. When Britain refused to support Prague, France abandoned Czechoslovakia. The realist expectation of weak commitment was fulfilled. The League of Nations is perhaps the most famous example of institutional failure. Collective security required both consensus and resolve. When challenged by Japan, Italy, and Germany, the major powers proved unwilling to commit the forces to the League necessary to make its sanctions workable.

In contrast to conflicts within the U.S. Congress over the rules that govern trade legislation, trade and security issues in the international arena take place within relatively weak institutions. The recent replacement of GATT by the World Trade Organization is an example of a governance change designed to strengthen an institution where the dispute itself took place within a relatively weak institution. GATT was a large multilateral contract among its members to accept certain principles of trade. For compliance, it relied largely on self- enforcement. As an institution, GATT specified few processes with which to manage disagreements. These spluttered in bilateral conflicts familiar to what students of international politics would expect. Trade disputes led the large trading countries to want stronger procedures for handling disputes among them, while the smaller countries sought ways of constraining the behavior of the more powerful ones. The WTO was the result. This is a rather familiar story of many countries seeking benefits from cooperation, understanding that, to do so, they will have to accept limits on their capacity for unilateral action.

To manage the negotiations from GATT to the WTO, the countries had only a weak institution, GATT itself. GATT did have regularized processes for meetings, an institution of sorts—what international-relations literature has called a regime. This institution could make commitments for discussions—the various GATT rounds—but it could not force decisions. There was a dispute-resolution mechanism, but it was quite weak. Thus the GATT round that led to the WTO must be seen as the result of a massive collective negotiation, where the members are committed to a regime—the regime of free trade and dispute resolution—and are in the process of creating an institution to do so. The existing institution plays little role in shaping the creation of a new one. The actual institution created arises from a complex bargaining process of interactive self-interest, shaped by the interest groups within each country mediated by each country's institutional framework. The formation of NAFTA is a similar story—an institution created by the United States, Canada, and Mexico that these countries can break at will, though not without cost to the stable relations among them. The institution was created by direct trilateral negotiations without the shadow of an existing institutional machinery (Hall and Taylor 1996).

The European Union (EU) provides an interesting example of progression from weak to stronger institutions, and a good case for exploring the analytic disputes about institutional design, development, and strength. The European Economic Community (EEC), the Union's original name, was created as an act of delegation by independent countries to a central authority. Does the Union therefore have power over the members? Formally speaking, any member country can leave the EU when it wishes. The EU lacks any coercive instrument to prevent secession. Thus it is quite unlike the United States at the time of the Civil War, whose Northern members had the will and resolve to compel the Southern states to remain, thereby redefining the terms of membership in the Union. Thus, realists argue, the European Union continues to be an agent of principals who are free to disobey.

This is formally correct. Members can leave, and the EU itself lacks coercive power. It remains exceedingly unlikely that member states would mobilize military power to keep members inside. Yet, it would be costly for members to leave. They would lose the advantages they had in joining in the first place. Within each country there are interest groups with much to lose from departure. They will fight to prevent this from happening. The European Union is strong, therefore, in that departing from it requires a cost members do not wish to pay; their desire for compliance acts as the EU's coercive instrument for compliance by its constituent members.

In recent years major governance quarrels in the European Union have revolved around deepening (extending the scope of community powers, most notably to monetary union) and expanding membership. There have also been governance issues that arise over the exercise of authority and strategic behavior using military force in such places as Yugoslavia and the Persian Gulf. Clearly the EU is limited in its ability to extend institutional scope by the need for compliance by its constituent parts, which have to agree on these extensions. The conflict over doing so is rather ordered, however; that is, the rules governing these debates over changing community governance are fairly clear. Procedures inside each country and for the community as a whole are regularized. Some argue that the democratization of these procedures slow down the process of decision making and weaken the community. Lisa Martin argues to the contrary that democratic approval, while perhaps slowing the process of agreement, builds greater commitment, credibility and strength when it finally occurs (Martin 1994; Richards 1997).

Procedures and processes may themselves alter governance institutions over time. The European Court of Justice has built authority through the ability of the legal community in the various countries to extend jurisdictions and powers through doctrinal development over many decisions. Each country could always challenge these jurisdictions and powers, but the political costs of doing so gradually rises as constituencies come to like the benefits provided by institutions of the community (Burley and Mattli 1993; Garrett 1995; Garrett and Tsebelis 1996; Garrett 1992; Mattli and Slaughter 1995). On matters of trade, governance quarrels within the EC increasingly resemble those within a country—they take place within understood mechanisms and processes.

Most of the examples of weak institutions cited in this section come from the international arena. There are indeed many such examples to be found, but this does not mean that institutions are always strong in domestic politics. Civil wars mark a sharp breakdown of domestic institutions, and these are rather more common than a strict distinction between domestic and international can sustain. Even within some "stable" countries, the reach of state authority in certain domains is weak: the drug trade, urban gangs, rural "militia," to cite a few American cases. Since the U.S. Constitution does not specify the internal rules of procedure, even within the rather formalized arena of the U.S. Congress drastic change can occur, as the revolt against Speaker Cannon in 1910–11 suggests. At any given moment, the rules rest on majority support, which can bring, and has brought, about change.

These several examples—cartels, the League of Nations, GATT, the WTO, the EU—explore governance debates in a framework of weak institutions, moving toward a stronger one as we examine the EU. To the extent the institutions are weak, their processes are not able to be decisive in shaping the outcome of any dispute. Under such conditions, how are governance disputes resolved?

Without institutions, strategic interaction involves the deployment of actor capabilities toward each other. Actors in a strategic interaction between countries have varying amounts of leverage: military strength and organization, economic might, population, technology, geographic location. Within countries, actors have varying capacities to mobilize populations, to commit credibly, to exercise will and resolve, to lead, to motivate, and to exert leverage through strikes, boycotts, disinvestment, capital flight, campaign contributions, media and advertising, voting, or force. They have different skills in signaling, communication, reasoning, and calculating. They have different shorthands of ideology and "priors," different sets of grand strategies and tactical doctrines. They vary in ideological pull across boundaries, in emotional ties or antagonisms, in historical context.

All these factors influence strategic interaction. They do so, of course, even when institutions are strong. But without institutions, the strategic setting is more fluid and these other capacities and attributes become all the more decisive. In the late nineteenth century, for example, France and Russia formed an alliance to balance Germany. They gave some institutional form to it: staff talks among generals. Loans and trade helped to provide economic self-interest to back up the geo-political concern. The strength of the commitment between the two countries rested completely on mutual self-interest. The British stayed aloof until Germany menaced the mouths of the Scheldt River, the traditional British indicator of threat to its own self-interests. On the eve of World War II, when Chamberlain concluded that British interests did not require a Czech contribution to balancing Germany, the meaning of the French commitment to Prague dissolved. Without a Soviet threat, what is today the meaning of the U.S.-Japan Security Treaty?

NATO is the most institutionalized security system in the world today, perhaps ever. Strong disagreements exist among its members about enlargement to the East, and quarrels occur over symbolic issues like the nationality of commanders. The procedures for managing these disagreements seem weak, subordinate to separate calculations of self-interest. France has managed to stay out of the command structure without any serious damage either to the credibility of NATO's commitment toward her or French engagement with its allies.

In the framework of loose or weak institutions, governance disputes resemble bargaining by wholly independent actors. It is in situations of this kind that institutions cannot adequately explain quarrels over institutional structures.

Collective Action and Information Costs

So far, the discussion has derived the importance of governance quarrels from the motivation to create institutions, and then turned to the issue of how such quarrels are resolved. The first step was to question the institutional context within which the quarrel takes place. The next step asks why one institutional arrangement is chosen over others. Institutions are created to solve problems. More than one institution may do so. Several different institutional arrangements can eliminate cycling, thus several different arrangements may meet the requirements of Pareto optimality, a point Krasner (1991) has applied to the subject of international relations. What factors determine which among a range of Pareto optimum solutions is selected? Two issues require examination: The first explores the collective-action problem raised by institutional creation; the second explores the assumptions about information that underlie the act of institutional creation or disintegration.

THE COLLECTIVE-ACTION ISSUE

Institutional building is costly. Forging agreement is difficult; if it were easy, institutions would rise and fall all the time. The costs of forming an agreement pose a collective-action problem. Someone must pay those costs if agreement is to be attained. The very thing that motivates the formation of an institution—a way of overcoming collective-action problems—also inhibits its realization. An argument about the benefits of an institution does not, by itself, explain its creation, since such reasoning fails to solve the collective-action problem used to justify the formation of the institution in the first place. The way the collective-action problem is overcome will influence the choice of specific institutions from a range of optimal possibilities.

Collective-action situations themselves influence the choice of institutions; that is, the nature of the incentives that motivate action have themselves a substantial impact on institutional design (Wilson 1973). Group size and the nature of the public good are particularly important variables. If the group is small and the public good can be provided by a single actor, then the institutions chosen are likely to emerge by unanimity or majority rule and will reflect the proclivities of that single actor, hegemon, majority, or k-group (Snidal 1985). If the good is provided by selective incentives, then how the individuals get drawn into the organization by personal benefits influences the type of institution chosen.

Most recently, strategic-action theorists have used the concept of joint product to explain institutional creation: Actors may have self-interested motives for developing an institution in addition to a collective one. Broz (1997) uses this idea to explain the origins of the gold standard and of central banking. The gold standard provided a public good, namely, a system for managing international finance. To create and operate it, some country needed incentives to pay the transaction costs of leadership. Hegemonic stability theory ascribes this role to the British, who, as the leading industrial economy, had the interest and the means to pay the costs of leadership. Britain was not the only important actor, argues Broz. The French had their own incentives, albeit a different one. Britain sought stability in the value of money, while the French sought insulation of the domestic economy from external fluctuations. Each country's particularistic motive produced a public good.

A similar account can be given on the origins of central banking. It is not hard to demonstrate the collective benefit of a stable central banking institution, but who would have the incentive to pay the transaction costs of creating it? Broz finds the answer in the interest of financiers in major centers like New York and London who were able to appropriate enough of the benefits to have an interest in organizing the institution (Broz 1998).

Joint product provides the individual incentives needed to overcome the collective-action problem of providing the public good of institutional creation. At the same time, joint product helps explain which institutions will be chosen. If, as Krasner has noted, there is more than one efficient institution at the Pareto frontier, which differ in how they distribute the benefits of efficiency, we need to know which among them is chosen. Part of the answer lies in the paying of the collective-action costs. Those with a strong interest to pay the costs of creating an institution will be able to influence the specific features it will have. Since the institution chosen arises out of political process, the specific details of arrangement will reflect the political processes noted above in the discussion of strong and weak institutions.

The role of politics is particularly important when the institution chosen is not Pareto optimal. Arguments from efficiency assume that strategic interaction leads to the Pareto frontier. Arguments about distribution point out that there is more than one spot along that frontier. Institutional formation involves more than an economic drive to equilibrium. It also requires a political equilibrium—an arrangement that suits actors' political requirements. As John Richards (1997, 1999) has shown in his exploration of the evolution of the international aviation services regime, the political equilibrium may be different from the economic one.

INFORMATION: PERFECT AND COSTLESS?

How do actors decide what institution realizes their objectives? A simple model of preferences would look directly at actors' goals: Actors pick the institution that gives them what they want. Closer inspection of this point reveals the problem of information. To pick the institution that corresponds to preferences, actors have to understand quite well all the connections among all actors in the system in all circumstances: their preferences, beliefs, actions, and so on—all the cause and effect possibilities of strategic interaction, over time. To make these calculations accurately, actors need both the ability and the resources to get complete information. This is a formidable information requirement.[3]

Information is costly. This is one of the powerful motives for creating institutions in the first place. No one, no matter how independently wealthy, has the resources to get all the available information about all decisions that effect them. Instead, they rely on agents, or representatives, to gather and evaluate information for them. For the principal, the one who selects the agent, the problem of monitoring arises: how to make sure the agent does what the principal wants and keep agency costs to a minimum (McCubbins, Noll, Weingast 1987, 1989). In designing institutions, principals are motivated to structure the system so as to produce results that accord with their goals. The authors of the American Constitution wanted to avoid tyranny, which they conceived as arising from the executive; to prevent it, they created checks and balances among the branches of government, and federalism between the nation and the states. In our era, Congress worries that the president will neglect human rights or drug issues in foreign affairs; to influence policy, Congress requires the executive to certify that various countries are making progress in these areas.

With a complex reality and costly information, creating a new institution can be a formidable challenge to the designers' cognitive skills. Many aspects of reality have to be integrated into a coherent whole. When institutions are weak, the process is especially difficult because there are no

---

[3] More sophisticated analysis examines information shortcuts or shorthands: ways that voters or other decision makers find substitutes for full information to predict patterns of behavior among agents or representatives. See Lupia and McCubbins 1998; Lupia 1994; and Gerber and Lupia 1997.

institutional devices to structure the process itself. It is particularly instructive, therefore, to look at grand moments of institutional design: the peace treaties after great wars, the creation of new international institutions such as the League of Nations, the UN, the IMF, GATT, the World Bank, and constitution writing within countries.

Constitution writing is rarely classified as an international event, yet its context is similar. In constitution writing, like civil war, the distinction between domestic and international politics is blurred. Groups within a country have to write a new set of rules, often without any, or only weak, institutional structures to bound the process.

Take one thousand people from five different countries and place them on identical continents in different worlds. Will they write the same constitution? Not likely. They will each bring their own "priors" to the governance dispute, priors that arise from their personal histories, experiences, and reading. The more complexity, uncertainty, and cycling in the writing of a constitution, the more these priors influence the way governance disputes are understood and resolved. Take ten different hegemons and give them the power the United States had after World War II. Will they create the same international institutions? Realists would say yes; others would sharply disagree. A look at how constitutions were written both domestically and internationally is instructive in showing the interplay of forces at work.

Within a decade of each other in the late eighteenth century, French and American politicians drafted new constitutions. To do so, each had to analyze a wide range of issues: the nature of human beings, the character of their respective societies, the structure of their economies, the extent of foreign threat, relations with cultural minorities, among other issues. In doing so, they did not sit down, tabula rasa, with a purely deductive formal technology of constitutional theorems to design a political system. Rather, they turned to a body of ideas about society and institutions reflective of their era, the political philosophy of their time and place: Montesquieu, Locke, Hobbes, and their interpretation of the constitutions of Greek and Roman antiquity.

Each set of leaders drew on similar inspirations but faced different situations and experiences. The would-be Americans imagined a society of independent economic actors, well educated in civic virtues, capable of reason and moral judgment. They thought of issues as interests, differences of opinion as faction, tyranny as arbitrary rule by an executive. The overall constitutional machinery expressed a broader bargain about the nature of society, its problems and good governance (Dahl 1956). The French political leaders interpreted things differently: They saw society full of reactionary forces, poorly-educated masses with limited civic virtue, and many foreign enemies. Their constitutional constructs were thus different from those of the Americans. In both cases, the authors of the respective constitutional bargains brought to their task a set of assumptions about people, society, issues, and politics, and a set of priors about what makes up good institutions (Higonnet 1995).

The comparable moments in international relations can be found in the famous conferences after great wars—those at Vienna, Versailles, Potsdam. The victors of those titanic struggles had an opportunity to shape a new set of arrangements with which to secure their future. Faced with many possibilities, what did they do? They analyzed. They examined the causes of war, the nature of past and future enemies, the requirements for peace—the same things scholars do. And just as scholars disagree, so did the negotiators in these settlements. Each came to these discussions with a past, a set of theories with which to bring order to the chaos of options.

Kissinger (1957) has rendered famous the contrast between Vienna and Versailles in this regard. The leaders at each great conference saw international relations quite differently. At Vienna, they thought like realists, and so constructed a state system of balancers, including the defeated French, the instigators of a quarter century of war. At Versailles, conversely, Wilson used "second-image" analysis: War was caused by domestic arrangements, by dictatorship. As Arno Mayer (1959) pointed out, Lenin also focused on domestic politics as the cause of war; for him it was capitalism. In each case, the leaders' different theories would surely have resulted in different treaties. Kissinger and realists generally blame World War II on the faulty reasoning of Versailles and credit the long European peace of the nineteenth century on the realists' balanced reasoning at Vienna. Contemporary theorists of the democratic peace challenge this thinking by attributing international behavior to a domestic political characteristic.

Neither peace treaty was quite so pure in its attributes. Leaders at Vienna were quite aware of domestic institutional arrangements and found them important. Despite the realist logic that prevailed in 1815, the European concert intervened to alter the political systems of countries. Foreign ministers of the concert powers blamed war on revolutionary and democratic domestic politics, and deployed force to protect monarchies; disagreement over how far to go in these interventions caused the European concert to break up. At Versailles, conversely, there were accommodations to realist premises of power balancing, demanded by various allies who did not agree with Wilson. The French insisted on a mutual defense treaty with the United States, which Wilson disliked but signed; it was never ratified in the United States (Lake 1999, chap. 4).

After World War II the great powers again mixed models of causality in their policies, blending realist and second-image analysis. Both the United States and the Soviet Union wanted their respective allies to resemble them in domestic systems: The Soviets created people's democracies, the United

States sought to strengthen the constitutionalist democracies in Western Europe. Each applied a strategic calculus to the other's systems: Allies with similar domestic systems were more reliable than a sharply different institutional arrangement would be.

In its sphere of influence outside the Soviet bloc, the United States was able to structure key elements of the global trading and security system: GATT, the IMF, the Marshall Plan, NATO, the security treaty with Japan, the European community. The Americans had substantial power in shaping these arrangements. Their ideas mixed self-interest with a projection onto the world of the American model, drawn from beliefs about institutions, world society, and international affairs that arose out of their understanding of the American experience. The American model was open trade in a strong set of international institutions—"embedded liberalism," as Ruggie (1982) named it. In realist reasoning this was the policy one would expect, given the United States' position in the world: the greatest military power, with an overwhelming share of world economic output. Free trade punctured the empires of America's allies and opened the world to American companies who faced no effective rivals. The institutions provided the rules for trade and finance in a type of competition Americans were likely to win. Alliances like NATO linked the members into a security system that defined obligations.

At the same time, American policy reflected other influences. Realist reasoning could also justify a different approach, a policy of domination and control, an empire, rather more in the Soviet model. Lake (1999, chap. 5) calls attention to the little known case of U.S. policy toward Micronesia, where the United States established imperial control. Toward Europe and the Soviets, there was extensive debate on policy: control Germany, as the Morgenthau Plan recommended, isolationism, accommodation of the Soviets. The outcome reflected a complex interplay of domestic politics, ideology about international relations, and realist calculations (Goldstein 1993; Goldstein and Keohane 1993; Burley 1993). Soviet behavior after 1917 and after 1945 arouses similar debates (Mayer 1959). Ideas and interests interact to simplify the information requirements of immensely complex institutional design episodes.

It is at this point that the rationalist analysis of strategic interaction, with a focus on Bayesian updating and learning, intersects with the literature on cognitive models, ideology, and the interpretation of identity and meaning (see Lake and Powell's discussion in chapter 1 of this volume). Governance disputes often involve situations of some ambiguity, where discretion is possible and judgment is required, situations where information is imperfect and costly. Ideas about situations help solve problems of uncertainty and lack of information; in a well-known article, Kreps (1990a) shows how "culture" solves coordination problems in corporations. Ideas lower search costs for information; where there is much uncertainty, unprecedented situations for which precedent is an imperfect guide for the future, simplification and lowering search costs are particularly valuable. Philosophies of government shape the process of institutional design by influencing the evaluation of preferences, the criteria of success or failure, and the framework of "updating" (Jervis 1970, 1976; Katzenstein 1996a, 1996b; Apter and Saich 1994).

Ideas become an indispensable part of strategic interaction because they form the basis of common language, or common conjecture (Goldstein and Keohane 1993). Game theoretic analysis of rational interaction assumes that the actors share some assumptions about how the world works, so they can make calculations about one another's probable behavior under specified conditions. Ideas about institutions and governance are thus a core element of strategic action. Ideas about institutions are themselves a type of "specific asset," an investment in knowledge. Political actors will have investments in ideas about how institutions work, ideas it is rational for them to use.

THE IMPACT OF INSTITUTIONS ON PREFERENCES AND STRATEGY

In the short term, within a single "box," to use the metaphor Lake and Powell developed in chapter 1, actors within governance disputes have stable preferences and beliefs, and thus clear strategies by which they choose institutions. In the longer term, however, it is clear that institutions alter the game as the actors succeed in altering institutions. Choices within a particular box affect attributes of the larger strategic setting "outside" the box. Here, we need to explore some of the feedback effects from past decisions on future conditions, a topic Miles Kahler examines further in the next chapter.

As actors invest in institutions, they see that as a result of their previous actions, the conditions of the interaction among them start to change. The rules of the institutions alter the actors' incentives. Consequently, actors may change their strategies. They may give up guns in place of policeman, accept contracts to be enforced by courts, pay taxes for education, and so on. As they undertake these changes, they evolve. They develop loyalties, attachments, perspectives. They move from individuals to citizens or subjects of a larger arena. They construct new selves. They go through a process of discovery and adjust their strategic interaction as conditions alter incentives and policy preferences. As this happens, the interaction of preferences, strategy, and governance structures is reciprocal. Governance mechanisms create a complex process of interaction where institutions and strategies influence each other (Gerber and Jackson 1993).

In this way, the strategic-choice and constructivist approaches intersect. The development of institutions allows the construction of new selves, indeed encourages it, if not actually requiring it. Without the institutions, these new constructs would not develop. This is the process observed when nations are formed out of diverse populations, for example, as individuals ceased being Norman or Bourgignon and became French (Weber 1976). Is this happening in Europe today? In creating the European Union, actors invest in strategies that create an environment that differs from the world that might exist had they not done so. As they come to depend on the Union, they can alter their behavior because of its existence (Rogowski 1989; Frieden 1988, 1991; Magee et al. 1989; Verdier 1994). As they alter their behavior, they themselves are altered internally. Strategic interaction sees this as revising strategies to attain a preference in light of new conditions that alter the probabilities of outcomes. Some constructivists would call this "forming new identities." The analytic dilemma turns on whether one is analyzing the short term, where it is reasonable to hold the elements of a strategic setting fixed, or the long term, where these elements obviously change and where one begins the first move. Durkheimians start with a system and move toward the unit; methodological individualists start with a unit and move toward the system. In the long term, it may be difficult to tell the difference between these two approaches.

A similar process can be observed when institutions disintegrate. Civil wars are conspicuous examples, the breakup of Yugoslavia being the most recent tragic case. So long as authority appeared strong, individuals could develop an identity as Yugoslavs, as members of a larger collectivity. People lived in Yugoslavia according to peaceful rules of conduct. The nation's institutions punished violence or other aggressive actions enacted by its citizens. Then political actors began to challenge the rules, demanding various changes. As the demands for change grew, confidence in the existing arrangements began to erode. Individuals, groups, and leaders could no longer be sure that acts of violence would be punished. Political "entrepreneurs" saw that acts of violence could provide advantages— for example, ethnic cleansing to homogenize territories. When that began, even friendly neighbors, critical of violence, began to fear for their own safety. Under the new conditions, friend and foe were no longer defined by class or political affiliation but rather by ethnicity, as defined by religion. As the governance structure was challenged, calculations of strategic interaction evolved to rework strategies about society and public policy. Preferences may have remained constant, but a vast change in strategy occurred from multi-ethnic tolerance to ethnic-based enmity (Laitin 1998;

Fearon and Laitin 1996; Lake and Rothchild 1996). In a tightly knit society the ties that bind its members are taken for granted, so much so that analysts ignore them—which is precisely the constructivists' complaint. When societies break apart, the conditionality of these bonds becomes more evident. People accept institutions because they assume that various arrangements will be honored. When evidence indicates that these commitments are not to be honored, institutions' preferences and other goals may change swiftly.

Analysts have modeled this process as a "tipping game," where individual preferences depend on the choices of others. As Laitin (1998, 326) suggests:

> Under conditions of oppression, people systematically engage in "preference falsification," in which they publicly reveal their support for the regime, or at least their apathy to politics. They lie not only to survey researchers but to their neighbors as well. If friends and neighbors each decide to conceal their true hatred for a regime unless it is safe to do otherwise—and consider safety to be only in large numbers—there can be long periods of quiet under conditions of profound enmity. Unpredictable events—in this case Gorbachev's signal that Soviet troops would not be used to support the East European communist regimes—can bring enough people (those who are willing to reveal their true preferences if only a small number of compatriots do so as well) into the streets to set off a cascade of protest. In May, there was order in Eastern Europe with no expectation whatsoever of imminent revolution, but by October all the East European satellite regimes had fallen.

Fearon and Laitin extend this reasoning to model ethnic conflict in Yugoslavia and elsewhere (Laitin 1998). Suzanne Lohmann (1994) models these shifts as an "informational cascade," where a few events provide important information that motivates massive action; she applies this reasoning to the collapse of the East European regimes of the Soviet era in 1989 (see also Hirschman 1993).

Civil wars pose important challenges to foreign-policy makers. Should they back the "legal" government or the insurgents (Lipson 1997)? Germany chose to recognize the independence of Croatia early in the Yugoslav crisis. Many critics argue that this ignited the breakup, which then launched the polarization process that led to civil war. Should Germany have known what would happen? Did German policy makers understand that identities, values, and strategies would change following their actions? Many experts on the region thought there were grave risks in making any change to the constitution of Yugoslavia that did not include mechanisms for managing ethnic relations. It is not unusual that expert advice is not followed. Did Germany know and accept the results, as the assumption of perfect information would assume? Or were German policy makers, and many other actors, not calculating clearly on the moves ahead (Walter 1994, 1997, 1998)?

Institutional design arises in ending civil wars, as well as in starting them. Civil wars may become intractable because the parties have difficulty trusting each other in the institutional arrangements of a settlement. Each side will turn to an institution that guarantees order and rights, but only if it has confidence that the institutional mechanism will hold. Barbara Walter (1998) argues that "domestic groups choose to battle 'to the death' before they reestablish order because any power sharing arrangement would, by definition, require them to relinquish any independent military forces and this fact makes them too helpless to survive attack and too weak to enforce long term cooperation." The parties to a dispute may be willing to negotiate a settlement but cannot be sure of its enforcement: They are unwilling to agree to power sharing arrangements that would make them vulnerable to betrayal by the other side. In these cases, argues Walter, the problem of civil war resolution is not, as many argue, irreconcilable conflicts, historical hatreds, conflicts of interest, greedy elites, or security dilemmas but rather the difficulty of constructing institutions that are able to enforce the agreement. Walter shows that this is where external intervention can have an effect, namely, by helping to guarantee the institutional arrangements of a peace settlement during the transition period necessary to build up confidence. In that situation, the outside forces act like the institutions of a constitution to structure the terms of interaction until enough "capital" has been invested and enough specific assets have accumulated in the settlement for it to become "self-enforcing."

To stop the killing in a Hobbesian state of nature, each side must trust that the other will exercise restraint. This can only happen if both sides accept an institution with the capacity for enforcement. They need not trust not each other, then; they need only trust that the institution will have the capacity to enforce the rules. In a constitutional order, that means accepting some alternation of power following established procedures; in an autocratic polity, it means accepting a Leviathan.

In the long run, strategy and institutions interact. In the next chapter Kahler examines this problem at greater length. In the context of the governance problem, actors form strategies in the framework of a particular institution. They also try to change institutions in their favor; other forces (e.g., technology, earthquakes, demographics) may be at work altering institutions as well. As the institutions change, so will strategies. This interactive process may be gradual and profoundly interdependent, making it difficult to know just where the strategic or institutional elements begin or end (Gerber and Jackson 1993).

CONCLUSION

Governance disputes lie at the intersection of conflicts shaped by rules and conflicts shaped by actors' capabilities. Frieden's essay in this volume (chapter 2) develops the logic of an argument about strategic interaction derived from preferences. To realize their policy objectives, actors must evaluate how these objectives interact with other actors' preferences so as to produce a strategy effective in a situation in which the actions of others matter. Morrow, in chapter 3 of this volume, analyzes the features of these interactions according to the type of game they produce. Rogowski, in chapter 4, examines what happens when the interactions are structured by different kinds of institutions. This chapter explores what occurs when institutions that manage disputes become themselves the objects of conflict. Here, it is assumed that political actors have awareness and the capacity to shape the structures of their interaction; Kahler, in the next chapter, explores the implications of eliminating the assumption of awareness.

Governance quarrels matter to the extent that institutions are important. Institutions structure power relations, so actors have every incentive to care about these institutions. They will deploy resources to shape institutions to their liking. As institutions develop, actors invest in them. The greater and more specific the investment, the larger the stake in any arrangement and the stronger the institution. If institutions are strong, they will shape the outcome of any governance quarrel. If institutions are weak, other resources of power come into play, such as the force of arms, powers of propaganda and persuasion, leadership skills, and economic leverage. To form institutions and to alter them poses collective-action problems. These can be overcome if there is a joint product, that is if some actors have a strong enough reward to pay the transaction costs of leadership.

Institutional formation and change poses information challenges. If information is complete and all aspects of the future can be fully anticipated, actors are playing a fully informed game where all aspects of the institutional arrangements being discussed are thoroughly grasped. If information is imperfect, if the future cannot be fully anticipated, then actors will have to turn to a variety of devices for linking together their preferences and strategies—for example, information shorthands, ideologies, prior convictions, philosophies about good and bad institutions—which construct a common knowledge among the players and reduce the information challenge to manageable proportions. These shorthands or ideologies come to influence the outcome of the strategic interaction in a governance dispute.

This instrumentalist approach to understanding governance disputes helps sort out arguments in international relations over the role of institutions, system, power, culture, and meaning. Realists doubt the importance of institutions in influencing behavior; they question the rewards institutions reap and the power that the investment of specific assets in them contributes to their persistence. Constructivists doubt the adequacy of self-interest that underlies the notion of specific assets in fully capturing the attachments actors form to the institutions around them. The Durkheimians among the constructivists, or among any system theorists, doubt that preferences form prior to a system. These alternative approaches lead to different understandings of a governance quarrel.

To some degree, the differences among these views are empirical: In some situations, the realist assumptions about institutions captures reality quite well; in other cases, institutions seem far more powerful. In some cases, the power of systems to shape the character of actors within those systems seems evident, whereas, in other situations, the system is constructed by actors whose characters are already formed.

The distinction between international relations and domestic politics can be recast as an empirical point about the strength of institutions. The governance struggle differs markedly in the factors that enter into play according to the strength of institutions. Where these are strong, governance arguments are greatly influenced by institutional procedures; this is likely to be the case in domestic systems but can also arise in international relations where institutions are strong. For this reason, quarrels within the European Union resemble domestic politics far more than they do the relations among states in wartime. Conversely, where institutions are weak, other power resources take on more importance, which can happen in both domestic and international settings. For this reason, countries experiencing civil war resemble international relations more than they resemble stable domestic politics.

Research cannot proceed effectively by putting all variables into play. As the editors of this volume note, methodological bets are vital. It is best to grasp the logic of each approach, follow it, and then explore what elements of reality it can or cannot model.

CHAPTER SIX.

Evolution, Choice, and International Change

MILES KAHLER

INTERNATIONAL relations has largely ignored evolutionary theories, which have become centers of vigorous investigation and debate in the biological sciences, in economics, and in philosophy. This skepticism has historical, empirical, and theoretical roots. Through a misreading of intellectual history, evolutionary theories have been tainted by their association with Social Darwinism and a particular image of international politics as a conflict-prone jungle. In addition, recent controversies surrounding sociobiology have left the mistaken impression that a deployment of evolutionary theory necessarily entails accepting a strong genetic influence on human behavior.

Equally important, the post-1945 international system does not appear to lend great support to a dynamic of variation and selection. Despite the birth of dozens of new and weak states, those weak states have, by and large, survived in much larger numbers than a crude evolutionary model might suggest. Even in a longer sweep of time, the survival of inefficient institutions remains a central puzzle in economic and international history. On a cursory reading of history, particularly recent history, the forces of selection appear weak or distorted. Finally, strong theoretical arguments have been made against a simple transfer of evolutionary theory from the biological to the social realm. In this view, evolutionary theories cannot be applied in more than a metaphorical way in the social sciences or international relations.

The advantages of an evolutionary approach, if a rigorous one could be developed, are equally clear. Evolutionary models impart a dynamic element to international relations theory and give it greater leverage in explaining historical change. Given the importance of the environment in "moving" evolutionary processes, evolutionary theories hold the promise of rehabilitating systemic theory and placing it on a sounder footing.

The author wishes to thank Jack Hirshleifer, John McMillan, Lou Pauly, and the others who contributed to *Strategic Choice and International Relations* for their comments on this chapter. Timothy Johnson provided excellent research assistance.

Whatever their ultimate success in stimulating theoretical development and empirical applications, evolutionary analogies jar our current assumptions and framework, forcing refinement and redesign.

Most important for this volume, evolutionary theory suggests limits to models of strategic choice as well as extending and enriching those models. An evolutionary approach carries to its limit one of the conceptual experiments described by Lake and Powell. Relatively spare claims about actor attributes permit both the relaxation of rationality assumptions and an examination of the explanatory power of the actors' environment. By widening conceptions of the strategic environment, evolutionary theories both underline and undermine a narrower definition of environment as a population with a limited menu of actions and information. Evolutionary theory also expands the scope of strategic-choice theory to a wider array of international settings and offers an avenue for explaining some persistent puzzles in strategic-choice accounts, such as selection among multiple institutional equilibria. Finally, evolution complements strategic choice by adding a dynamic driver to models that rely on equilibrium outcomes.

The first step in assessing evolutionary theories and their applications in international relations is establishing a benchmark, drawn from the natural sciences, for an evolutionary framework. Since social scientists have awarded evolution a wide array of definitions, establishing a common understanding from the outset is essential. The next section presents several applications, drawn largely from economics, of an evolutionary approach in the social sciences. Apart from assessing the strengths and shortcomings of these applications, this section also establishes the complementarities and tensions between an evolutionary and a strategic-choice framework. In the third section, three applications of an evolutionary approach to international relations are compared to alternative, nonevolutionary explanations. Each is concerned with population in international relations: how institutions evolve, why the average size of states has changed over time and why units of a particular kind (sovereign territorial states) have become dominant in modern international relations. These explorations lead to conclusions on the prerequisites of a successful research program inspired by evolutionary approaches to international relations and the benefits of integrating evolutionary and strategic-choice frameworks.

DEFINING EVOLUTIONARY THEORY: DARWINIAN NATURAL SELECTION AND ITS RIVALS

The "Darwin industry" in the history of science has both enriched our understanding of the evolution of evolutionary theory and undermined some long-standing and popular preconceptions about Darwin's role in the Darwinian revolution. Many controversies marked and continue to mark the working out of the Darwinian revolution in evolutionary biology. The rivals of Darwinian evolutionary theory have precise (and often more powerful) theoretical parallels in the social sciences.

Darwin, despite his central creative role (which has not been seriously undermined) did not invent evolution: In alternative forms, evolution was widely accepted before Darwin.[1] Darwin's essential contribution was proposing natural selection as the main mechanism by which evolution and the origin of species had come about. Natural selection remains the core of the Darwinian research program. In the theoretical break represented by natural selection, variation is not directed and appears independently of any adaptive advantage; selection working through the environment shapes that variation toward adaptedness. Causality shifts from the organism (where it lay in the principal rivals to Darwinian theory) to the environment (Depew and Weber 1995).[2] The mechanism of natural selection was suggested to Darwin, it seems, by two analogies: the artificial selection of stock breeders and the Malthusian model, drawn from political economy, of competition for survival within a population. The shift to "population thinking" was another part of the contribution that Darwin (and Alfred Russel Wallace, who arrived at a similar model at about the same time) made to the theory of evolution (Mayr 1982). Concentration on populations reinforced the gradualism of Darwin's image of evolution, in which macro-change (the origin of species) occurred through a host of micro-changes within a population set in a particular environment.

Darwin's *The Origin of Species* ultimately shattered the hold of theistic theories of evolution on the scientific community, but his revolution was an incomplete one. Peter J. Bowler (1983, 7–8) makes clear the power of Darwinism's rivals into the early twentieth century: the inheritance of acquired characteristics embodied in neo-Lamarckism, which offered powerful support for a progressive view of life and history; orthogenesis, in which evolution is driven by the unfolding of forces within organisms; and mutation (or saltation) in which species are born through large and sudden "leaps" of change. The power of these alternatives, particularly neo-Lamarckism, was such that only a fortuitous alliance between Darwinism and the neo-Mendelians, who founded the modern science of genetics, carried the day. Genetics provided a definitive explanation of

---

[1] This account of the development of evolutionary theory is based on Young 1992; Depew and Weber 1995; Bowler 1983, 1988; and Mayr 1982, 400–488.

[2] Depew and Weber (1995) argue the importance of the Newtonian model of physics in pressing Darwin toward an emphasis on "external rather than internal causes."

the principal source of variation in the neo-Darwinian synthesis of the twentieth century, rendering Lamarckism irrelevant to the new biological sciences. Lamarckism was also undermined by a deeper flaw in its logic— characters were acquired in response to new environmental conditions and then could be inherited without further influence from the environment (Bowler 1983, 76–77). This non-Darwinian variation in the plasticity of inherited traits points to a dilemma in transferring Darwinian models to social and cultural phenomena. Some social and cultural traits or behaviors are transmitted virtually without change, paralleling the heritability of traits in the Darwinian model; others can change dramatically over relatively short spans of time.

What, then, in skeletal form, does an evolutionary model on Darwinian lines require? In its barest form, it requires several crucial decisions. The first is a determination of the *relevant population or level* at which selection occurs. Here, classical Darwinians are adamant: Selection takes place at the level of the individual organism (or, more recently, the gene). Group or species selection is rejected. Although this neo-Darwinian consensus holds, the possibility of a hierarchy of selective processes that would include macroevolutionary "species sorting" or "species selection" has been raised by those who question the ability of the classical Darwinian model to deal with the paleontological record (Gould 1992, 60–63). Some perceive the Darwinian status quo as even more unsettled and predict that Darwinism may come to apply only to a middle range of processes at the level of organisms and populations; macroevolution and microevolution (below the level of the organism) may be governed to a lesser degree by selection and adaptation (Depew and Weber 1995, 15).

Any transfer of a Darwinian model to the social sciences must make similar judgments. One might argue that any evolutionary process must ultimately select on individual modes of behaviors or routines carried out by individuals (Matthews 1993:164–65). On the other hand, one could argue (in parallel with those espousing a hierarchy of evolution in the natural world) that selection or "sorting" of firms, organizations, or states is not reducible to the individual level.

Second, the *sources of variation* within a population and replication across generations must be identified. Although Darwin accepted the existence of variation in natural populations, the principal source of that variation, genetic mutation, had to wait decades for its identification. In social life and international relations, sources of variation in individual behavior or organizational routines are less difficult to identify, although the sources are more varied. More controversial is the existence of directed variation as individuals, firms, or states respond to environmental changes. The possibility of learning that is incorporated into social "genotypes" and reproduced across generations introduces a Lamarckian element into many evolutionary theories in the social sciences.[3]

Many social-science models of evolutionary design address the issue of replication by positing a high degree of inertia in human and institutional behaviors. That inertia is attributed to bounded rationality, reliance on routines, or path dependence. Although inertia of this kind may plausibly serve as a proxy for biological replication, it risks confining variation too much. Also, variation (innovation) in such models is often induced by environmental pressure, deviating from the random and undirected variation of Darwinian theory.

Third, the *selection environment* for the population in question must be identified. In classical Darwinism, intraspecific competition (on a model similar to that of Malthus) is the overriding feature of the selection environment: Since population size would increase exponentially if all members reproduced and the resources on which the population relies are relatively fixed, a "fierce struggle for existence" occurs in which only a fraction of each generation survives (Mayr 1982, 479–81). In the social world, vague references to competition or a "market for institutions" substitute for careful analysis of the features of a competitive environment. As Jack Hirshleifer (1987b) points out, in many social settings (such as most markets), certain types of competition familiar in nature (interference and predation) are ruled out. Market competition is limited to the "more innocuous forms of scramble" (depletion of resources). In fact, according to Hirshleifer, market competition is a three-sided competition—against a rival for the opportunity to engage in exchanges with a third party (consumer or supplier). As one moves further from a pure market environment to the politicized markets of most societies or to institutional environments, the selection environment and the dynamics of competition grow murkier. Many controversies in international relations revolve, in part, around the definition of the relevant selection environment for states. For realists, competition is defined by the military competition among great powers (in which lesser military powers play little or no role); for liberals, the environment may be defined more broadly to include economic actors (such as multinational corporations) that may interact strategically with states or by changes in economic parameters, such as relative prices, that may have effects on the differential success of states over time.

Adaptation, a fourth element at the core of the Darwinian research program, has been criticized by some biologists as Panglossian storytell-

---

[3] Larmarckian findings also creep back into the natural world. Two investigators studying animal behavior have recently argued that learned behaviors can be passed stably across generations (although not, of course, incorporated in the genotype) (Angier 1995).

ing, in which virtually every feature of an organism can be "explained" as an adaptation by a superselectionist (Gould and Lewontin 1979). Even convinced neo-Darwinians have admitted the careless use of adaptation and have cautioned against imputing adaptive value to each and every element of the phenotype. Traits may be "tolerated by natural selection but not specially shaped for life in a particular adaptive zone" (Mayr 1988, 136).

In applying evolutionary approaches to societies or international relations, adaptationist accounts are even more open to question. Although critics of adaptationist excess in biology may argue that there are constraints on adaptation because of body plans or other artifacts of evolutionary history, they would not deny the power of natural selection in inducing adaptation. The arguments for a developmentalist explanation in social or economic evolution are much stronger, since the power of environmental pressures to force adaptation is not so readily conceded. Rather than critics who argue against explaining *all* social phenomena as products of adaptation to selective pressures, many social scientists are likely to contest *any* role for environmental pressures in shaping the features of organizations, institutions, or states.

Finally, classical Darwinian theory has espoused *gradual change* as its model, following Darwin's dictum against evolutionary change by "leaps." The rate of evolutionary change became the subject of a widely followed (and often misunderstood) controversy within evolutionary biology, the question of punctuated equilibrium. In contrast to the classical Darwinian emphasis on steady, incremental evolutionary change, Stephen Jay Gould and Niles Eldredge proposed a model of periods of rapid speciation followed by periods of relative stasis (Somit and Peterson 1992). The debate later became embroiled in controversy over the hierarchy of selection noted above. Although punctuated equilibrium was quickly picked up by social scientists, its implications for evolutionary theories in the social sciences are, in fact, less important than the other constituents of Darwinian theory.

The term *evolutionary* has often taken on the connotation of gradual in the study of history and society; "evolutionary" approaches to economic reform, for example, have recently been contrasted to "shock treatment." Nevertheless, the "saltationist" view that history is also shaped by ruptures and variability in the rate of change has always been a powerful one. Although the gradualist view is still the predominant Darwinian one, more rapid change need not overturn an evolutionary theory if it does not at the same time undermine the underlying variation-selection-adaptation model of natural selection.

Darwin's theory of natural selection, as interpreted by the neo-Darwinian synthesis, erased assumptions of progress and intentional design in the natural world. Each of these issues continues, in different ways, to haunt Darwinian intellectual transfers, however. The assumption of human progress, carefully segregated from its biological analogue, proved to be a much more difficult artifact to eliminate in the social sciences and history. Outside the natural sciences, interest in evolutionary theory was often driven by its perceived progressive implications. Echoes of progressive assumptions can be heard in recent accounts of institutional evolution toward more efficient outcomes. Design, although not theistic design, has also lingered in unexpected ways. The belief in purposive design and its importance in human artifacts of all kinds—particularly institutions— does not contradict an evolutionary account, but it must contend with unintended evolutionary change that takes a course different from that intended by purposive agents (Hirshleifer 1987b). Tension between optimizing choice and institutional evolution through competitive selection reappears in efforts to link a Darwinian evolutionary view to a strategic-choice perspective (Matthews 1993).

The logic of Darwinian theory was not recognized in an abrupt, Kuhnian scientific revolution. It was worked out over decades as new scientific constituencies found in Darwin's ideas the missing pieces of different puzzles they confronted. Even its austere outlines remain controversial and contested, although estimates of the importance of recent assaults differ widely (Depew and Weber 1995; Dennett 1995). Those persistent controversies confirm, however, that the adaptations made by social scientists who import evolutionary theory are not simply an inevitable softening through misunderstanding.

Although a biologically based template for evolutionary models provides a useful point of departure, it should not be used as a tool to weigh and find wanting the softer adaptations of evolutionary theory found in the social sciences. In line with the pragmatism of strategic-choice theory, the success of those adaptations can only be estimated by their usefulness in explaining important international outcomes. Precisely which constituents of Darwinian theory are omitted or relaxed by social scientists and the logic of those efforts at redesign are the subjects of the next section.

CHOICE AND EVOLUTION IN THE SOCIAL SCIENCES

Darwinian theory had striking and well-documented connections to contemporary political economy. Darwin's famous reading of Thomas Malthus in 1838 and his appropriation of competition under conditions of scarcity were awarded an essential place by Darwin himself in the elaboration of natural selection. Others detect in Darwin's treatment of diversity another borrowing: Adam Smith's division of labor. Darwin's shift from an essentialist view of species as units to a selectionist approach based on populations of individual organisms grounded his theory in a fashion similar to economics (Depew and Weber 1995).

Despite these inherited similarities, Darwinism and the social sciences have diverged for much of their histories. Although social philosophers and social scientists claimed to be evolutionists, few were Darwinians. Perhaps natural selection's uncertain fate in biology permitted the social sciences to borrow an evolutionism that resembled Darwinism's rivals more closely than Darwinism itself. The overriding importance of the environment in the Darwinian scheme has presented one drawback to the transfer of Darwinian models. Skeptics well versed in Darwinian theory, such as John Maynard Smith (1972), have argued that Darwinism could assume a relatively fixed environment that populations could not change; human history, in Smith's view, cannot sustain that assumption without question, an assumption that is further undermined by economic and social development.

The overwhelming environmental determinism of Darwinism is difficult for social scientists to accept. At the same time, another basis of Darwinism—undirected, random variation—is also a difficult starting point for the social sciences, particularly those who deploy a strategic-choice approach. The purposive, designing character of human action means that variation often takes place to meet environmental change or challenge, and social or cultural variation will not be purely random. If a population and a selection environment can be clearly defined, these issues—the weight of the environment in determining outcomes and the potentially directed character of variation in human societies—must be confronted in any application of evolutionary theory to the social sciences. The issues replay the conceptual experiment of Lake and Powell by forcing attention to the importance of the environment as opposed to actor beliefs and preferences.

Despite the difficult methodological issues a theoretical transfer poses, evolutionary theories have demonstrated perennial appeal for one overriding reason: Darwinism offers a model of demonstrated power in explaining irreversible (noncyclical) change, analogous to historical change. At the same time, the Darwinian model requires nonheroic assumptions regarding the rationality and information-processing capabilities of populations.

Evolutionary theories in the social sciences that resemble the Darwinian model can be arrayed on two dimensions: the relative weight they assign to the selection environment in determining outcomes and their reliance on either populations displaying fixed behavioral repertoires or purposive, rational actors who "read" the environment and learn from past experience or from other players. One cluster of "hard Darwinian" approaches mimics natural selection by concentrating attention on selection pressures on large populations, with few concessions to individual foresight or choice. Evolutionary economics relaxes both the environmental and behavioral assumptions, the latter by accepting directed rather than random variation. Evolutionary game theory remains closest to a frame of strategic choice, melding nonheroic rationality assumptions with outcomes in which particular strategies coexist or dominate. These evolutionary approaches share populations that typically consist of institutions (often firms); they aim to explain the "differential growth and survival of patterns of social organization." "Inheritance" can be supplied by the "deadweight of social inertia, supported by intentionally taught tradition." Variation is incorporated by mutations in the form of "copying errors," imitation, and rational thought (Hirshleifer 1982, 221).

"Hard Darwinism"

Armen Alchian's (1950, 211) account of firm competition, an "extreme random-behavior model without any individual rationality, foresight, or motivation whatsoever," is an early exemplar of the "hard Darwinian" model transferred to economic competition. His model is designed to demonstrate that, given assumptions about the selection criterion, in this case "realized positive profits," rational or optimizing assumptions about the agents are not required. Firm success may well be the result of luck or chance. This model, if its stringent conditions are accepted, does not rule out judgments on the viability of different firms: "With a knowledge of the economy's realized requisites for survival and by a comparison of alternative conditions, [the observer] can state what types of firms or behavior relative to other possible types will be more viable, even though the firms themselves may not know the conditions or even try to achieve them" (Alchian 1950, 216).

Alchian's Darwinian model stands at one end of this array of evolutionary models (emphasis on competitive selection by the environment, no requirement of rational or optimizing behavior on the part of agents), but he admits the possibility of individual efforts at adaptation through purposive, foresighted behavior. (Of course, there is no guarantee that such behavior will be selected.) Like other evolutionary theorists, under conditions of uncertainty, he suggests that "rough and ready" imitative rules of behavior are one likely alternative; another is innovative trial-and-error behavior. Outside an evolutionary framework, John Steinbruner's (1974) cybernetic model of decision making incorporates a similar model of simple learning from a limited repertoire of environmental cues; learning takes place only in the sense that a unit's behavior changes systematically. Also drawn from foreign-policy analysis is a nonlearning model that Philip Tetlock labels "autistic": wholly nonadaptive with no effective feedback from the environment (Breslauer and Tetlock 1991). Although Tetlock's version assigns the environment only a very small role in the determination of outcomes, such a model of individual behavior could be implanted in a Darwinian model (as it is in Alchian's) with the crucial change that final *outcomes* are determined by environmental selection rather than internally driven change.

Few applications of evolutionary models have adopted a hard Darwinian approach. Organizational ecology, which attempts to transfer explicitly biological categories to the study of populations of organizations, is an important exception (Carroll 1984; Hannan and Freeman 1989). "Population thinking" and an emphasis on the environment as a powerful explanatory variable are important constituents of this Darwinian approach to organizational selection and survival. Another key and controversial assumption is inertia. Organizations are not viewed as highly plastic or malleable; managers or leaders are predicted to have little long-term effect on the survival prospects of institutions they direct. Given these assumptions, organizational ecology sets itself apart from, on the one hand, explanations of organizational change through learning or adaptation in response to environmental change and, on the other, change based on random transformation in response to internal dynamics. In the view of organizational ecologists, "most of the variability in the core structures of organizations comes about through the creation of new organizations and organizational forms and the demise of old ones" (Hannan and Freeman 1989, 11–12).

Although organizational ecology seems to transpose the Darwinian model neatly to the organizational world, the preceding declaration suggests a central ambiguity: what it is that changes, is created, or dies. An ecological approach would take the rise and fall of populations in competition with other populations as the core research question. Some organizational ecologists, however, seem intent on explaining some equivalent of the origin of species (of organizations)—the evolution of organizational forms. Unfortunately, as their critics have pointed out, no clear organizational taxonomy exists to define when a new "species" has emerged (Young 1988).[4]

Apart from asserting powerful forces of inertia within organizations, organizational ecology also lacks a convincing model for the equivalents of inheritance and reproduction. An emphasis on inertia also overrides a careful examination of the sources of variation and ultimately "speciation" in organizational form, although one hypothesis relates organiza-

[4] For a response on the taxonomy issue, see Carroll 1984, 78–80.

tional innovation to the movement into new resource spaces (parallel to allopatric speciation in nature) (Romanelli 1991).

The most telling criticisms of the organizational ecology approach, however, have centered on two issues that arise repeatedly when Darwinism is transferred to the social sciences. Organizations, as human constructions, can influence their environment; specifically, they can create resources. The intense competitive struggle over resources that is part of the organizational ecology perspective must, therefore, be demonstrated or qualified (Young 1988). The issue of human agency and the ability of organizations to direct their adaptations consciously and successfully has undoubtedly created the greatest unease, however, particularly among those who make a living by advising organizations on their strategies. The view from organizational ecology is clear, if unproven: Adaptation is not directed. As Hannan and Freeman declare: "In a world of high uncertainty, adaptive efforts by individuals may turn out to be essentially random with respect to future value" (1989, 22). This radically skeptical view about the ability of organizations to learn in an adaptively advantageous way is perhaps the most unsettling of the implications of this and other Darwinian applications in the social sciences.

Evolutionary Economics

Evolutionary economics, as elaborated by Richard R. Nelson and Sidney G. Winter, moves another step away from natural selection in the array of evolutionary approaches. Unlike the "hard" Darwinian models just described, Nelson and Winter's enterprise aims to explain economic change or "the dynamic process" that lies behind change in a variable over time by shifting emphasis toward an adaptive agent and adding simple learning to the model. Nelson's (1995) definition of an evolutionary model accepts that the variable in question is subject to random variation and "systematic selection forces" that "winnow" on the variation. Nelson and Winter (1982) are critical of the optimization and equilibrium frameworks of conventional economics, but they argue that "blind" and "deliberate" processes can be interwoven in an evolutionary account. As a result, their evolutionary theory is "unabashedly Lamarckian": Variation in behavior can be stimulated by adverse conditions (directed variation), and variation can then become embedded in organizations (inheritance of acquired characteristics).

The population of interest for Nelson and Winter is a population of firms or other large, complex organizations engaged in the provision of goods and services for an identifiable clientele. At least rough measures of good and bad performance can be established for the population. (The scope of their theory could therefore apply to many other large organizations, including nation-states.) Their version of evolutionary economics is devoted to explaining economic change, particularly technological change, and offering a new understanding of economic growth. Nelson and Winter argue that disaggregation to the level of differential survival and growth in a particular population of firms should provide a better explanation of these economic outcomes than conventional theory.

Although Nelson and Winter move away from the random variation and environmental selection of hard Darwinian models, they also keep their distance from an optimizing view of firm behavior as well. Routines, "regular and predictable behavioral patterns of firms," are central to their conception of "organization genetics"; routine provides in more empirically defensible form the "inertia" posited by organizational ecologists. Routines provide the fixity across "generations" of organizations that evolutionary theories require. They are also the source of variation on which the selection environment can operate, for within the classes of routines are those that can modify the operations of the firm, changes that are modeled as "searches" (Nelson and Winter 1982). Searches that produce new behavior are the sources of innovation, which lies at the heart of any theory of technological change.

Here as well, however, Nelson and Winter walk a line between a model of foresighted adaptation to change and complete inertia or random search. The firm (or its leadership) may select options, but deliberate, maximizing choice is not part of their model. Instead, their model of innovation includes bounded rationality and a cybernetic style of search by existing firms or by potential entrants to an industry stimulated by changing environmental conditions. Innovation can have a multiplier effect through a process of imitation, a further deviation from a purely biological model. Their selection environment diverges from a simple one of market competition under conditions of scarcity. The market is the core of the selection environment, since successful innovation leads to higher profits, further investment, and firm growth (in turn, shaping larger patterns of economic growth). Relatively unsuccessful firms lose market share and profitability, and shrink. On the other hand, Nelson and Winter stipulate several additional elements in a complete model of the selection environment: the costs and benefits that enter the calculus of a firm deciding on an innovation; the way that consumer and regulatory preferences define "profitability"; the relationship between "profit" and the expansion or contraction of the organization; and the mechanisms of imitation (Nelson and Winter 1982, 262–63). This effort to flesh out the constituents of the environment is one of the most innovative features of Nelson and Winter's evolutionary model.

This version of evolutionary economics, designed to further an important research agenda, seems a useful corrective to both an austere Darwinism or a conventional optimization model. Unfortunately, its relaxation of Darwinian assumptions retains an ad hoc flavor. Evolutionary economics has, somewhat counterintuitively, attempted to explain innovation and technological change using a model of firm behavior that remains strongly inertial and undirected. Unfortunately, defining its central constituents is difficult. Routines are central for Nelson and Winter, but the degree of fixity required to qualify as a "routine" is difficult to estimate: Routines must change in the face of poor performance, or adaptive organizational change would be impossible. If routines are too plastic, however, then the constancy required in an evolutionary model falls away. In similar fashion, Nelson and Winter accept that the environment for firms is changeable—fixity cannot be assumed as it typically is in nature— yet the features that can be pulled from the environment as key predictors of firm performance are very difficult to estimate empirically. The differentiation required in the definition of a selection environment could lead to increasingly individualized "environments" and undermine the evolutionary notion of a population confronting a relatively uniform environment.

Evolutionary Game Theory

Evolutionary game theory, a wide bridge for exchange between biology and the social sciences, also provides an evolutionary approach that incorporates and qualifies a starting point in strategic choice. Evolutionary game theory has been borrowed directly from one of the most fertile frontiers of evolutionary biology, where game theory has provided a means to explain the evolution of behaviors (or, more broadly, phenotypes) in settings where "success depends on what others are doing" (Maynard Smith 1982, 1). Payoffs are related to reproductive success (an increase in fitness); since strategies are attached to individual members of nonhuman populations, evolutionary game theory in biology is "game theory without rationality" (Rapoport, cited in Sigmund 1995, 167). As Binmore and Samuelson (1992, 286) describe:

> In evolutionary game theory, a game G is seen as being played repeatedly. Each time it is played, Nature chooses its players from a population whose composition changes over time. The players do not think about how to play G. They are endowed with strategies by a process of mutation and selection that tends to eliminate strategies that are relatively less successful.

The relevant "environment" in these cases is defined as other members of a population, often, though not always, members of the same species.

Although the presence of more than two strategies may result in complicated and unstable outcomes between competing populations, two alternatives will produce either domination of one strategy (and its adoption by the entire population), bi-stability (each strategy is a best reply against itself, and initial advantage leads through reinforcement to dominance of one or the other), or coexistence, in which both strategies persist (Sigmund 1995).

Of course, the existing strategies are constantly challenged by new strategies introduced through mutation. John Maynard Smith developed the important concept of an evolutionarily stable strategy (ESS) to describe a strategy that cannot be invaded by another, mutant strategy as the result of natural selection. Determining whether and when an ESS emerges (it is far from inevitable) has been central to the research program spawned by evolutionary game theory's treatment of biological populations.

For economists and other social scientists, evolutionary game theory has provided a response to two somewhat different difficulties in strategic choice: bounded rationality (injecting more "realism" into game-theoretic assumptions about the information-processing capabilities of players) and multiple equilibria (Samuelson 1993; Morrow 1994a). If evolutionary biologists began with hard-wired populations that were the equivalent of automata, social scientists worked back from demanding definitions of rationality to far more limited notions. Evolutionary game theorists have introduced behavioral hypotheses as a means of modeling bounded rationality and learning of a simple sort: inertia (uncertainty and adjustment costs); myopia (which incorporates Alchian's imitation); and mutation (a small probability that a player will change strategies at random) (Kandori, Mailath, and Rob 1993). These hypotheses introduce enough consistency in agent behavior for selection to operate. Equilibrium selection is driven, in some cases, by mutations introduced into the agent populations or by "mistakes" made by the boundedly rational agents in the learning process (Samuelson 1993).

The interest of biologists in mutual aid or cooperative behavior—a puzzle given the "selfish gene" basis of competition among members of a species—further stimulated interest in the prerequisites for these outcomes and reasons for the robustness, stability, and initial viability of particular strategies, particularly Tit-for-Tat (TFT) as a strategy in the Prisoner's Dilemma game. In the work of Robert Axelrod, Jack Hirshleifer, and others, this research agenda was transferred to the social sciences and international relations (Axelrod 1984; Hirshleifer and Martinez Coll 1988). Although an active research program based on increasingly complex simulations continues, the results of those simulations, despite their suggestiveness for social and international phenomena, have increasingly called into question the broad original claims made for the superiority of TFT. Other empirical applications of evolutionary game theory have produced interesting and often counterintuitive results. In their modeling of financial market behavior, Blume and Easley (1992) discovered that the link between rationality and fitness was weak, further eroding the automatic identity of optimizing behavior and competitive fitness that once was accepted. Their model was also able to suggest selective advantages for particular types of learning. In an application with profound importance for social evolution, H. Peyton Young (1991) has modeled the evolution of conventions on the basis of no common knowledge and minimal rationality: "Society can 'learn' even when its members do not." Spatial proximity, which reduces the costs of recognition, has been demonstrated as highly important in the emergence of cooperation among animals and plants (Nowak, May, and Sigmund 1995, 80–81). Axelrod also noted the significance of clustering for initial invasions of TFT into hostile populations. These findings echo the tentative findings of Kurt Gaubatz (1993) that democracies have tended to form clusters historically (apart from a brief period in the interwar years), even though that clustering has not produced advantages in capabilities vis-à-vis nondemocracies.

Despite these suggestive applications of evolutionary game theory, the limited transfer from this species of strategic choice to empirical research agendas may illustrate weaknesses in the evolutionary analogy that resemble those in other evolutionary approaches. Those questions concern defining the population, describing the sources of variation in the models, specification of the environment, and justifying the limits imposed on the rationality of agents.

Although populations, defined by strategies, are relatively easy to delineate in evolutionary models of this kind, those populations typically consist of atomistic individuals; in the case of many simulations, real individuals. No social structure or decision rules for acting collectively are introduced, which also makes direct application to social actors more difficult (Hirshleifer and Martinez Coll 1988). These models do not provide explanations for the degree of original variation among strategies in a society or its sources. The introduction of variation in the populations through mutation is generally ad hoc: The rate at which mutations occur in a social or economic setting is difficult to estimate. One of the key differences between biological and social settings is the probable rate of mutation: In the former, they are relatively rare; in the latter, they may occur so frequently that existing equilibria do not have time to adjust between their appearance (Binmore and Samuelson 1992). Outcomes are often highly sensitive to sequencing and rate of entry of new mutants and their strategies. A shift in competitive pressures that results in an ESS may, through degeneration in the frequency of particular strategies, permit invasion by another competitor to which it had previously been immune

(Young and Foster 1991). If mutants can introduce any completely new form of behavior, mutants can then alter the game being played as well as the frequency of particular strategies (Mailath 1992).

As has been the case in other evolutionary approaches, specification of the selection environment has proven difficult in both game simulations and social and historical settings. As Blume and Easley (1992) point out, in financial markets and other economic situations, the fitness criterion in a given environment (embodied in the payoffs) must be chosen carefully. Many apparently robust strategies have proven to be highly sensitive to environmental conditions, when environment is defined as populations with different strategies. Doubts regarding the early findings of TFT's dominant position under many environmental conditions have emerged with additional simulations. Hirshleifer argues that the success of TFT in furthering cooperation through evolution is "highly situation-dependent." Altering some of Axelrod's initial conditions favors other strategies or permits a stable equilibrium in which several strategies coexist (Hirshleifer and Martinez Coll 1988). Hirshleifer and Martinez Coll (1992, 272) argue that typically a wider menu of strategies will survive in many environments, coexisting, "each doing relatively well in some environmental contexts but not in others." Recent simulations suggest that a much less demanding strategy (in terms of probability of error or cost of complexity) of win-stay, lose-shift (labeled Pavlov) may be a more widespread basis for the evolution of cooperation in nature than TFT (Nowak and Sigmund 1993).

Environment in a social or historical setting may include more than populations of players, however. How that larger environment feeds into the payoff structure and discount parameters is rarely made explicit. Hirshleifer, for example, makes changes (such as introducing an elimination rather than a round-robin tournament) that suggest a "harsher" or less forgiving overall environment. Such key environmental adjustments might correspond to changes in military technology (the sucker's payoff becomes complete destruction rather than future economic disadvantage or some other economic penalty) or a growth in trade (increasing the payoffs for cooperation).

As described earlier, evolutionary game theory also permits the relaxation of stringent rationality assumptions. The naive and fixed quality of "strategy" (taken to mean "a specification of what an individual will do in any situation in which it may find itself") eliminates the need for sophisticated recognition, reasoning, and learning abilities (Maynard Smith 1982, 10). Applications of evolutionary game theory in the social sciences have incorporated simple learning behavior, and some have even determined the relative fitness of different types of learning. The realistic qualities that bounded rationality add to evolutionary models are also necessary for the inertial and consistent quality of behavior in those models. As Morrow (1994a, 204) suggests, however, bounded rationality has several meanings: It requires precise definition and justification before it is deployed in evolutionary models. The plausible limits on human reasoning will change from environment to environment: Such a typology remains to be constructed.

Although simulations of strategic interaction that follow rough Darwinian precepts and evolutionary game theory have provided tantalizing analogies to social and international interaction, a research program linking strategic choice and evolutionary dynamics is only now taking shape. As Anatol Rapoport (1988) warns, it is premature to offer policy prescriptions on the basis of simulations confined by such restrictive (and apparently sensitive) conditions. Nevertheless, applications of evolutionary game theory provide a promising avenue for melding realistic reasoning assumptions, strategic choice, and a dynamic provided by selective pressures acting on populations of actors.

EVOLUTION, INSTITUTIONS, AND THE UNITS
OF INTERNATIONAL RELATIONS

Preceding chapters in this volume have demonstrated the central place that strategic choice has long occupied in international relations. An evolutionary vocabulary has also been part of international relations, but, until recently, evolutionary theories have not been. Kenneth Waltz (1979), for example, asserts that selection and socialization are the two principal mechanisms through which structure affects behavior in international politics. In his treatment of selection through competition, he employs a radically Darwinian vocabulary at some points (rationality means "only that some do better than others—whether through intelligence, skill, hard work, or dumb luck") but never elaborates a clear intervening indicator of differential "success" (apart from simple survival), a clear portrait of the competitive environment, or an assessment of how the selection environment varies over time.

Robert G. Gilpin's (1981) influential treatment of change in international politics is more cyclical than evolutionary. In his account of rise and decline of hegemonic powers, the sources of change are endogenous to particular states; pressures from other states do not figure directly. Limitations on change and expansion include the "generation of opposing power," but emphasis is placed on internal processes that set limits to the expansion of scale: centrifugal forces within the state and structural changes in its economy.

The evolutionary theories described in the preceding section have been drawn largely from economics, where competitive selection of agents (particularly firms) has been an important theoretical contender with models based on optimization. The strengths of an evolutionary approach to world politics are best displayed in international change of a kind that Darwinian models explain in nature: changes in the characteristics of populations over relatively long periods of time (or many iterations of play). Three constituents of international relations have inspired alternative theories with evolutionary outlines: selection among alternative institutional equilibria, selection on the scale of the units, and institutional isomorphism among these units (selection that leads to the dominance of a particular "species" of units—sovereign territorial states—with a striking number of similar characteristics). These applications of evolutionary models to international relations also parallel one of the methodological bets of the strategic-choice approach described by Lake and Powell: Evolutionary models can be applied to different levels of analysis that present a "seamless web from individuals to international outcomes."

Institutional Evolution

Peter Gourevitch has described the emergence of institutions—domestic and international—as strategic equilibria among specified agents. Institutional change can be explained by endogenous change in preferences or strategic repertoires (through learning). An alternative source of institutional change is evolution: competitive selection among institutional equilibria over time.

One of the most influential and superficially evolutionary accounts for institutional change is that of Friedrich von Hayek. For Hayek, institutions and "spontaneous order" emerge through a process he portrays as parallel to natural selection, neither natural (genetically based) nor artificial (the product of conscious human design). Institutional order is the result of "a process of winnowing or sifting, directed by the differential advantages gained by groups from practices adopted for some unknown and perhaps purely accidental reasons" (Hayek 1979, 155). The emergence of order bears some resemblance to the evolution of cooperation through "blind" selection on self-interested strategies, but Hayek's analogy is clearly the market system and its ability to marshal the particular informational advantages of individuals and coordinate their activities. Hayek's view of institutional evolution also resembles Darwinian evolution in his occasional anti-teleological declarations: Unlike his bêtes noires (among them, Karl Marx), Hayek does not believe we can comprehend the direction of history or suggest any laws of evolution.

Unfortunately, Hayek's allusions to natural selection remain just that. He does not present a coherent evolutionary theory for institutional development. The sources of continuing variation and institutional innovation are obscure (Hodgson 1993b). Hayek posits a vague "market for institutions" in which groups (his is a theory of group selection in the cultural and institutional sphere) are advantaged and disadvantaged by means unspecified in an environment that operates according to other than market criteria. (The eradication of entire cultures through war and conquest, for example, hardly fits with Hayek's relatively benign, "bottom up" view of human evolution.) As Nelson (1995, 82) describes, Hayek resembles other theorists of institutional evolution in failing to specify how selective mechanisms work, whether they are purely selective or involve some learning (beyond simple trial and error), and why they benefit society as a whole rather than the particular and powerful interests of groups within society. Finally, Hayek's attitude toward rationality remains ambivalent: hostile to all rationalist "grand designs" imposed from above yet intent on mobilizing intervention against such collectivist designs when evolution goes astray (Hodgson 1993b, 183–85). Apparently, "blind" evolution must finally be corrected by reason and learning, learning based, in this case, on Hayek's reading of the twentieth century.

The evolving neo-institutionalism of Douglass C. North represents another influential account of institutional change that incorporates implicit evolutionary assumptions. In his early work North's arguments about institutions are driven explicitly by considerations of efficiency: The creation of more efficient economic organization is the key to understanding the success of the West in comparison to other regions in the early modern era (North and Thomas 1973). The evolution of more efficient economic organization in Western Europe, in turn, was driven by underlying changes, particularly the expansion of trade and changes in military technology, that increased the optimal size of political organization. North's early statements have an inevitabilist and functionalist quality, in which these changes point toward the emergence of nation-states. International military competition lurks in the background of the account, but as the last chapters of *The Rise of the Western World* suggest, there was no convergence (apart from scale of political unit) on isomorphic internal institutional arrangements. The Netherlands and England were both the most efficient political economies in Europe and outliers because of their relatively small scale. Although North claimed that international competition provided a "powerful incentive" for convergence among the principal states of Europe and there was some convergence on a larger scale (even this is disputed), there was little convergence between the domestic institutional arrangements of those who forged ahead economically and those who fell behind. Failure to converge on the most efficient institutional design has become the central problem in North's most recent work.

North (1994) has now explicitly abandoned his argument that institutions necessarily evolve in the direction of allocative efficiency. Institutions reduce uncertainty, but there is no guarantee that they will provide an efficient framework for human interaction. Unlike Hayek, North (1990) is aware that persistent institutions are all too often highly inefficient and conducive to economic stagnation. Instead of assuming a selective tendency toward more efficient institutions, North now attempts to explain why economic stagnation in the context of inefficient institutions can persist so long, for centuries in many cases. His model continues to rely on competition and the market, although he admits that political markets are very different from economic ones.

At the core of his explanation for the failure of competitive selection, an inability to winnow out inefficient economic and political organization, is the notion of adaptive efficiency: Rules that permit societies to "acquire knowledge and learning, to induce innovation, to undertake risk and creative activity of all sorts, as well as to resolve problems and bottlenecks of the society through time" (North 1990, 80). The core explanation for adaptively inefficient societies appears to be institutional path dependence (or lock-in), on the one hand, and cognitive barriers to social learning, on the other. The competitive environment, vaguely defined in early North, has virtually disappeared in late North, where the explanations for differential economic performance are wholly endogenous, linked to the weight of the past (path dependence) and cognitive and ideological filters that obstruct collective learning. These predispositions for institutional inertia could form the basis of a selection argument; for North, they are explanations for institutional stasis and economic failure.

The virtual disappearance of the selection environment in North's revised account of institutional evolution only confirms the criticisms leveled against the neoclassical view of institutions. Defining a relevant competitive environment is made more difficult by the very broad definition awarded to "institutions"—"humanly devised constraints that shape human interaction" (North 1990; Nelson 1995). But it is far from clear that the competitive environment—which continues to receive bows in the new institutionalist literature—is of central concern. As James Caporaso (1989, 154) argues, the new institutional history at best flirts with creating an evolutionary theory for institutional change, which would require "a language shift from efficiency to adaptation, from utilities to selectors, and from conscious choice to blind (unforesightful) probes." Rather than reinstating ill-defined analogies to competitive markets, an evolutionary approach would call into question the market analogy and set to work examining the selectors (Nelson's selection environment) at work in institutional change. Assessing the weight of that environment and delineating its contours has hardly begun: "We have very little understanding of how this kind of a selection environment works, and how it defines 'fitness.' We have no reason to believe that such selection environments are stringent, or stable, much less that they select on 'economic efficiency' " (Nelson 1995, 83).

Evolutionary game theory has provided a somewhat different view of institutional emergence and the possibility of stable institutional equilibria. Axelrod's (1986) treatment of the evolution of norms resembles his earlier simulations of the evolution of cooperation in the n-person Prisoner's Dilemma game. Rational behavior is not assumed; a small probability of mutation in the populations is added; "reproductive success" is awarded to the more successful players. He adds a central assumption that stable norms depend on some probability of enforcement, which entails costs for both the target and the enforcer. The pattern that emerges, under certain initial assumptions of willingness to defect (with a risk of detection) and willingness to punish within the population, is growing norm-observant behavior (under threat of punishment), decline in the punishing population (because of the enforcement costs), and a subsequent rise in violation of norms—in short, stable norms fail to emerge. The norms game achieves stability only with the introduction of a meta-norms game in which those who fail to punish defection are themselves punished (and this outcome is dependent on a sufficiently high level of vengefulness, i.e., a high probability that defection of either kind will be punished!). Whether sufficient levels of vengefulness in support of meta-norms are approached in human populations is an empirical question that Axelrod does not answer.

Ulrich Witt (1989) develops an evolutionary alternative that is more Hayekian in inspiration: Institutions are propagated in the absence of strategic behavior through diffusion and imitation effects alone. The utility of adopting an institutional or normative innovation in this model is dependent on the relative frequency of other adopters in the population. In certain cases, propagation will occur "spontaneously" because of the individual benefits of the population, and a stable institutional equilibrium will be reached. In other cases, the critical mass of adopters cannot be reached without the intervention of "diffusion agents" who serve to propagate new institutions by inducing "a sufficient number of other agents to expect that collective adoption will come about, so that the expectation becomes self-fulfilling."

Finally, Young (1991) develops a model for the emergence of self-enforcing conventions that does not depend on deductive reasoning or the positing of a focal point. Rather, expectations over time converge on an equilibrium because of the feedback effect of past play. Young demonstrates that these expectations will converge in an evolutionary fashion on one equilibrium, a stochastically stable equilibrium, if there is sufficient stochastic variability (representing experimentation or mistakes) in the players' responses.

Each of these approaches to the evolution of norms, conventions, and institutions contains different assumptions regarding rational behavior, strategic interaction, and a stable or randomly fluctuating environment. Those differences, in turn, reflect the variety of institutions and the strategic context underlying them (the need for enforcement, for example, or the possibility of spontaneous and self-interested adoption). An evolutionary model of institutions provides a means of explaining the emergence of single (or limited) institutional alternatives among the many multiple equilibria that exist in the context of behavior that, at best, exhibits bounded rationality.

Evolution and the Scale of Units

From the end of feudalism until the end of World War II the scale of units in world politics appeared to increase, reaching its peak in a world conflict conducted by gigantic (by historical standards) political units—empires and superpowers-to-be. Following 1945, decolonization brought a rapid decline in the average scale of nation-states, a trend that has received a recent additional inflection with the end of the Soviet Union and Yugoslavia. Several theories have been proposed to account for this pattern. David Friedman (1977) bases his theory on the calculus of a fiscal maximizer: Territory is valued for the increase in tax revenues that it promises (net of collection costs). Taxes on different bases (land, trade, and labor) have different implications for this calculus. In Friedman's analysis, trade and labor offer potential tax resources that can "escape" an individual ruler: Trade will be either undertaxed or overtaxed if trade routes fall in different jurisdictions; labor can move to another jurisdiction if it is taxed. A relative increase in these two sources of tax revenue will lead to efforts at extending territorial control (or expanding ethnic homogeneity) in order to maximize revenue. Friedman argues that the collapse of trade in the early feudal period encouraged the fragmentation of political units that were wholly dependent on land for revenue. As trade expanded in the late medieval period, political units grew in size, and ethnic groups were increasingly found within one political unit.

A different logic informs a recent article by Alberto Alesina and Enrico Spolaore (1997). Their assumptions include democratic polities in which a population's preferences over public goods must be satisfied by their leaders. Tension arises between economies of scale in the provision of public goods and the probability that a larger population will be more heterogeneous in its preferences over the public goods provided. One implication is that a world of democratic polities, in which the population's preferences must be conceded, will display smaller scale in its units than a world of dictatorships. A second implication flows from the advantages of increasing scale and the preferred means of capturing those benefits: As economic integration increases (barriers to trade decline), the size of the country is less significant. Therefore, Alesina and Spolaore contend that the size of nations will vary inversely with the degree of economic integration among them.

Absent from both these accounts is any consideration of the competitive environment of these units: Friedman's model may assume a competitive reason for revenue maximizing; Alesina and Spolaore concede that the role of military threats and defense spending must be added to their model. Their opposed predictions on one key relationship—the effects of increasing trade on size of political units (Friedman predicts an increase in size, Alesina and Spolaore a decline) is related to this failure to take into account competition from other units. In some circumstances, the most advantageous means to capture the gains from increasing trade is to capture or subordinate other political units (both the early modern period and the late nineteenth century seem to confirm this relationship); in other periods, such as the late twentieth century, territorial control is disconnected from the gains of economic integration.

A third model comes closer to incorporating the competitive environment into an explanation of scale through the variable of military technology. Richard Bean (1973) links apparently exogenous changes in "the art of war" to an increase in the optimal size of the state during the period from 1400 to 1600. The introduction of cannons and particularly the adoption of standing armies (rather than feudal levies) increased the revenue demands of the state (and directly diminished the chances of internal resistance). Economies of scale could be achieved through distributing public goods provision over a larger tax base; a larger territory would also increase the gains from trade. In Bean's account the process of state expansion had an inner face (centralization) and an outer face (consolidation of smaller units into larger ones).

Leaving aside the actual degree of consolidation in these centuries (some fragmentation also occurred), Bean's account is weakened by its failure to address the selective and competitive processes that may have encouraged the increase in scale. The standing army of infantry was hardly a new technology: The demand of sovereigns for this old-new military instrument bears explanation; a change in the competitive environment is a plausible candidate. The advantages of larger scale stipulated by Bean are dependent on a fixed administrative and fiscal technology (innovation in revenue raising could be enhanced in smaller units, as it was in the Netherlands and England) and the absence of offsetting costs to increased scale. In fact, a central argument of economic historians has been the importance of changes that accompany increased scale and centralization: Too much centralization could embed inefficient institutions that were deleterious to long-term growth. An overpowerful sovereign had no incentive to concede the protection of property rights and other institutional innovations conducive to long-term growth (North and Thomas 1973). An optimal size, given existing military technology, might be attained through means that reduced long-run selective advantage. Rather than positing that "competition will tend to eliminate firms whose size is outside the optimal range" (through disintegration or absorption), this casual market analogy requires explication. The selection environment may have induced the shift in military technology as well as setting both upper and lower bounds on the scale of viable political units. Given the continued survival of a multitude of small polities in Europe after 1600, the intensity of competition itself must also be called into question.

The Evolutionary "Fitness" of the Nation-State

The adaptive advantages of the sovereign territorial nation-state are raised in Bean's account of early modern Europe. Although he emphasizes an increase in the scale of political units, the population of Europe also witnessed a shift in the type of political unit. Just as scale increased through the mid-twentieth century, so the frequency of the sovereign territorial nation-state grew to a dominant position against its competitors. With the demise of the last multinational empire, the Soviet Union, there were no competitors, with the possible exception of a European Union that might or might not evolve toward federation. Competitive pressures are one explanation for institutional isomorphism, and two recent explanations for growing isomorphism among political units in early modern Europe rely on competitive dynamics and evolutionary models.

Charles Tilly (1975, 1990) has long emphasized the role of military competition in the creation of the modern state system. He has diverged from many other investigators in rejecting a simple straight-line evolution from the medieval monarchy to the modern state. Instead, Tilly (1990) sees divergent paths and attempts to explain both variation in the kinds of states that have appeared in Europe since the Middle Ages and their eventual convergence on the nation-state model. Two alternatives were particularly prominent: one based on capital and cities, the other on coercion and states. Condensing his far more intricate argument, Tilly maintains that "war made states, and vice versa." War was responsible for the variation in political units, a Lamarckian argument that variation was stimulated by an environmental challenge, in this case, the threat of military conflict. War was also critical in the selection out of alternative forms. The crucial advantage of city-states (capital) was undermined with the spread of commercialization and capital accumulation to larger political units. At this point, Tilly's argument is close to that of Bean: A shift to standing armies meant that far greater resources were required to survive in a competitive setting. Small-scale, decentralized states were at a distinct disadvantage.

Hendrik Spruyt (1994) has advanced an alternative to Tilly's explanation that is even more explicitly evolutionary in its structure. Like Tilly, he posits variation in political forms in the late Middle Ages, but the variation is not stimulated by the environmental challenge of military conflict. Rather, it results from an exogenous change in the economic environment: the growth of trade, which acts on different internal political alignments to produce different outcomes. Change in the medieval environment produced three "synchronic alternatives" that competed over the next centuries: sovereign territorial states, the city-states of Italy, and the city-league (represented by the German Hansa). Spruyt carefully specifies the key dimensions on which these alternative forms varied— degree of internal hierarchy and demarcation of authority by territorial parameters.

Compared to Tilly, Spruyt's explanation of the selective advantage enjoyed by the sovereign territorial state awards performance in military conflict with competitors a less important role. The apparently Darwinian role of military success disguises, in Spruyt's view, the more fundamental organizational advantages of the state. The state could mobilize military resources more effectively than its rivals, but only because of its superior institutional structure. That structure also granted it other advantages in the environment of early modern Europe. Spruyt advances three different mechanisms of "selection," although two of these do not fit within a hard Darwinian frame. The sovereign territorial state's internal organization permitted it to mobilize resources more effectively and granted it other external advantages, such as greater credibility in committing to international agreements and an enhanced ability to prevent free-riding. Although this explanation for the selective advantages of the territorial state extends beyond Tilly's emphasis on mobilization for military conflict, it is compatible with Tilly's view.

Spruyt's second mechanism tilting toward isomorphism is not a competitive one but institutionalist. Drawing on the sociologist Anthony Giddens, Spruyt proposes mutual empowerment that favors the state against the city-state and the city-league: a process of creating a state-favoring environment and rendering illegitimate those rivals that did not possess its features of territorial demarcation and internal hierarchy. Although this mechanism is construed by Spruyt as more cognitive or normative in its operation, it also resembles such biological mechanisms as kin recognition that extend the realm of cooperative behavior.

Finally, a third mechanism (really two different processes) is shaped by the competitive external environment only indirectly; competition may spur imitation of more successful institutional forms (compatible with a broadened evolutionary model) and accelerate the exit of social actors from less successful units (less compatible with an evolutionary model). Each of these mechanisms favored the sovereign territorial state over its rivals; although they might contribute to survival in the Darwinian context of military conflict, they were separable in their effects.

Tilly and Spruyt provide convincing and partially compatible explanations for variation and convergence in political forms in Europe. Both confront the familiar difficulty of evolutionary theories in assessing the weight of the selection environment to the outcome in question: Neither can explain why convergence was incomplete until very recently. City-states survived into the modern era; that only one city-league existed makes it difficult to draw firm conclusions about the viability of that form. Not only did city-states survive, some—particularly the federation of city-states labeled the Netherlands—became dominant powers in the new era, a fact that poses problems for both Tilly and Spruyt.

Although the introduction of variation into these evolutionary accounts is valuable, one might also remark that the range of variation was even greater than Tilly and Spruyt allow. In particular, neither pays close attention to the failure in Europe of the political form that had long been dominant in the rest of the world: empire. As E. L. Jones (1987) remarks: "A long-lasting states system is a miracle. Empires are more understandable since they are formed by straightforward military expansion with obvious rewards for those engaged in it." The size of empires continued to grow even as the modern territorial state emerged as an institutional competitor (Taagepera 1978). Like Bean, Tilly and Spruyt are better at setting a lower bound to the mobilizing abilities of emerging states than they are at setting an upper limit.

More troubling is the question of the selection environment. Tilly's reliance on the military environment is straightforward, and his linkage of the territorial state and a greater ability to mobilize resources is plausible. Neither Tilly nor Spruyt examine the economic environment, however; this is particularly puzzling in Spruyt's case, since he claims that exogenous economic change produced the burst of variation that begins the competition among these rivals. Assessing the non-Darwinian mechanisms that Spruyt introduces is also difficult, particularly the importance of mutual empowerment: Additional evidence of its deployment against the state's organizational rivals is necessary. In general, it is not clear whether Spruyt sees these other mechanisms as subsumed under a broader Darwinian dynamic conducive to survival or whether they stand independently.

Finally, the role of rational and foresighted behavior in these models of competition among rival political forms is not clear. By incorporating mechanisms such as imitation and social choice (selection from "below"), Spruyt's model could include elements of strategic behavior that affected ultimate outcomes in a way that a purely Darwinian model would omit. For both Tilly and Spruyt, the answer to this question hinges on whether directed adaptation of core institutions in the competing variants was possible or whether path dependence locked in initial institutional designs. If statehood reduces to scale (and it comes close to doing so in Tilly's account), then such self-directed transformation is unlikely. If the outlines of the territorial state are based on a centralized and territorial political structure, then directed modifications are conceivable. Whether, under conditions of uncertainty, the selective advantages of particular institutional forms were clear-cut requires more investigation, however. Did political units during the critical centuries engage in little political experimentation, in undirected random experiments, or in consciously chosen adaptations?

CONCLUSION: EVOLUTIONARY THEORIES AND THEIR RIVALS

The explanations offered by Tilly and Spruyt provide excellent examples of an evolutionary logic applied to an important problem in international relations. The design of their arguments fits the broad definition of an evolutionary model given by Richard Nelson: an explanation of the movement of a variable across time; a means of generating variation and a mechanism for winnowing on that variation; and "inertial forces" that provide "constancy" in the survivors. Their accounts also suggest a research agenda suited for evolutionary theories: large populations interacting with relatively fixed environments across long stretches of time. Simply stating this description of an agenda offers one explanation for the lack of an evolutionary research program in international relations. Theorists in international relations have been fixated on the post-1945 international system and immediate policy issues arising from the cold war; "grand" theorists have been more preoccupied with explaining supposed eternal patterns rather than dealing with international change. Rather than large populations, international relations has, by and large, concentrated its attention on the great powers and often the superpowers.

"Population thinking" does not come naturally to the field. The *longue durée* has seldom been more than a decade or two.

The Scope of Evolutionary Theories

Evolutionary theories will only find a larger audience in international relations if the field expands its historical reach (as Spruyt and Tilly have done) and the scope of the problems it considers. Pushing the arguments of Spruyt and Tilly to the even larger universe of political units in existence at the beginning of European expansion and explaining the relative success of those units over time as they were drawn into the vortex of military and economic competition is only one possible avenue of research.

Evolutionary game theory raises the possibility of concentrating on state strategies and the selection of particular strategies by the competitive environment. The contemporary convergence of economies on market-oriented and neo-liberal policies has been explained by the bargaining leverage of international investors and financial institutions; simultaneous, endogenous choices for market-oriented policies are also candidates in explaining this shift. An evolutionary model provides a competing explanation: the relative success of states adopting strategies more open to an increasingly liberalized international economic environment. In some cases (the Soviet Union), failure meant demise; in others, successful change in strategy meant an increase in resources and international status. Developing models that select on strategies will require a more sophisticated typology of strategies, one that moves beyond the choice in Prisoner's Dilemma simply to "cooperate" or "defect" and is grounded in the historical choices governments make.

Widening the scope of international relations beyond a state-defined international environment and populations of states will also enhance the utility of evolutionary approaches. International changes that form part of the environment of states—the evolution of international industrial networks, the emergence and disintegration of dominant languages, patterns of migration—should be incorporated in a redefinition of the environment; evolutionary theories might then become more plausible explanatory contenders.

In the broadest terms, betting on the value of evolutionary theories means placing a wager on how the world works. As Lake and Powell suggest in chapter 1 of this volume, theory should be deployed pragmatically, allowing that every theory represents a necessary simplification of reality. Quasi-Darwinian processes are not the only means of explaining historical change; as Hirshleifer (1987b, 220) points out, "revolutionary" (rather than gradual) and "designed" (rather than unintended) change may be playing a larger role in social life because of underlying economic and social changes. Whatever bet one makes in a larger research program, however, it seems likely that certain research problems in international relations will remain potential candidates for an evolutionary approach.

Methodological Choices

Several important methodological issues run through the applications of evolutionary theory reviewed above. The most important is the link between evolutionary models and a strategic-choice approach to international relations. Assumptions of rationality and foresight are incorporated in some evolutionary approaches, but for most, rational behavior is not required. The "hard" Darwinians believe that the applicability of Darwinian arguments depends on "tightness of coupling between individual intentions and organization outcomes" (Hannan and Freeman 1989, 23). Organizational ecologists take as their starting point that individual intentions make little difference to long-term organizational success or failure. Others, such as Nelson and Winter, retain an element of directed variation and simple learning in their models. Evolutionary models are capable of conceding many different readings of the existence of rational and foresighted behavior at the individual or institutional level; they cannot assign that behavior overwhelming explanatory weight, however, or the importance of the selection environment in creating unanticipated outcomes would recede sharply. In the applications described, directed variation and adaptive learning are the two points at which the introduction of at least bounded rationality can contribute to the explanatory power of the models. On this dimension, the refinement of evolutionary models parallels the deployment of learning as one source of change in the broader class of strategic-choice models. One of the appeals of evolutionary models, however, remains the relief that they provide from demanding assumptions of rationality in explaining international outcomes.

A second methodological requirement is an explanation for variation in the population. For international relations, that requirement is less demanding than the need for a substantial degree of inertia to ensure consistent behavior across time as a field for selection to occur. Here once again, relaxing rationality assumptions contributes a measure of required replication in behaviors and strategies.

A third methodological challenge is the characterization of the environment. Biologists argue over the weight of the environment in explaining adaptations, but the introduction of "constraints" in their controversies implies constraints imposed by past evolution and the existing design of an organism—the "internal" is the constraint. In the social sciences, with a strong bias toward endogenous explanations for change, "constraints" are imposed from the outside on what is essentially an inside story. For evolutionary theorists in social sciences, the starting point among evolutionary biologists—their conceptual bet that adaptation is explained by selection on traits by the environment—must be defended.

Constructing adaptationist explanations in the social sciences is made far more difficult by the poorly specified notion of environment. As Lake and Powell describe, the strategic-choice approach makes a methodological bet on a partial equilibrium approach, one that "simplifies problems by ignoring some feedback effects." Evolutionary approaches must make such choices about the relevant selection environment explicitly and defensibly. To the degree that evolutionary language is employed in international relations, the environment is frequently defined as other states in their roles as military competitors. Although this definition dovetails with the strategic-choice approach, it may omit crucial elements in the selection environment. For new institutional historians, a vague analogy such as the "market for institutions" has sufficed. Several routes could permit a more careful and rigorous specification of the relevant selection environment. Hirshleifer's typology of competition in biological populations suggests one route for refinement: a typology of competitive strategies that are "permissible" in particular settings. Some measure of the intensity of competition and the determinants of that intensity would also contribute to more convincing applications of evolutionary theories.

Finally, both evolutionary theory and theories that rely more on conscious design by agents are haunted by the question of contingency. Stephen Jay Gould's treatment of the Burgess shale argues the implications of this alternative vigorously (and incorrectly in the eyes of other theorists) (Gould 1989). Alchian (1950) poses a similar possibility in his recounting of the Borél experiment. Alchian uses the Borél example to argue for the ability of economists to use an evolutionary model for explanation, even if random and undirected behavior is the field for selection. Gould draws a very different conclusion: that for some outcomes, a plausible adaptationist story cannot be constructed. To his eye, the exotic forms discovered in the Burgess shale might well have been as successful as other inhabitants of the Cambrian seas whose ancestors (among them, us) survived. The environmental shocks that have imposed mass extinctions periodically changed the rules of selection so radically that it is difficult for Gould to conceive of a gradualist evolutionary story to account for winners and losers. In dramatic form, Gould raises the issue of rate of environmental change and whether a rapidly changing environment can sustain an adaptationist account. Jon Elster (1989, 80) has applied the same argument against employing selectionist arguments in the social sciences: "The social-selection argument may work in slowly changing peasant societies in which there is time for tools and routines to reach local perfection. It is unlikely to have much explanatory power in complex, rapidly evolving economies." It is important to note that Elster is arguing against an evolutionary argument for optimal adaptation.

Evolutionary Theory as an Antidote

Whether evolutionary approaches find a prominent place on the future research agenda of international relations or not, they will continue to be useful as antidotes to unthinking assumptions that guide our research. First, they force researchers to account for the effects of observed purposive behavior and learning, rather than assuming it will have the effects intended. One cannot assume that the amount of attention that agents devote to their environment and to devising "adaptive" strategies to deal with environmental challenges is directly related to successful learning. In early modern Europe, learning and adaptation was relatively rapid in the sphere of military technology and much less rapid (if evident at all) in the realm of political and economic institutions. Moving learning and directed adaptation out of the realm of hand waving requires specification of feedback loops and the ways that learned behavior enters future interactions with other players and the environment.

Even more important is the attention that evolutionary theory forces on initial variation. Social scientists employ and enjoy models of straight-line development, internally determined. Concentrating on the winners and ignoring the evolutionary alternatives that were unsuccessful or did not survive is an unfortunate habit and one that is impossible in any serious evolutionary program.

These useful correctives to common theoretical pitfalls provide both an unexpected fit with and clear divergence from approaches to international relations that are often seen as rivals to strategic choice. Cognitive models also explain why adaptive learning fails and why selection runs roughshod over agents that attempt to interpret and adjust to their environments. As described above, North's explanations for the failure of economies to converge on more efficient institutions rely increasingly on cognitive insights. Unlike most cognitive models in international relations, however, the population basis of evolutionary theories renders individual cognitive differences less important in explaining outcomes.

Constructivists award a significant role to the social environment in their explanations of international outcomes. In their view of the malleability of actors and their identities, however, constructivists diverge sharply from the evolutionary perspective, which requires a "hard" population base on which the environment can act. More paradoxically, Darwinian models bring to the fore two themes that the postmoderns in international relations have stressed. A hard Darwinian model is resolutely anti-teleological: No overarching narrative for the direction of history exists, particularly no notion of progress defined in conventional Western terms. As already noted, a Darwinian model also forces attention on voices and alternatives that may have been smothered in the loud and triumphal music of today's "winners." Evolutionary theory implicitly endorses postmodern attention to repressed discourses. It also serves to counter the skewing of historical narrative to match the power and interests of those whose selective advantage has included an ability to manipulate history itself.

CHAPTER SEVEN.

The Limits of Strategic Choice: Constrained Rationality and Incomplete Explanation

ARTHUR A. STEIN

GAME THEORY, especially as applied in microeconomics, has been bally-hooed as the savior of the study of international politics and attacked as its destroyer.[1] It will, proponents argue, provide the firm analytic founda-tions on which to build a rigorous science. This volume itself reflects such hubris. But like other innovations, this one has been shunned as well as welcomed. If its supporters have the zeal of religious converts, its detractors reflect no small degree of mindless defensiveness. This essay highlights the strengths of a strategic-choice approach, which lie in its flexibility and rigor, but also elucidates its weaknesses, which lie in its excessive simplification, causal incompleteness, and post hoccery.

My task in this essay is both that of defender and critic of the faith. I emphasize the strengths of the approach but also detail its core weak-nesses. I argue that some typical criticisms are actually of particular mod-eling choices rather than of the approach itself. But I also delineate a set of more fundamental weaknesses. As would be expected of a believ-ing agnostic asked to play the role of church ombudsperson, I conclude that though limited and incomplete, the approach is both useful and unavoidable.

A strategic-choice approach is particularly suited to the study of inter-national relations.[2] Long before the development of strategic interaction

This paper was written with the financial assistance of the University of California's Institute on Global Conflict and Cooperation and UCLA's Academic Senate. The author thanks Alan Kessler for research assistance. My thanks to the volume editors and contributors, and to Jim Caporaso, Amy Davis, Jim Fearon, Steph Haggard, Alan Kessler, Lisa Martin, Paul Papayoanou, Beth Simmons, Cherie Steele, as well as anonymous referees of Princeton Uni-versity Press.

[1] This is also happening in other subfields of political science and, indeed, other disci-plines.

[2] The area of economics most devoted to strategic choices has been regularly monitored by political scientists who mine it for intellectual nuggets. Economists, who typically assume competitive markets, often ignore strategic interaction, assuming that individuals and firms simply take markets as given and do not make strategic choices. But economists do see firms

models, the field of international relations (like classical diplomatic history) focused on the interests of states and how interactions affect choice and strategy. Similarly, a strategic-choice approach begins with purposive, intentionalist, rational explanations of behavior and adds the component of actor interaction. The actors' choices reflect not only their preferences and the constraints they confront but also the existence of other actors making choices. Not surprisingly, therefore, game theory's formal tools for analyzing strategic choice quickly found application in the study of international politics.[3] That it met so ready an audience and was synonymous with key assumptions in the field also meant, however, that its impact was not revolutionary.[4]

This chapter highlights the benefits and strengths of a strategic-choice approach to the analysis of international politics. First, the approach provides the benefits of mathematical modeling: rigor, deduction, and inter-

---

as making strategic choices when there are but few of them, and political scientists have looked to economists' work on duopoly and oligopoly for analogues to international politics. International-relations scholars were affected by the work of economists in the late 1940s and early 1950s on monopolistic competition. This is quite evident in Waltz (1959), who cites the work of Fellner and Chamberlain. It is also evident in Kaplan's (1957) characterization of different international systems, which comport with economists' characterizations of different kinds of markets (Boulding 1958).

The connection between economists and international relations has resulted in many economists being taken to the bosom of international-relations scholars (Viner, Hirschman) and to economists addressing international relations issues directly (Schelling, Boulding).

[3] Economists played a central role in World War II in the military application of operations research and strategic gaming (Shubik 1992; Kaplan 1983; Bernstein 1995). Game theory in the immediate postwar period was sustained by military spending and immediately applied to strategic security issues long before it was embraced by economists (Leonard 1992; Mirowski 1991).

The relevance of game theory to international politics was noted in two of the most important books in international-relations theory written in the 1950s. Waltz (1959) and Kaplan (1957) both refer to game theory. Indeed, Kaplan's book includes an appendix on the subject. Economist Thomas Schelling published, in 1960, his classic *The Strategy of Conflict*, applying game theory to issues of international conflict. A special issue of *World Politics* in October 1961, devoted to theoretical work on the international system, includes two essays by economists, both on game theory (Schelling 1961; Quandt 1961). Two other essays in that volume also discuss game theory (Kaplan 1961; Burns 1961), making the number of contributors to the 1961 special issue discussing game theory almost half the total. By 1985 another special issue of *World Politics* devoted to international cooperation dealt almost entirely with game theoretically based work.

For a discussion of the isomorphism of game theory and international relations, see Stein 1990. For a review essay, see O'Neill 1994. One can argue that strategic choice is not an approach to, but a definition of, international politics. The focus here is on the former.

[4] In contrast, a strategic-choice approach came much later to, and was far more revolutionary in its impact on, other subfields of political science, such as electoral politics or public law, in which sociological perspectives dominated (and still do). For the spread of rational choice and game theory into political science, see Rogowski 1978; Riker 1992; and Ordeshook 1986; also see Miller 1997.

nal consistency. In addition, its flexibility allows it to be applied very broadly. Indeed, its flexibility is such that many of the criticisms typically leveled at it are actually about specific modeling choices rather than fundamental criticisms of the approach per se. I argue, that is, that many criticisms imply alternative modeling choices rather than an alternative approach, so that criticisms characterized as fundamental are more typically squabbles within a church. Scholars must make strategic choices in applying strategic-choice models to the study of international politics. Scholars must be self-conscious about critical modeling assumptions and intermediate steps rather than simply parrot the substantively driven assumptions made in other fields. The approach is generic, but particular scholarly choices make it meaningful. There is, in other words, an art to applying the science of choice.[5]

Yet, the chapter is skeptical as well as affirming, for the approach has serious limitations, both generically and specifically as applied to international relations. I argue that the core assumptions of the model are ideal ones, originally made with a normative intent and that there are fundamental problems in the use of such models for explanation. Indeed, the use of such models for positive explanation either is viable only because the models are self-fulfilling or fails because the models make problematic simplifying assumptions about human capabilities. When the models are expanded to achieve greater verisimilitude, they become indeterminate and incomplete—consistent with a variety of outcomes and a variety of plausible models and paths to any particular outcome.

THE ART OF THE SCIENCE OF CHOICE: MODELING AND POST HOC EXPLANATION

Given the flexibility of the approach, constructing models of strategic choice is an art rather than a science, requiring scholars to make an array of choices about the nature of the actors, their preferences, their choices, their beliefs, and so on.[6] These scholarly choices can be debated.

Purposive Explanation and Actors in International Relations

A strength of the strategic-choice approach is its applicability to any actor. Economists apply it to individuals and to firms. In the case of interna-

---

[5] Aumann (1985) sees both game theory and mathematical economics as art forms. Much the same can be said of mathematics in general.

[6] This point is more general in that science is a logic of justification rather than a logic of discovery.

tional relations, it can be applied to people, bureaucracies, nations, and others. Thus it effectively finesses the unit-of-analysis debate in international relations. Moreover, the strategic-choice approach explains the existence of collectivities in terms of the interests that brought them into being and thus provides microfoundations for aggregation and delineates the requisite assumptions for the application of the approach to collective actors.

Explanations of behavior in the social sciences typically begin with reference to intentions (whether of individuals or larger social aggregates like firms, interest groups, or governments).[7] Scholars treat actions as purposive and so assess actors' interests, options, and calculations in explaining them. More specifically, purposive intentionalist explanation is one standard approach to the study of international relations.[8] Explanation of a government's action often starts by addressing that government's interests, and the "national interest" lies at the heart of classical models of explanation in the field.[9]

Concomitant with intentions is the question of whose interests: who are the actors whose intentions serve to explain their actions. In the debate among scholars of international politics over the appropriate unit of analysis, some scholars reduce international politics to human behavior and explain world politics as the result of individual choices. For them, the relevant unit of analysis is the individual, and state policy is ultimately reducible to the actions of individuals. Explaining foreign policy and international politics means explaining leaders' choices. Critical questions are reformulated to frame the question in such terms. Explaining the origins of World War I devolves to explaining the confluence of the personal choices that resulted in war: the ambivalent signaling of Lloyd George, Ferdinand's decision to attack Serbia, Bethmann-Holweg's decision to issue a blank check to Austria-Hungary, and so on.

Others find the relevant behavioral units to be aggregations of people. Economists treat firms as actors; international relations scholars treat states the same way. They see foreign policy as collective action and deem

---

[7] For a discussion of rational-choice theory as a subset of intentionalist explanation, see Elster 1986.

[8] It is this very centrality of purposive explanation that places the discipline of economics at the heart of the social sciences. For a discussion of the evolving meanings of economics and political economy, see Groenewegen 1991. The centrality of purposive explanation in the social sciences makes possible both the importation of economic ideas now so prevalent in political science and elsewhere (this volume being an excellent reflection) and the imperialism characteristic of recent economic theorizing. Economists have applied their models to all sorts of decision problems (Becker 1976; Hirshleifer 1985; Radnitzky and Bernholz 1987; Radnitzky 1992; Baron and Hannan 1994).

[9] Graham Allison (1971) began his critique of standard international-relations theorizing by elucidating this approach and dubbing it "model I." The link between balance of power,

the collectivities to be actors. Often dubbed "the unitary-actor approach," this perspective treats international politics as the result of state policy. Explaining the origins of World War I is then reduced to a determination of the confluence of state choices, like the British failure clearly to deter and the German blank check to Austria, that resulted in war.

Not only is strategic-choice analysis silent on the unit-of-analysis issue, applications of the approach effectively expand it by disaggregating the person. Scholars working in this research tradition have given us "the rational gene" and conceptualized weakness of the will as an "intrapersonal prisoner's dilemma." Such social and natural scientists reduce the explanation of behavior to a unit of analysis more fundamental than the human being. Just as psychoanalysts are prepared to disaggregate the human being into the constituent components of ego, id, and superego, these theorists of strategic choice are prepared to see those components as engaged in a strategic game against one another.

The very flexibility of the approach means that critics often focus on modeling choices rather than challenge purposive explanation in general. Critics of the state-as-actor perspective, for example, equate strategic-choice analysis with a focus on unitary states. Since proponents of bureaucratic politics explanations do not view states as integrated entities that can be modeled as having preferences and making choices, they offer an alternative unit of analysis, the bureaucracy or organization, and then focus on how its preferences, interests, choices, and interactions determine a state's foreign policy. But bureaucratic politics explanations, although billed as a process alternative to purpose, simply shift purposive explanation to a different (albeit still aggregated) level of analysis.[10] Organizational interests replace national interests, and interacting bureaucracies replace interacting states. Hence bureaucratic politics arguments can be modeled using strategic interaction as readily as the perspective they criticize (Bendor and Hammond 1992).

A strategic-interaction approach also breaks down the level-of-analysis problem in international relations. Scholars have argued that scholarship in the field could focus on individuals, states, or the international system, and, more important, that the levels of analysis could not interact or be combined.[11] Analysts would have to choose, they argued, between undertaking a true systemic study or one that was reductionistic (focusing on individuals or states) because they could not combine domestic politics

---

typically thought of as the key theory in the field, and a purposive explanation is provided by Morgenthau's famous statement, "interests defined as power."

[10] See Allison 1971 and the subtle changes in Allison and Halperin 1972. For critiques and discussions, see Art 1973; Ball 1974; and Perlmutter 1974. For an excellent paper applying rational actor models to Allison's formulation, see Bendor and Hammond 1992.

[11] Some scholars add bureaucratic politics as an additional level of analysis (Jervis 1976).

and the international system. In contrast, a strategic-choice approach can be seen as a vehicle for integrating the levels of analysis, demonstrating that some levels act as constraints on choice at other levels and that micro-foundations for macro-outcomes are essential.[12] Moreover, the framework provides the ability to move across levels of analysis, to move from individuals' preferences to states' preferences and to international outcomes.[13]

Indeed, strategic-choice models can be so broadly applied that they can be, and have been, applied to an array of actors, including people, firms, and states. Moreover, the interactions analyzed can involve combinations. The models can be applied to the interactions of actors at different levels of aggregation: individuals with states, and states with international organizations, multinational organizations, and nonstate actors (the Palestinian Liberation Organization, for example).[14] Using a strategic-choice approach thus allows the assessment of interactions across levels of analysis.

Although a strategic-choice approach is silent on the unit-of-analysis question, it does stipulate the necessary assumptions for its application to larger aggregates. The actors in a strategic-choice framework are presumed to have consistent utility functions and to be capable of choice, perception, and calculation. These specifications provide more precise meaning to the notion of unitariness. For states to be seen as actors in a strategic-choice sense, they must be unitary in more than that a decision by such actors implicates everyone in the collectivity. A nation that declares war on another implicates all its members in that decision. But that meaning of unitariness is insufficient for a strategic-choice approach, which requires that aggregate actors be unitary in that they have a definable utility function.[15]

---

[12] I make this argument in a more extended fashion in Stein 1990, esp. 175–84.

[13] The thrust of this discussion is that levels of analysis can be, and typically must be, combined in an explanation of some outcome—that independent variables at different levels of analysis can be combined. But there is another sense in which a level-of-analysis problem remains: At what unit and level of analysis should one choose to explain. Put another way, at what level of analysis should one couch the dependent variable. To take a concrete example, one can choose to explain why President Kennedy responded to Soviet missiles in Cuba and selected a blockade or why the United States responded to Soviet missiles and adopted a blockade or why a bipolar system periodically generates superpower crises that are resolved short of war. Each question can be answered by combining levels of analysis, but the questions differ.

[14] For a different conception of problems in game theory with the notion of a player, see Güth 1991.

[15] The long-standing application of purposive explanation to states as actors in international politics means that the whole field, not just strategic interaction analyses, must confront the question of the viability of treating such aggregates as actors. Few if any scholars are troubled by discussing national interests, a few more are taken aback by discussing the utility functions of states, but many more balk when a psychohistorian asserts that "nations

Not only can the strategic-choice approach deal with actors at different levels of aggregation, such models explain the existence of aggregate entities by providing explanations both for why actors create institutions and the consequences of institutions for choice. Self-interested actors, whether individuals, firms, or states, create institutions to deal with collective-action problems and the suboptimalities associated with autonomous choice.

As Rogowski demonstrates in chapter 4 of this volume, institutions are mechanisms for collective choice, and their design significantly determines the nature of that choice. The collective choices of institutions can be affected by their constituent members, and so issues of franchise and membership are central to their design. The specific mechanisms by which the preferences of constituent members are aggregated also significantly determine outcomes.[16] And, as Gourevitch demonstrates in chapter 5 of this volume, that institutions and their design matter means that they are significant and important foci for political struggles. Thus, although the approach assumes the nature and utility functions of actors as given and does not address how they change (from empires and city-states to states, for example), it can be used to explain the strategic-choice bases of changes in institutional form.[17]

In short, a strategic-choice framework provides microfoundations for macrobehavior. It links levels of analysis by treating aggregate entities as the products of individual choice (Gourevitch) and collective choice as the consequence of different mechanisms for the aggregation of individual preferences (Rogowski).

The interest of purposive self-interested autonomous actors in mechanisms for collective action breaks down the realist/institutionalist divide in international relations. Many scholars have contrasted realism and institutionalism as two alternative approaches to the field; the former emphasize autonomous choice under anarchy, and the latter stress the role of international institutions. The strategic-choice approach developed in this volume transcends this intellectual split by explaining institutional creation, design, contestation, and collapse as the products of autono-

---

have psychologies, just as individuals do; they have dreams and fantasies that can be analyzed; they have urges that arise from childhood fears and traumas of their populace" (*New Yorker* 1995, 55–56). Yet analytically (in the scientific, rather than psycho, sense), extending interests and purposive calculation to states is perhaps as questionable as extending them to psyches. For a discussion of the problem of social choice and aggregate entities, see Sen 1995.

[16] The centrality of rules and procedures to outcomes is the key conclusion from Arrow's (1951) Nobel-prize winning work and is a core motif of the literature on social choice.

[17] More broadly, as the title of an edited volume suggests, organizations can be seen as games (Binmore and Dasgupta 1986).

mous choice. Actors create, maintain, argue about, and attack institutions. Their self-interest in different settings explains all these responses.

Taking Preferences Seriously

Strategic interaction analysis is also flexible because it is built on the foundation of subjective utility and so can encompass a variety of preferences and bases of calculation. Whether the units of analysis are individuals, firms, or states, the analysis begins with some articulation of their preferences.[18] Ironically, this theoretical flexibility is not always evident in scholarly practice.

In chapter 2 of this volume, Jeffry Frieden delineates the ways that scholars ascertain the preferences that animate their analyses. Frieden stresses an analytic preference for positing actor preferences or rooting them in some deductive theory. Further, he points out, it is better to explain change (whether across actors or for one actor over time) by reference to changing circumstances rather than changing preferences. This avoids the circularity associated with explaining behavioral change by preference change when our knowledge of preference change comes from observing behavioral change. Despite the predisposition of strategic-choice theorists for fixed preferences, Frieden shows that we can explain changes in behavior by changes in preference if we have some independent means by which to ascertain the change in preferences.

However arrived at, whether held constant or allowed to change, preferences are central to the analytic enterprise. Yet, scholars of international relations have disagreed about how to characterize actor preferences. Given the focus on subjective utility in a theory of choice, it is ironic that scholars typically posit the interests and preferences of actors rather than investigate them empirically. There is a long-standing tradition in international relations of imputing the national interest. Classical realists argue that all states have a core national interest of assuring their physical and territorial integrity and so act to maximize their power.[19] This assumption was to play the role in studies of international relations that the assumption of wealth maximization played in economics. But power maximization came to be seen as either an unfalsifiable assertion or a falsifiable and false one (Rosecrance 1961).

---

[18] As already mentioned, some criticisms of strategic choice are actually criticisms of intentionalist explanation. After all, causal explanation is provided in the natural sciences without reference to intention and purpose. It is possible to conceive of a social science that similarly ignores the preferences of individuals and groups of individuals. But this line of criticism has not developed in the field.

[19] The maximization of power is at the heart of Morgenthau's (1948) work.

The neorealist revolution replaced power maximization with an assumption that states minimally act to assure their own survival.[20] Yet, this assumption is neither self-evident nor adequate. Assuming the primacy of survival as a minimum is not enough to provide an unambiguous basis for decision. It is not self-evident because what constitutes survival must itself be defined. Survival raises issues of self-definition and identity. Some states fit the classical realist vision of focusing solely on physical and territorial integrity. But other states define their survival more broadly, including such issues as ideology and ethnicity (Stein 1995). Moreover, the presumption of a minimal concern with state survival is simply inadequate. It confines the field to be able only to address those international relations in which states' survival is on the line, and this ignores too much of international relations.[21]

Further, in international relations (and in other fields), imputing the same interest to all actors has drawn criticism and led to calls for inducing subjective national interests and not just assuming objective interests.[22] This view holds that actors' formulations of their interests, the nature of their utility functions, must be investigated directly. This problem is at its most interesting among anthropologists, who must choose whether to explain the behavior of people and groups within the framework of their own worldviews or by applying concepts that have no meaning to those people whose behavior is to be explained.[23]

This debate mirrors the controversy in international relations between generalists (or theorists) and regionalists in the study of international relations. During U.S. involvement in Vietnam, for example, debates raged not only about appropriate policy but about the knowledge necessary to

[20] The difference between positing the maximization of power and minimally assuring survival is the main, self-consciously articulated distinction between classical realism and neorealism (Waltz 1979, 1990).

[21] This animates Krasner's (1978) inductive search for the national interest. Krasner begins by arguing that the core realist assumption about state preferences is inadequate to explain the bulk of a great power's foreign policy.

[22] Rosenau (1968) distinguishes between subjective and objective assessments of the national interest; Krasner (1978) distinguishes between deductive and inductive means of assessing the national interest.

[23] See the distinction between emic and etic in Harris 1979. This anthropological problem has entered political science in discussions of peasant behavior (Scott 1975, 1976; Popkin 1979). The problem also arises for historians, who confront the issue of being constrained by what was self-consciously known by those in the past.

There is a long-standing argument about the universality of economic exchanges and the existence of premodern modes of calculation and assessment (Finley 1973; Polanyi 1944; Kindleberger 1974; Humphreys 1969). For a refutation of the argument for classical economies, see Conybeare 1987, chap. 4. The issue is hotly debated among economic anthropologists, who refer to it as the substantivist-formalist controversy. For an essay that links these strands, see Lowry 1979.

make policy. Theoretically oriented scholars were prepared to apply the lessons of game theory and deterrence to the American intervention in Vietnam. John McNaughton, assistant secretary of defense in the Johnson administration, asked his old friend, Thomas Schelling, to apply his ideas about bargaining and signaling and coercive warfare to the problem of intimidating North Vietnam through the use of U.S. air power.[24] In contrast, regionalists are horrified by the ahistorical and acontextual use of general arguments. In this case, they held that a knowledge of Vietnamese history, society, and culture were essential to understanding how to interact with the North Vietnamese.

In addition to the issue of how to ascertain states' utility functions is the question of what to include in them. The larger issue is what sorts of preferences about states will be assumed in the study of international relations. The analytic predisposition of adherents of strategic-choice models is to keep the utility functions as spare as possible. But a core question for the field is how spare can assumptions of state preferences be. No matter how compelling the analytic desire for a simple stipulated preference, the preference functions of states will have to be expanded in order to explain the range of observed international relations.[25]

Much of the work in the field of international political economy, for example, simply borrows assumptions about state preferences from international trade theory and holds that states are interested in maximizing national wealth. But as recent criticisms of this work point out, foreign economic policy is driven by both security and material concerns. This is the heart of Gowa's argument that foreign economic policies have *security externalities* and that security interests as well as economic ones underlie foreign-trade policies (Gowa 1989; Gowa and Mansfield 1993). Similarly, security policies have *wealth externalities*, and these figure in the formulation of state security policies. Concerns about the effects of security policies and military spending on a state's export prospects and future economic growth have been and remain key elements in the formulation of national security policy. Scholars are focusing on how material and security interests combine in the formulation of foreign economic policies and even of security policy (Frieden 1994b; Papayoanou 1996, 1997, 1999; Skålnes 1998, 1999; Steele 1995; Weber 1997).

---

[24] Significantly, Schelling had no idea where to begin (Kaplan 1983).

[25] Much the same has occurred in other subfields of political science. Scholars who have run up against the limits of what they can explain in American politics simply by positing that politicians have a preference to be reelected have begun to expand politicians' utility functions to include policy preferences. Similarly, positing that voters have a simple preference for maximizing income has proved inadequate, and more recent work combines voters'

Conjoined with the issues of how to define and assess preferences is the question of whether preferences can change. Analysts often treat preferences as fixed and unchanging.[26] Some even hold that changing preferences pose a problem for a theory of choice. Yet, it is possible to model how preferences are formed and how they change (Kapteyn, Wansbeek, and Buyze 1980; Hansson 1995; March 1978; Schelling 1984).[27]

Scholarly debate about the nature of preferences, the basis for inferring them and their malleability, is within the church and constitutes no challenge to strategic interaction analysis per se. Making one set of modeling choices (bets, in the language of Lake and Powell in chapter 1 of this volume), preferring to keep preferences unchanged and explaining by reference to changing constraints and opportunities (Frieden's chapter 2), does not mean that other modeling choices imply a fundamentally different view of causality.

STRATEGIC CHOICE AS MATHEMATICAL MODEL, MATHEMATICS AS THE LANGUAGE OF SCIENCE: MODELING AND INTELLECTUAL BRUSH CLEARING

The main benefits ascribed to the use of a strategic-choice approach in international relations are those of any mathematical model, greater analytical coherence and rigor. Game theory, which is the basis of the strategic-choice approach discussed in this volume, is a branch of mathematics, and its strengths are those all mathematical modeling imparts.[28] Mathe-

---

interests in their own incomes with some general preference (held in varying degrees by different voters) for equity.

[26] Stigler and Becker (1977) make a strong argument for this position. Frieden's essay in this volume (chapter 2) makes this case for international relations.

[27] The issue of preference change is related to that of the dependence of preference on belief. Chapter 1 of this volume takes the orthodox position of keeping these separate, but there are important cases in which preference depends on belief (Hausman and McPherson 1994).

The issue of preference change is related, too, to the question of whether actors themselves change and whether they are capable of taking into account anything other than present aims. It is not just that actors heavily discount future payoffs but that they have no sense of, or interest in, their future selves and simply pursue present aims (Parfit 1984; Walsh 1994). Is the IBM that made business machines in the first half of the century the same company that made computers in the second half of the century when the products, organizational structure, and leadership had all changed? Similarly, is the middle-aged corporate executive the same person as the hippie of two decades earlier? Can they be said to share the same preferences? Can the young hippie be thought of as making choices with calculated temporal consequences?

[28] The father of the theory of games, John von Neumann is, by at least one reckoning, one of the greatest mathematicians of all time (Paulos 1991). His important work, *The*

matics is the language of science.[29] It adds precision and rigor and makes assessments possible that simply are not possible in ordinary language.[30]

Moreover, mathematical models are formally true.[31] Hence the empirical adequacy of game theory, indeed of formal and mathematical work more generally, is not at issue. The statements formally derived within an axiomatic structure are formally true and need not be empirically assessed.[32] But because the central role of empirics involves the isomorphism between analytic and modeling assumptions and the underlying reality being assessed, many of the disputes over strategic choice actually concern the specific modeling decisions scholars make.

Further, although mathematics is substance-free, specific uses fill this generic tool with meaning, and verbal formulations of substantive problems translated into formal (or numerical) terms must be subsequently translated back.[33] Quite different substantive domains may be studied using similar mathematical tools, but the use of similar tools need not imply common substantive links. Specific kinds of mathematics have been developed with particular substantive issues in mind, but the tools can be applied in other domains as long as the problems are isomorphic. Newton developed the mathematics of calculus in order to study planetary motion, but calculus is applicable to any question involving how fast something

---

Theory of Games and Economic Behavior, focused on economic behavior largely because of the impact of his coauthor, Oskar Morgenstern, the economist (Leonard 1992; Rellstab 1992; Schotter 1992; Mirowski 1992). But the earlier roots of game theory are all in mathematics (Dimand and Dimand 1992). Ironically, during game theory's early history at Princeton, the mathematics department encouraged, and the economics department frowned on, the new enterprise (Shubik 1992).

[29] Galileo expanded this point further when he wrote, "The book of nature is written in the language of mathematics; without its help it is impossible to comprehend a single word of it" (quoted in Pinker 1997).

[30] The renowned economic game theorist, David Kreps (1990c), offers a rather restrained and limited picture of the contributions of game theory to economics. Indeed, the contributions he lists are not specific to game theory at all but are generic ones applicable to mathematical modeling generally.

[31] Indeed, the different appellations applied to this enterprise in political science include "formal theory" and "mathematical political theory."

[32] This discussion finesses debates in the philosophy of mathematics.

[33] Not all mathematical possibilities have real-world counterparts. Many games can be analyzed as hypotheticals, but relatively few have been studied because they model important social reality. Kenneth Boulding once decried modern mathematical economics as "a quantum mechanics for an unknown universe." Mathematicians disagree about whether their constructions exist in their minds or in the world. For an introduction to such issues in the philosophy of mathematics, see Barrow 1992; Davis and Hersh 1981; and Paulos 1991.

is changing or how much a changing quantity totals.[34] One should be wary of assuming that two domains are comparable simply because some models are usable in both. That calculus can be applied to elections and planetary motion does not mean that the domains are not fundamentally different.

Similarly, game theory is generic in character and has also been widely applied. In addition to its extensive use in economics (Kreps 1990b, 1990c; Tirole 1988; Fudenberg and Tirole 1991; Binmore 1992; Rasmusen 1989; Osborne and Rubinstein 1994), it has been used in social psychology (Colman 1982; see also Kelley and Thibaut 1978), political science (Brams 1975; Ordeshook 1986), international relations (Brams 1985; Brams and Kilgour 1988; Nicholson 1992), and philosophy (Braithwaite 1955; Gauthier 1986; Parfit 1984; Lewis 1969).[35] Indeed, game theory has become widely applied in biology to interactions between animals (Maynard Smith 1976, 1982, 1984, and comments that follow 1984; Dugatkin and Reeve 1998).[36] In all fields, every application involves modeling choices, and most scholarly debates are about such choices.

Still, the core assumptions of game theory would appear to demand greater constraints on their use than other branches of mathematics. In arithmetic, for example, little need be assumed about objects and events in order to count, add, subtract, multiply, and divide them. In contrast, applying a strategic-choice model would seem to presuppose more stringent substantive assumptions. The actors in a strategic model must be sentient creatures capable of comparison, assessment, and choice.

Yet, the components of a strategic-choice approach are not so constraining as to limit its applicability to human beings alone. That game theory can be used to model animal behavior[37] implies neither that inten-

---

[34] On the centrality of the substantive importance of the study of moving bodies for critical developments in mathematics, see Kline 1985; for the simplest description of differential and integral calculus, see Paulos 1991.

[35] For an imaginative application to literary interpretation, see Brams 1980.

[36] For discussions of the analogous quality of economics and biology by economists, see Hirshleifer 1977, 1978a, 1978b; and Samuelson 1978, 1985.

[37] Hammerstein (1989) notes that, surprisingly, a model presuming human rationality has not only found wide applicability in the study of animal behavior but seems to do a better job explaining it than it does human behavior. For a review of game theory and evolutionary biology, see Hammerstein and Selten 1994.

The Kahler essay in this volume (chapter 6) beautifully demonstrates the issues associated with the use of evolutionary models in international relations. In their hard biological form, these models dismiss intentionality, but Kahler discusses the ways that such models have been imported into the social sciences and the attendant modifications that see a role for directed variation and adaptive learning.

tionality can be attributed to animals nor that intentionality need not be part of game-theoretic explanations in the social sciences.[38] That noncooperative games can be applied to pretrial bargaining, legislatures, and international politics does not mean that the domains are not analytically and theoretically distinctive.

The central benefit of mathematical modeling is its logic and coherence, its internal consistency. These are not trivial advantages in an intellectual domain beset by analytic sloppiness. The analytic consequences can be readily grouped into three types. First, formal modeling can demonstrate *nondeducibility*—that the deductions argued to follow from certain premises do not actually do so. As has been argued in recent years, for example, assumptions of anarchy do not by themselves lead to a deduction of the conflictual nature of international politics.[39] Second, formal modeling can demonstrate *multifinality*—that multiple outcomes flow from the same premises. The multiple equilibrium problem discussed below provides one example. Third, formal modeling can demonstrate *equifinality*—that there are alternative paths to the same outcome. The example often given, as in chapter one of this volume, is that a concern with relative gains can emerge from a purely self-regarding calculus without the need to change the underlying utility function.[40] These consequences of mathematical modeling have proved powerful enough to transform the scientific enterprise, both natural and social.

THE NORMATIVE-POSITIVE PARADOX

Ironically, the strategic-choice approach offered here as a retrospective explanation for behavior and outcome began as part of a normative enterprise intended to improve decisions, not to explain them. The use of such normative tools and ideal types for positive explanation is inherently problematic—they are either true or false because of their self-conscious application. Moreover, modifying these tools to make them more isomorphic with reality, and thus more useful for explanation, has generated a knowledge of the incompleteness and indeterminacy of such models.

Game theory has been used in international politics, as elsewhere, both to explain behavior and as a tool for improving the quality of decisions. The predominant focus in this volume, and thus for most of this essay, is on the use of strategic choice as an explanation for international politics.

[38] In a similar vein, the use of a conception of equilibrium in the natural and social sciences does not imply that economic equilibrium means the same thing as physical equilibrium (Phelps 1991).

[39] For my formulation, see Stein 1990.

[40] For my take on this, see Stein 1990, chap. 5.

But to its progenitors and original practitioners, game theory has been a normative tool, one devised to make decisions more rational.[41]

A Normative Enterprise: Constrained Actors
in Search of Rationality

Probability, logic, decision theory, and game theory were all developed to improve human decision making. They were not developed as accurate representations and reconstructions of what people actually do but as tools individuals should apply to achieve more rational decisions than they otherwise might.[42] People were assumed to be purposive but limited in their capacity to be fully rational. Decision-making tools were thus desired, created, recommended, and adopted. The logician Gottlob Frege argued that logic addresses the way people "must think if they are not to miss the truth" (Lowe 1993).[43] Similarly, probability theory has its roots in gamblers looking for an edge. On their own, people were seen as poor intuitive statisticians prone to mistakes, and the use of probability theory could improve their decisions.[44] Psychologists' findings about the heuristics and biases of human judgment underscore the point; in the words of Kahneman and Tversky (1973, 237): "In making predictions and judgments under uncertainty, people do not appear to follow the calculus of chance or the statistical theory of prediction. Instead, they rely on a limited number of heuristics which sometimes yield reasonable judgments and sometimes lead to severe and systematic errors" (see Kahneman, Slovic, Tversky 1982). These fields all began with a normative orientation rather than a positive one; they were intended to improve human decision making and were not intended to explain what people actually do.

---

[41] The only value to which decision theorists and game theorists were committed was rationality: optimizing and maximizing actor preferences.

[42] Nozick (1993, xi) characterizes the contrast between two perspectives regarding people and their rationality as expressed by two of the greats: "Descartes attempted to show why we should trust the results of reasoning, Hume questioned the rationality of our doing so."

[43] The contrary position was held by Locke who argued that people have minds that do not require instruction in logic. Knowledge of the rules of logic can help, but the mind can reason in logical terms even absent a knowledge of logic. This is akin to the argument in modern macroeconomics that individuals calculated rational expectations even before the elaboration of the model and the mathematics that made it tractable.

[44] Some early probability theorists saw their enterprise as capturing intuitive reasoning, or, as Pierre Laplace put it, probability theory was "only good sense reduced to calculus" (Laplace 1951 [1814], 196). When probability theory conflicted with intuition, it was the theory that needed reformulation (Daston 1980, 1988).

Similarly, the use of game theory can be seen as a normative tool useful for decisions.[45] Just as the telescope extends what one can see beyond the range of the unaided human eye, so game theory extends what one can logically assess beyond the means of the untrained and unaided human brain. Seen as such a tool, game theory (and decision theory) may be quite useful for making decisions but cannot be used to explain decisions made by actors in the past who did not have this knowledge.[46]

Ironically, though, what started as a normative enterprise has become a positive one. Tools once created to improve the quality of otherwise imperfect human decision making are now being used to explain choice. The social constructions of humans wishing to improve the quality of their cognitively constrained mental faculties, both bounded and semi-autistic, are now being used retrospectively to explain past human choices.[47]

Decision- and game-theoretic explanations of choice are thus inherently problematic in that they make inappropriate assumptions about the capacity of individuals and groups to make rational individual and social choices. The models were developed as normative instruments because individuals were seen as wanting to be rational but constrained in their ability to be rational. Applying such models as positive explanations, then, has led to the assault on rational choice by cognitive psychologists. As discussed below, individuals' presumptive ability to make rational choices has been systematically attacked by work in cognitive psychology showing that individuals deviate from the requisites of individual rationality.

Finally, that formal work was developed with an avowed normative objective of improving the quality of decision making implies that it is absurd to criticize it as inherently conservative. Yet, one criticism of formal work in economics and political science is that it is conservative since it takes the world and its constraints as given and so ignores alternative possibilities.[48] In international relations, rational-choice theory is seen as

---

[45] Nozick (1993) argues that it is inadequate even as a normative construction and that the standard normative view of conditions that a rational decision should satisfy must be expanded to include the symbolic meaning of actions.

[46] One can push the point further. Perhaps game theory is not an experimental apparatus being used to explore the world but a tool that can itself generate structure, as a computer algorithm might. If so, game theory is creating something new. On experimental tools, see the discussion in Barrow 1992, 261.

[47] Camerer (1997, 167) points out that "it is remarkable how much game theory has been done while largely ignoring [the] question [of whether it is meant to describe actual choices by people and institutions]" and goes on to note that even when it "does aim to describe behavior, it often proceeds with a disturbingly low ratio of careful observation to theorizing."

[48] The critique is also related to the politics of the modern age. Earlier generations of economists were vociferous critics of socialism and communism. Some of those writing in the public-choice arena in the last two decades have been staunch critics of the welfare state.

blocking the prospects for envisioning and creating a world that transcends the anarchic and conflictual system of competitive nation-states.[49] But this criticism applies to current practice or practitioners rather than to the nature of the intellectual tool. Nothing in the nature of strategic choice generates a particular political, as opposed to analytic, perspective. Indeed, people developed the perspective in order to overcome their natural limitations and better fulfill their natural desires.

Bounded Rationality, Political Autism, Knowledge, and Self-Validating Theory

Strategic-choice explanations will certainly be correct in explaining the choices of actors who self-consciously and correctly use strategic-choice theory in making their decisions. A socially constructed edifice of rationality created by self-interested and purposive beings will function as a self-validating or self-fulfilling theory when actors use a model of the world to make their choices and to explain the behavior of those who make choices using such a model.

But since the model is a normative ideal, its use as a positive explanation will sometimes prove wrong when it is applied to cases in which actors do not use the model self-consciously. Since the models were constructed by those who deemed themselves crippled rationalists who needed decision-making tools to make better decisions, using the models to explain the decisions of those who did not use them will prove problematic at least some of the time.

The very use of rational-choice models in positive explanation has opened the door for cognitive psychologists to demonstrate all the ways in which people are crippled rationalists who fail to achieve the normative ideal captured in rational-choice theory.[50] The psychologists' assault is not on purposive explanation per se. Abelson (1976) argues that social psychologists subscribe to a "limited subjective rationality" that qualifies standard notions of rationality by recognizing that people may have dis-

---

[49] Some feminists and Marxists view rational choice as hostile to their agendas and have gravitated to the seemingly more hospitable intellectual soil of constructivism or postmodernism. Yet, rational choice can as readily be used by Marxists and feminists (there are many of the former and few of the latter) as by conservative proponents of decentralized market exchange.

Note that these labels are only specific to a stylized and caricatured depiction of modern political alignments. In an earlier time, political liberals were the staunch proponents of decentralized markets against conservative statist supporters of mercantilism. For the evolution of liberal views of the state and exchange, see Stein 1993.

[50] For an accessible history of the cognitive revolution, see Gardner 1985.

torted notions of reality and may filter information. The qualifications capture the mental-processing rules that people actually use in place of formal logic.

A key implication of these criticisms is that careful attention must be paid to the human ability to process information and to how people conceptualize the world in which they function. To reflect reality, formalizations of choice must necessarily be built on accurate behavioral foundations.[51] In addition, context not only matters, it may be all important.[52] The substantive nature of actual choices may be an essential element of decision.

But the criticisms emerging from cognitive psychology do not constitute attacks on purposive explanations per se but on their assumptions about rationality. Psychologists, who have argued that human beings do not have the cognitive ability always to carry out the requisites of rational choice, focus on the heuristics and shortcuts people use to process information and make decisions.[53] They have also clearly demonstrated the importance of context to decision making. Unlike economists, who emphasize the generality and universality of rational choice, psychologists point to situational factors. Their experimental work clearly shows, for example, that individuals do not perceive gains and losses symmetrically. People take risks to avoid certain losses but are risk averse with regard to gains. Thus how options are framed, as losses or gains, is critically important in determining actual choice (Tversky and Kahneman 1981, 1987).[54]

[51] Perhaps the greatest such problem posed by psychology for modern game theory is whether people are Bayesian rational. Formal models of incomplete information games depend on Bayesian updating (Mariotti 1995), yet the empirical evidence is that most people are not naturally Bayesian.

[52] The existence of constraints on cognitive ability (Oaksford and Chater 1993) and the context-dependence of cognition (Stevenson 1993) are widely recognized, and psychologists do want to ground theory in cognitive process (Shafir 1993). Some economists, too, see the importance of incorporating actual reasoning (Rubinstein 1991) and stress the importance of bounded rationality and of empirics (Binmore 1988). Or, as Simon (1990) puts it, the invariants of human behavior lie in cognitive mechanisms for choice.

[53] Economists were originally quite skeptical of many of these psychological assaults but have now conceded many of their points. A good way to trace this is in the work of Charles Plott (Grether and Plott 1979; Plott 1987). One implication has been the burgeoning field of experimental economics and the use of small group experiments to assess economic arguments (Smith 1992).

The key work is that of Tversky and Kahneman 1974. Economists have debated how troubled they should be that people do not function in the ways assumed by economic theory (Friedman 1953; McClelland 1975, 136–43; Lagueux 1994). Most defensively, Plott (1987) accepts the problematic nature of the psychological evidence on economic assumptions but argues that the enterprise be continued in the absence of a viable alternative.

[54] Still another example of the importance of context is provided by the argument that people make decisions sequentially using some aspect of the options available to them. Econ-

Critical choices between peace and war can also reflect framing. Leaders who see a choice between war now and war later, rather than between a cooperative gesture and a military response, are much more likely to take an escalatory military step during a crisis (Snyder 1978). The decisions that led to World War I were made by leaders who saw no alternative (Farrar 1972).

The constraints on rationality include human emotions, as well as how brains process information, for people have passions as well as interests (Hirschman 1977).[55] Economists have developed utilitarian explanations for the existence of our emotions and argue that self-interested beings find emotions quite helpful (Frank 1988, 1993; Hirshleifer 1987a, 1993).[56] Nevertheless, the utilitarian basis of emotions does not undercut the perverse implications of emotionalism for rational-choice explanations of behavior.[57] Again, formal theorizing with a normative focus may be driven by a desire to minimize the impact of emotions on decisions—to facilitate interests and minimize the ability of passions to get in the way—but positive theory that seeks to explain what people actually do must incorporate the impact passions, as well as interests, have on choice.[58]

Not only are humans boundedly rational and emotional, they are also somewhat politically autistic. They do not make appropriate attributions, especially in social settings. A classic example comes from the actor/observer literature, which finds that people typically attribute their own choices to structural constraints but attribute others' choices to prefer-

---

omists would argue that each of three equally valued options would have a one-third probability of being chosen. Tversky (1972) argues that this is nonsensical when two of the options have a common feature—for example, different recordings of the same symphony—and the third is quite different (a book, for example). Tversky's argument is that a person would first choose between a book and a recording and only then select between recordings; so the odds of selecting the book are one in two, and the odds associated with each recording are one in four. Again, it is not a model of calculated choice that is being questioned but the specific presumptions of the process.

[55] Hirschman (1991a, 357) argues that turn-of-the-century economists rejected the "instinctual-intuitive, the habitual, the unconscious, the ideological and neurotically-driven"—that is, turned away from the "nonrational that characterized virtually all of the influential philosophical, psychological, and sociological thinking of the time." In so doing, they emptied their concepts, most specifically self-interest, "of their psychological origin."

[56] One philosopher argues that impulses have utility in finding salient solutions to coordination problems (Gilbert 1989b). Others argue that habitual and routine behaviors can be seen as rational (Hodgson 1993a). Simon (1978a) points out that even psychoanalytic theory contains a functional component and a sense of rationality (contrast with Cohen 1976).

[57] Human emotions need not be seen as antithetical to rational choice; indeed, they may be essential to any human ability to comprehend and evaluate gain and loss (Damasio 1994).

[58] Some game theory does include the possibility of unexplained deviations from presumed rationality (threats that leave something to chance, trembling hand equilibria).

ences, predispositions, and character. International relations are rife with such political autism. The security dilemma describes how states reduce their own security by not taking the reactions of others into account when they take steps to improve their security. The belief that one's own actions are merely reactions to others' provocations, when those others' actions are not understood as reactions themselves, is a form of political autism.

Hence using strategic choice as an explanation requires making insupportable assumptions about individual capability. People are crippled rationalists, wanting to make rational decisions but constrained and limited by their own psychology: by their emotions and cognitive processes.

Yet self-interested purposive beings also use the knowledge at their disposal to improve the quality of their decisions—to improve on the limitations of their biology. They create tools, like computers, and develop knowledge, including game theory, in order to do better.

This means that *actors' knowledge, including that of social-science theory, must be incorporated into the explanation of choice and outcome.*

Knowledge of strategic choice (and economics) is self-fulfilling and self-validating. These bodies of knowledge were created by people who wanted to do better, and they provide guidelines for doing just that. When self-interested actors apply them, their knowledge claims are true precisely because they are used. The self-conscious normative use of economics makes economics a self-fulfilling truth as a positive theory.[59]

By contrast, *knowledge of psychology is self-falsifying.* Although economists and psychologists agree on the desirability and utility of purposive explanation, the former presume rational choice, the latter question it. The work of psychologists focuses on the ways that people fall short of the ideal model of rational choice. Much psychological work, therefore, including that in international relations, proffers recommendations on overcoming peoples' shortcomings that make the theories self-falsifying. Studies of crisis decision making typically find that stress adversely affects decisions, but they conclude with recommendations on how to avoid the impact of stress and achieve more rational decisions (Holsti 1989; Janis 1982). The implicit, if not explicit, message of much psychological work is that being sensitive to cognitive distortions can improve the quality and rationality of human decision making.[60]

A complete model of choice and behavior must necessarily include the knowledge actors have about the world. Since people can be aware of, and

---

[59] In recent bidding for government cellular phone rights, all the bidders hired game theorists to advise them on bargaining strategy, and, not surprisingly, the game-theoretic prediction for the bidding worked quite well.

[60] Much the same can be said of psychoanalytic theory. Once individuals became aware of the factors driving their behavior, the analysts held, they would be able to deal with them.

indeed can make use of, social scientists' theories about their behavior, explanations of their behavior need to incorporate people's knowledge and beliefs about how the world works and the implications of such knowledge for their decisions. This means that some knowledge claims become true because of their self-conscious application by the subjects of the theory, and other knowledge claims become false because of their subjects' conscious awareness of them.

Positive Verisimilitude and Incomplete and Indeterminate Explanation (The Multiple-Equilibria Problem)

One solution to the problem of using a normative model for positive purposes is to expand the formal model to make it more isomorphic with the reality being explained, that is, to make it less of an ideal for which humans strive and more reflective of constrained human beings with constrained information. In fact, scholars have modified the nature of rationality presumed in strategic-choice explanations.[61] Early critics focused on the presumably unbounded nature of rational explanation, which posits that actors assess all possible options and maximize. Even reflective game theorists recognize this, or, as one major game theorist puts it, "homo rationalis [a species that acts purposefully and logically] is a mythical species, like the unicorn and the mermaid" (Aumann 1985). Economist Brian Arthur characterizes the domain of rational explanation in similarly dismissive terms: "If one were to imagine the vast collection of decision problems economic agents might conceivably deal with as a sea or an ocean, with the easier problems on top and more complicated ones at increasing depth, then deductive rationality would describe human behavior accurately within a few feet of the surface" (Arthur 1994, 406).[62]

Troubled by the synoptic quality of rationality, Herbert Simon and others replace it with a notion of bounded rationality. Simon, for example, argues that actors satisfice rather than maximize, that they stop their process of assessment when they hit on a minimally acceptable option. At issue here is not an alternative to purposive explanation per se but to its

---

[61] For many who accept the logic of purposive explanation, the notion of rationality still draws wrath. Although the discussion that follows treats criticisms analytically, understand that some criticism stems from the connotation of the word *rationality*. Rational-choice explanations do contain some assumptions in addition to those of intentionalist explanation (Elster 1985, 1986).

[62] Arthur (1994, 406) goes on to suggest that deductive rationality would apply to a simple game such as tic-tac-toe but that "rational 'solutions' are not found at the depth of checkers, and certainly not at the still modest depths of chess and go."

character.[63] Rather than being hyperrational, individuals are boundedly rational, and bounded rationality has emerged as a growth industry within rational-choice scholarship.[64]

The recognition of the inadequacy of decision theory and game theory as positive explanations has sent scholars in the direction of making these models more isomorphic with the reality being modeled. The simplistic assumptions of early models—simultaneous choice by two actors, each choosing between two options and having complete information about strategies and payoffs—were replaced by subsequent refinements that dealt with sequential choice and incomplete information.[65] These refinements expand the problem of multiple equilibria and thus explode the indeterminacy associated with the models. Further expanding the models to achieve greater verisimilitude (e.g., adding options and actors, etc.) quickly reaches the limits of mathematical tractability, but even if these problems are eventually solved, the solutions will surely expand the range of indeterminacy.

As currently developed, strategic situations of the slightest complexity are plagued by multiple equilibria and multiple solutions concepts. Many recent solution concepts have been developed in order to reduce the number of equilibria generated by simpler criteria.[66] But the mere existence of multiple equilibria (as well as multiple solution concepts) implies that knowing the players' strategies and payoffs is inadequate completely to determine a unique outcome. In other words, structure and choice are indeterminate because they are explanatorily incomplete.[67] This *strategic*

---

[63] The way Simon (1976, 1978a, 1978b) and others put it is to distinguish between different types or aspects of rationality (Evans 1993). Simon's distinction is between substantive and procedural rationality.

[64] See Conlisk 1996; and Lipman 1991, 1995. Aumann (1997, 8) argues that equilibrium refinements that have been proposed to deal with the multiple-equilibrium problem "don't really sound like bounded rationality. They sound more like super-rationality."

[65] Game theory has been extended from perfect to imperfect information, from dealing with cases in which the payoffs sum to zero to those in which they do not, from assuming that utility (payoffs) can be transferred among actors to cases in which they cannot, from assuming simultaneous choice (normal or strategic form) to sequential choice (extensive form), from dealing only with the interaction of two actors to that of n actors, and from complete to incomplete information. Aumann (1992) extends game theory to cases in which actors need not assume that others are necessarily rational. For a description of advances, see Harsanyi 1977, 1988.

[66] For a discussion of the relationship among equilibria, see Morrow 1994a.

[67] The existence of multiple equilibria implies that the enterprise is inadequate for prescription and incomplete as explanation. The reliance of solution concepts on beliefs about unreachable states is also a problem. Some scholars confronting the issue of equilibrium selection and individual deviation from strategic rationality have even abandoned the formal enterprise and moved toward the use of experiments to assess the basis of human choice

indeterminacy principle represents the explanatory boundary of strategic choice and minimally implies that in cases with multiple equilibria, complete explanation will require conjoining this approach with something else. Strategic-choice explanations thus demonstrate their own theoretical incompleteness.

COMMON KNOWLEDGE, THE CONSTRUCTION OF CHOICE, AND POST HOC EXPLANATION

Strategic-interaction models presume that actors have common knowledge of the rules of the game, of each other, their choices, and the probability distribution of one another's preferences. The limitations associated with this modeling requirement are enormous and, in all but the most structured social situations, mean that explanation is invariably post hoc.

The essence of the strategic problem is the assumptions made about the common knowledge of the actors.[68] This was unproblematic when game theorists only studied games, like chess, and could assume the players had common knowledge of the rules. Much the same is true of highly structured social settings, as when a government establishes fixed procedures to regulate bidding between firms in an auction. But in many social settings, common knowledge is far more problematic. Can we, for example, even be certain that people mean the same thing when they use the same word?[69] This form of the problem is particularly important in international relations. At one point, Yasir Arafat, the Palestinian leader, created a roadblock in Israeli-Palestinian negotiations when, in addressing an Arab audience, he used the Arabic word, *jihad* (usually translated as holy war). A debate ensued about the meaning of the word in Arabic and its typical translation; namely, had Arafat alluded simply to a political struggle or to a holy war.

(Plott 1991). Those unwilling to depart from the formal enterprise are increasingly moving toward evolutionary game theory that does not depend on strong rationality assumptions (Binmore and Samuelson 1994; Van Damme 1994; Robson 1995).

[68] For the ongoing discussion of the meaning and necessity of an assumption of common knowledge about the rules of the game, see Lismont and Mongin 1994. This focus has brought together the frontiers of game theory with that of logic in philosophy (Bacharach 1987, 1994; Stalnaker 1994). For some implications of a deviation from common knowledge, see Geanakoplos 1992, 1994.

Putting oneself in another's shoes is biologically hard-wired. The autistic suffer from a neurological disorder that makes them largely blind to the existence of other minds and makes them unable to assess others' beliefs and intentions. Simon Baron-Cohen (1995) describes this inability to infer what others are thinking as "mindblindness."

[69] This is, in fact, a critical issue in the philosophy of language.

More broadly, how states come to see themselves as engaged in a particular game is itself important. Even if we assume that states know the targets, both direct and indirect, of their actions, it is not at all clear that states accurately recognize themselves as targets of others' actions. Scholars have debated the extent to which Truman's decision to drop the atomic bomb on Japan was intended as a signal to the Soviet Union. Conversely, in certain situations states incorrectly see themselves as targets of others' actions, or sometimes fail to recognize that they are targets.[70] Even more broadly, actions have audiences as well as targets, and actions taken for domestic audiences can have international consequences, and vice versa. The general point is that in certain games, it is not always self-evident who the actors are.

The issue of what is posited on behalf of actors extends to the nature of their choices. Typically, scholarly analysis stipulates the strategic choices actors confront. Yet, crafting alternatives lies at the heart of statecraft and creative diplomacy. When diplomats search for "formulas" to resolve conflicts, they are looking for options other than those that created the deadlock in the first place (Zartman and Berman 1982). Ulysses's choice could have been framed as between traveling within hearing distance of the sirens or navigating a path that kept him out of hearing range. It could also have been put as the choice between keeping his ears plugged (not hearing) or leaving his ears unplugged but paying the consequences. But Ulysses devised an alternative, one that effectively allowed him to eat his cake and have it, too.[71] This human creativity in structuring alternatives is completely outside the modeling of strategic choice. An analyst can elucidate the payoffs associated with various options and can explain choices and even detail circumstances in which actors find themselves aggrieved and would prefer to have different options than the ones they seem to have or be given. But the delineation of choice is a human activity, so one cannot know a priori whether actors will craft new alternatives and of what kind.[72] In other words, the analyst cannot know a priori that Ulysses will devise a way that will allow him both to listen to the sirens'

[70] Jervis (1976) argues that states often mistakenly see themselves as the targets of others' actions.

[71] Elster (1979) uses the story to demonstrate a case in which the possibility for rational choice exists before the fact rather than during it. Elster refers to this as "imperfect rationality."

[72] The point can be put even more broadly: actors do not know what their preferences are until they actually begin to analyze a problem. Anderson (1983) argues that during the Cuban missile crisis, the preferences of the members of the executive committee advising President Kennedy only emerged during their deliberations through the process of assessing options. For a debate on whether the mutual determination of wants and benefits poses a problem for decision theory or is merely an attack on the implicit view of how deliberations take place, see Kusser and Spohn 1992 and Broome 1994.

call and to avoid their deadly temptation. Post hoc, it is easy to explain Ulysses's choice. Strategic-choice explanation presumes a knowledge of the complete set of options and is thus post hoc.

Constructing options and transforming payoffs plays fundamentally with the conception of choice under constraints. Some actors are pragmatists who take constraints as given; others act as revolutionaries more interested in overcoming constraints. The exchange between U.S. President Jimmy Carter and Israeli Prime Minister Menachem Begin at Camp David illustrates a dialogue between a pragmatist and a visionary. Carter focused on the extant situation and what it required from the Israeli leader. Begin's response, irritating to Carter, was to lecture the U. S. president on Jewish history. His point was implicit but clear: Had he and others given in to presumed requisites of the day, the state of Israel would not have been created in 1948. Begin preferred to await better circumstances than to compromise with current reality. Alternatively, he could try to create an alternative future and reality, what Israelis refer to as "creating facts."

Actors cannot only create options and attempt to transcend constraints, they can also structure choices for one another. The Prisoner's Dilemma is, after all, a case of three actors making choices in which one of them, the district attorney, has the power to structure the options and payoffs available to the other two (Burns and Buckley 1974).[73]

Institutional design is also about structuring choice and creating new alternatives. Such designs, for example, can transform public goods into collective ones, and vice versa.[74] The most-favored-nation clause fundamentally alters the inherently private and divisible nature of trade and trade policy. States can and do pursue specific and differentiable trade relations with other states. Historically, trade agreements were signed by pairs of countries stipulating general terms for their bilateral trade. These illiberal tools, originally mercantilist devices states used to discriminate among their various trading partners, were completely transformed through the inclusion of the most-favored-nation clause. By guaranteeing that the signatories would extend to one another any preferences they offered third nations in subsequent treaties, this clause ensured that no state would be more favored; thus international trade agreements

---

[73] Relational power—the ability to affect another's payoffs—can be distinguished from metapower—the ability to structure another's options and payoffs (Baumgartner, Buckley, and Burns 1975; Baumgartner, Buckley, Burns, and Schuster 1976).

[74] Other elements of institutional design include the construction of private property rights in order to "marketize" some domain rather than regulate it and the construction of different oversight structures (the fire alarms/police patrols distinction).

changed from private discriminatory arrangements into accords that created a public good among a club of members.[75]

The constraints by which actors are limited or which they attempt to transcend vary in character. Physical and biological limitations differ from social ones. Without external assistance, human beings cannot fly. This inability to soar constitutes a tight constraint. Social constraints are less confining. Constructivists are correct, to some extent, in stressing human creativity and construction: Social structure is, in part, a product of human agency. The strategic-choice theorist has no problem explaining and modeling the strategic constructions of human beings. The norms and social artifacts that can be modeled as constraining choice can also be explained as the products of choice. Post hoc, there is little that cannot be included in the strategic-choice enterprise.

In using the simple building blocks of choice and payoff, models of strategic choice decontextualize calculation, relationship, and the international system. Everything about the respective actors and their relationship must be contained in the structure of the game (who goes when, what choices they have), their payoffs, their beliefs, and the information conditions. Power asymmetries between the actors, for example, are either irrelevant or their impact must be contained in one of these elements (the powerful may have more options than the weak, they may have better information, they may have higher payoffs, etc.). But power is not a direct factor in these models; it operates through the components of strategic choice delineated in chapter 1 of this volume.[76]

The same is true of relationships. Some states see one another as enemies; others see one another as allies. Does the existence of a prisoner's dilemma imply the same things in both cases? Because the alliance problem is a prisoner's dilemma (Snyder 1984) and the armament choice between enemies is also a prisoner's dilemma, does that mean there is no difference between alliances and rivalries in international politics?[77]

Here, too, the strategic-choice theorist can make accommodations. That game-theoretic modeling effectively treats actors on a par, in much the way the notion of sovereignty does, does not mean that prisoner's dilemmas between asymmetric powers cannot be modeled differently

---

[75] This is discussed in Stein 1984, 1990, and picked up by Ruggie 1992.

[76] The five elements of a strategic situation are "i) the collection of players; ii) the physical order in which play proceeds; iii) the choices available whenever it is a player's turn to move; iv) the information about previous choices made by others available to a player whose turn it is to move; and v) the payoffs to each of the players resulting from any play of the game" (Reny 1992, 103). As Philip Reny (ibid.) points out, this is so flexible that, "remarkably, one is hard-pressed to uncover a real-life strategic situation which cannot be usefully modelled [sic] by a carefully chosen extensive-form game."

[77] See the discussion in Stein 1990, chap. 6.

than those between states of relatively equal power, or that such games between allies cannot be modeled differently than those between rivals.

Strategic choice can be applied to actors and interactions at any level of analysis, but, in so doing, it decontextualizes the role of domain. The distinction between anarchy in international politics and hierarchy in domestic politics disappears. This generates important insights—that there are elements of anarchy in domestic politics and elements of hierarchy in international politics and that there exist wide swatches of international cooperation and domestic conflict. But it also misses something critical, namely, that the difference between legitimate authority in domestic politics and its absence in international politics is ignored in the blithe comparison of international conflict to pretrial bargaining within societies (cf., chapter 1 of this volume).

Formal theorists not only impute actors' preferences and choices, they also assume their bases for calculation and assessment. Although a smattering of studies employ alternative decision criteria, the application of a strategic-choice approach has typically treated expected utility as the basis for choice. But there are bases of calculation and assessment other than expected utility (not to mention the different ways expected utility has itself been formalized; see Schoemaker 1982).[78] The neorealist emphasis on a preeminent concern with survival can be read to imply a lexicographic utility function in which states act to maximize their chances of survival without engaging in any trade-offs among other interests (Stein 1990). This comports with the recognition that a variety of decision criteria are available for actors making purposive calculated choices.[79] Again, these can be incorporated in the structure of models of strategic choice.

Models of strategic choice are enormously flexible, and scholars can invariably construct post hoc models with an equilibrium outcome that matches the behavior actually chosen. Yet, except where the situation is quite constraining, the models can only be constructed post hoc. Even then, they do not typically generate one unique equilibrium and also face equally plausible contending models (ones that generate an alternative set of equilibria that include the observed outcome).

We have now come full circle. An approach created to improve human decision making has created an intellectual enterprise that falls short both

[78] A variety of paradoxes reflect different ways of arriving at a rational choice. More specifically, backward induction as the basis of rational choice generates certain paradoxes (Selten 1978; Binmore 1987; Pettit and Sugden 1989; Basu 1994; and, for their linkage with issues of common knowledge, Reny 1992).

[79] Seemingly perverse decisions by calculating actors are not new to political life. Radicals who oppose reform and support reactionaries in the belief that this will bring revolution sooner provide an intriguing example of the contorted calculations that underlie political decisions.

as normative recommendation and as positive theory, and for the same reasons. The limitations of human cognition in conjunction with the inherent constraints of uncertainty in a strategic setting result in models that, while still excessively simple, depend on strong common knowledge assumptions and decisive situational constraints and nevertheless result in multiple equilibria. Our knowledge of strategic reasoning gives us models that neither prescribe a unique strategy nor identify a complete explanation for any choice (even retrospectively, except in the simplest cases).[80]

The strategic-choice approach discussed in this volume has generic problems and limitations with international-relations manifestations.[81] Although the papers here demonstrate the utility of the approach, they also implicitly demonstrate that it does not resolve some core issues plaguing the study of international politics. At the end of the day, despite greater rigor, tighter conceptualization, and more precise specification, unresolved questions remain.

ALL BETS ARE OFF: WHITHER STRATEGIC CHOICE

This volume is written with a note of triumphalism.[82] The use of strategic choice is growing. The lag in importing an idea from an economics article into political science grows ever shorter. Every new development is assessed for its potential application in political science.

Yet, this is not the first coming of strategic choice.[83] Game theory made its way into international relations in the late 1950s, was accepted and

---

[80] The limitation of formal models beyond some level of complexity can be seen as related to Gödel's incompleteness theorem about mathematics more generally: that beyond some level of complexity, all logical systems are incomplete in that they contain propositions that cannot be proven true or false within the rules of that system.

[81] Sutton (1990, 507) argues that game-theoretic models in industrial economics, the very area transformed by game theory in the 1980s and which has been the inspiration for international-relations scholars, are similarly beset by problems of indeterminacy. He wonders "whether the old taunt is true, that 'with oligopoly, anything can happen,' " and continues to ask, "in 'explaining' everything, have we explained nothing?" To the extent that international relations, too, is a domain dominated by a small set of great powers engaged in strategic behavior, then it may also be a domain in which many outcomes are possible and in which many equally viable models can be developed. Sutton's description of game-theoretic models of industrial economics, that the "richness of possible formulations leads to an often embarrassingly wide range of outcomes supportable as equilibria within some 'reasonable' specification," could as easily apply to international relations.

[82] The combination of triumphalism and proselytizing exhortation suggests either a religious movement or a Ponzi scheme.

[83] It should be noted that the initial manifesto that organized this volume was written as if Schelling had had no impact in the late 1950s.

absorbed, and the field moved on and elsewhere. Two explanations can be proffered for the eclipse of game theory in the 1960s.[84] First, the formal tools seemed to have been fully developed. The apparent end of technical development, in conjunction with the incorporation of the extant body of findings, led international-relations scholars to other pursuits. More directly, the deterrence problem on which early game theory focused had been worked through, there seemed little more that could be said about deterrence in formal terms, and no other interesting applications for the method appeared to exist. Second, the assumptions that underlay the formal work on deterrence could be directly assessed empirically. Thus one response to game-theoretic studies of deterrence was to undertake empirical assessments of the nature of decision making. Scholars interested in deterrence questioned the assumption of unitary actors (directly leading to the development of the bureaucratic politics literature) and the presumed rationality of decision making during crises.[85] Empirical work on decision making in the late 1960s and early 1970s attempted to assess directly some of the assumptions of formal deterrence theory.

Formal game-theoretic work returned to the forefront of international relations in the late 1970s and early 1980s. It came after the quantitative work of the mid- and late 1960s had either been discredited or was no longer generative, when empirical work seemed excessively inductive and too little informed by theory, and when extant theorizing was flighty and undisciplined. By then, it also reflected new developments in game theory: the use of simulation (Axelrod 1984) and games with sequential moves (Selten 1975, 1978, on perfect equilibrium; Kreps and Wilson 1982, on sequential equilibrium).[86]

Two elements seem to drive developments in the evolution of international relations theory. One is the generative force of a research tradition. Approaches with numerous followers tend to have research agendas that drive intellectual effort. Eventually, though, these run out of steam—research avenues get fully spun out or reach the limits of the technologically

---

[84] A striking indication of this is the relative attention paid to game theory in two special issues of *World Politics* in the 1960s. As noted above, the 1961 volume paid considerable attention to game theory. The 1969 issue paid scant attention to that subject, however, concentrating largely on the wave of quantitative empirical work that had become the focus of the field's attention in the mid-1960s.

[85] For the evolution of work on deterrence, see Jervis 1979. As a historical note, the direction of Graham Allison's work was affected by Andrew Marshall, director of research for the defense department and a key figure at the RAND Corporation during the mid-1950s, when game theory and economic modeling were applied to strategic questions.

[86] Snyder and Diesing's 1977 publication was also an important event, although their work reflected the interest in decision making and empirical work that was a hallmark of the 1970s.

tractable and feasible. Absent new technical developments, scholarly interests and efforts shift elsewhere. Something like this happened to content analysis, simulation, and events data modeling, among other approaches. A similar occurrence seems evident more recently in the shift toward experimentation and evolutionary game theory among economists and some political scientists.[87]

The other important force changing the focus of scholarship in international politics is the real world. World War II and the events of the late 1930s dealt a death blow to the field's attention to international law. Changes in the perceived efficacy and utility of the United Nations have regularly fueled and dampened interest in international organizations. The perceived successes and failures of European integration have affected the study of regional integration more broadly. The Cuban missile crisis generated the literature on crises and crisis decision making and crisis management. The collapse of Bretton Woods and the oil crisis brought the return of international political economy. The rhetorical stridency, increased defense budgets, and collapse of détente in the early Reagan years brought a rebirth of security studies, a subfield that had atrophied in the mid- and late 1970s.[88] The end of the cold war is already having profound effects on the research interests of those in international relations. Whether the widespread use of game theory survives this shift will depend on the ability of strategic-choice theorists to address substantive issues of current concern.[89] Given that today's game theorists recognize the importance of behavioral approaches, and given the current state of formal theorizing, another cycle is not out of the question.[90]

Yet, there remain both new methodological developments not fully tapped and numerous potential agendas for the continued application of strategic choice in international relations. Many components of strategic interaction deemed important by common sense have been profitably illuminated by technical developments in game theory. Reputation and signaling are two that have been studied formally and applied to interna-

[87] The economists' turn toward evolutionary game theory can be seen in Binmore and Samuelson 1994 and Van Damme 1994. For a characterization of experimentation as behavioral game theory, see Camerer 1997. Also see the adaptive-learning approach discussed in Honkapohja 1993.

[88] Jervis's (1978) work on military doctrine helped drive the appearance of this new intellectual agenda, as did Robert Powell's revisiting of Schelling with the new developments in game theory.

[89] For example, will the formal work of Fearon, Cetinyan, and others, illuminate more about the impact of ethnicity in international politics than alternative approaches?

[90] The phenomenon of cycling between formal and behavioral work can be seen in the history of economics as well (Seligman 1971; Latsis 1972). Formal theorizing generates great insights, but pressures build both for empirical assessments of assumptions and for information about what formalists ignore.

tional politics. But even here, much work can yet be done. Concepts such as resolution, conviction, stubbornness, stamina, and probity are all elements of reputation that cannot yet be addressed by game theory (Shubik 1993, 220). Some of the continued vitality of the approach in international relations depends on such developments.[91]

What Alternative?

Explaining behavior by reference to purpose is a standard practice in the social sciences. Not surprisingly, therefore, many debates are within the approach of purposive explanation. Indeed, the formal tools discussed here are constructions of purposive human beings who wanted to improve the rationality of their decisions. Is there, then, any alternative outside, and different from, a purposive approach?

It is not clear what the alternative to purposive explanation is and whether any of the suggested possibilities lie outside purposive explanation. Harsanyi (1969) contrasts rational choice with functionalist and conformist explanation but then argues that rational choice provides an explanation for institutions and social values. Elster (1986) points to structuralism and social norms as alternative possibilities, although he finds the former implausible and the latter incorrect. Then, too, his potential alternatives have also been the focus of rational-choice explanation.[92]

Even the constructivist or postmodern alternative, which I cannot even sketch here, is hardly at odds with the rational-choice approach. It merely takes the primitives of strategic choice, the nature of the system and of preferences, as malleable and in need of explanation. But strategic choice can address these matters as well. The common law and norms, along with such other factors as private property rights and institutions, can be seen as constraining and framing choice. But they can also be studied as the products of human agency and choice.[93]

Further, parallels may be drawn between constructivism and postmodernism, on the one hand, and game theory and economics, on the other:

---

[91] The injunction "grow or stagnate" may not apply to political entities, but it does apply to intellectual enterprises.

[92] One can easily generate models of choice in which actors are, in effect, strategic dummies without choice (the view of structural models). One can also focus on the choices underlying social norms. Plott (1987) simply says there is no alternative to rational choice.

[93] A rational-choice basis can be established for tradition and norms, which are the alternatives often sketched in sociological thought. For discussions of rationality by some of the classic sociologists of the twentieth century, see Cohen 1976 and Lane 1974. For one assessment of when norms do or do not undercut rational choice, see Mortimore 1976. For my discussion, see Stein 1996.

Both emphasize doubt and uncertainty, and the open-endedness emphasized by postmodernism is also found in game theory (Heap 1993). Ironically, constructivists characterize a strategic-choice approach, despite its emphasis on choice and its normative roots, as structural and contrast it with one that emphasizes agency. Yet, a strategic-choice approach can elucidate both the situations in which actors have an interest in constructing political alternatives and the requisites for institutional design and construction in the modern world. One can even argue that there is a new-age quality to modern game theory: Discussions of the equilibria attainable in incomplete information games under some sets of assumptions and expectations come close to the argument that peace will come when we all think peace. In short, strategic choice emphasizes agency and can deal with social constructions such as norms and institutions.

CONCLUSION

Strategic choice is more than a language and a set of tools, but it is far less than a theory. It is more than a language because it has content and entails substantive assumptions. As a result, it is richer than calculus (a branch of mathematics specifically developed to study planetary motion but applicable to many phenomena that share nothing of a substantive nature). Yet, as an approach, strategic choice remains a largely empty vessel—not shapeless but in need of content if it is to have something to contribute. It is therefore specific applications of strategic choice, rather than strategic choice per se, that often draw criticism. The continued success of strategic choice lies in its indigenous development in confronting concerns specific to international politics. Yet, we know that complexifying the model to make it more isomorphic with reality typically makes it indeterminate and incomplete as an explanation. So our response, if asked if we should believe in game theory and strategic choice, should be that of the Zen master when asked if he believed in God. Sounding as if caught in a strategic game himself, he answered, "If you do, I don't; and if you don't, I do."[94] And our response to the question of whether a strategic-choice approach should constitute the foundation of explanation in international politics is "yes, one cannot do without it; and no, it is simply not enough by itself."

---

[94] Related by Abraham Kaplan (1967) to explain that he did not lack faith in models of rationality but wanted to say "however" to the faithful.

References

Abelson, R. P. 1976. "Social Psychology's Rational Man." In *Rationality and the Social Sciences: Contributions to the Philosophy and Methodology of the Social Sciences*, edited by S. I. Benn and G. W. Mortimore. London: Routledge and Kegan Paul.

Alchian, Armen A. 1950. "Uncertainty, Evolution, and Economic Theory." *Journal of Political Economy* 58:211–21.

Alesina, Alberto, and Enrico Spolaore. 1997. "On the Number and Size of Nations." *Quarterly Journal of Economics* 112:1027–56.

Allison, Graham T. 1971. *Essence of Decision: Explaining the Cuban Missile Crisis*. Boston: Little, Brown.

Allison, Graham T., and Morton Halperin. 1972. "Bureaucratic Politics: A Paradigm and Some Policy Implications." *World Politics* 24:40–79.

Alt, James, and Michael Gilligan. 1994. "The Political Economy of Trading States: Factor Specificity, Collective Action Problems, and Domestic Political Institutions." *Journal of Political Philosophy* 2:165–92.

Altfeld, Michael F. 1985. "The Decision to Ally: A Theory and Test." *Western Political Quarterly* 37:523–44.

Altfeld, Michael F., and Bruce Bueno de Mesquita. 1979. "Choosing Sides in Wars." *International Studies Quarterly* 23:87–112.

Amsden, Alice H. 1985. "The State and Taiwan's Economic Development." In *Bringing the State Back In*, edited by Peter B. Evans, Dietrich Rueschemeyer, and Theda Skocpol. Cambridge: Cambridge University Press.

———. 1989. *Asia's Next Giant: South Korea and Late Industrialization*. New York: Oxford University Press.

Anderson, Paul A. 1983. "Decision Making by Objection and the Cuban Missile Crisis." *Administrative Science Quarterly* 28:201–22.

Anderson, Perry. 1974. *Lineages of the Absolutist State*. London: NLB.

Angier, Natalie. 1995. "Heredity's More Than Genes, New Theory Proposes." *New York Times*, January 3, B13, B22.

Apter, David, and Tony Saich. 1994. *Revolutionary Discourse in Mao's Republic*. Cambridge, Mass.: Harvard University Press.

Arrow, Kenneth J. 1951. *Social Choice and Individual Values*. New York: Wiley.

Art, Robert J. 1973. "Bureaucratic Politics and American Foreign Policy: A Critique." *Policy Sciences* 4:467–90.

Art, Robert J., and Robert Jervis. 1992. *International Politics: Enduring Concepts and Contemporary Issues*, 3rd ed. New York: HarperCollins.

Arthur, W. Brian. 1994. "Inductive Reasoning and Bounded Rationality." *American Economic Review* 84:406–11.

Aumann, Robert J. 1985. "What Is Game Theory Trying to Accomplish?" In *Frontiers of Economics*, edited by K. Arrow and S. Honkapohja. Oxford: Basil Blackwell.

Aumann, Robert J. 1992. "Irrationality in Game Theory." In *Economic Analysis of Markets and Games: Essays in Honor of Frank Hahn*, edited by Partha Dasgupta, Douglas Gale, Oliver Hart, and Eric Maskin. Cambridge: MIT Press.

———. 1997. "Rationality and Bounded Rationality." *Games and Economic Behavior* 21:2–14.

Axelrod, Robert M. 1984. *The Evolution of Cooperation*. New York: Basic Books.

———. 1986. "An Evolutionary Approach to Norms." *American Political Science Review* 8:1095–1111.

Axelrod, Robert M., and Robert O. Keohane. 1986. "Achieving Cooperation under Anarchy: Strategies and Institutions." In *Cooperation under Anarchy*, edited by Kenneth A. Oye. Princeton, N.J.: Princeton University Press.

Bacharach, Michael. 1987. "A Theory of Rational Decision in Games." *Erkenntnis* 27:17–55.

———. 1994. "The Epistemic Structure of a Theory of a Game." *Theory and Decision* 37:7–48.

Baldwin, David A., ed. 1993. *Neorealism and Neoliberalism: The Contemporary Debate*. New York: Columbia University Press.

Ball, Desmond. 1974. "The Blind Men and the Elephant: A Critique of Bureaucratic Politics Theory." *Australian Outlook* 28:71–92.

Baron, David P. 1991. "Majoritarian Incentives, Pork Barrel Programs, and Procedural Controls." *American Journal of Political Science* 35:57–90.

Baron, David P., and John Ferejohn. 1989. "Bargaining in Legislatures." *American Political Science Review* 83:1181–1206.

Baron, James N., and Michael T. Hannan. 1994. "The Impact of Economics on Contemporary Sociology." *Journal of Economic Literature* 32:1111–46.

Baron-Cohen, Simon. 1995. *Mindblindness: An Essay on Autism and Theory of Mind*. Cambridge: MIT Press.

Barrow, John D. 1992. *Pi in the Sky: Counting, Thinking, and Being*. Oxford: Oxford University Press.

Basu, Kaushik. 1994. "The Traveler's Dilemma: Paradoxes of Rationality in Game Theory." *American Economic Review* 84:391–95.

Baumgartner, Tom, Walter Buckley, and Tom R. Burns. 1975. "Relational Control: The Human Structuring of Cooperation and Conflict." *Journal of Conflict Resolution* 19:417–40.

Baumgartner, Tom, Walter Buckley, Tom R. Burns, and Peter Schuster. 1976. "Meta-Power and the Structuring of Social Hierarchies." In *Power and Control: Social Structures and Their Transformation*, edited by Tom R. Burns and Walter Buckley. Beverly Hills: Sage.

Bean, Richard. 1973. "War and the Birth of the Nation-State." *Journal of Economic History* 33:203–27.

Becker, Gary S. 1976. *The Economic Approach to Human Behavior*. Chicago: University of Chicago Press.

Bendor, Jonathan, and Thomas H. Hammond. 1992 "Rethinking Allison's Models." *American Political Science Review* 86:301–22.

Benoit, Jean-Pierre, and Vijay Krishna. 1985. "Finitely Repeated Games." *Econometrica* 53:890–904.

Bergsten, C. Fred, Robert O. Keohane, and Joseph S. Nye Jr. 1975. "International Economics and International Politics: A Framework for Analysis." In *World Politics and International Economics*, edited by C. Fred Bergsten and Lawrence B. Krause. Washington, D.C.: Brookings Institution.

Bernstein, Michael A. 1995. "American Economics and the National Security State, 1941–1953." *Radical History Review*, no. 63: 8–26.

Binmore, Ken. 1987. "Modeling Rational Players: Part I." *Economics and Philosophy* 3:179–214.

———. 1988. "Modeling Rational Players: Part II." *Economics and Philosophy* 4:9–55.

———. 1992. *Fun and Games: A Text on Game Theory*. Lexington: Heath.

Binmore, Ken, and Partha Dasgupta, eds. 1986. *Economic Organizations as Games*. Oxford: Basil Blackwell.

Binmore, Ken, and Larry Samuelson. 1992. "Evolutionary Stability in Repeated Games Played by Finite Automata." *Journal of Economic Theory* 57:278–305.

———. 1994. "Drift." *European Economic Review* 38:859–67.

Blainey, Geoffrey. 1988. *The Causes of War*, 3rd ed. New York: Free Press.

Blechman, Barry M. 1966. "The Quantitative Evaluation of Foreign Policy Alternatives: Sinai, 1956." *Journal of Conflict Resolution* 16:408–26.

Blume, Lawrence, and David Easley. 1992. "Evolution and Market Behavior." *Journal of Economic Theory* 58:9–40.

Boulding, K. E. 1958. "Theoretical Systems and Political Realities: A Review of Morton A. Kaplan, *System and Process in International Politics*." *Journal of Conflict Resolution* 2:329–34.

Bowler, Peter J. 1983. *The Eclipse of Darwinism: Anti-Darwinian Evolution Theories in the Decades around 1900*. Baltimore: The Johns Hopkins University Press.

———. 1988. *The Non-Darwinian Revolution: Reinterpreting a Historical Myth*. Baltimore: The John Hopkins University Press.

Braithwaite, Richard Bevan. 1955. *Theory of Games as a Tool for the Moral Philosopher*. Cambridge: Cambridge University Press.

Brams, Steven J. 1975. *Game Theory and Politics*. New York: Free Press.

———. 1980. *Biblical Games: A Strategic Analysis of Stories in the Old Testament*. Cambridge, Mass.: MIT Press.

———. 1985. *Superpower Games: Applying Game Theory to Superpower Conflict*. New Haven, Conn.: Yale University Press.

Brams, Steven J., and D. Marc Kilgour. 1988. *Game Theory and National Security*. New York: Basil Blackwell.

Breslauer, George, and Philip Tetlock, eds. 1991. *Learning in U.S. and Soviet Foreign Policy*. Boulder, Colo.: Westview.

Brewer, John. 1989. *The Sinews of Power: War, Money, and the English State, 1688–1783*. New York: Knopf.

Broome, John. 1994. "The Mutual Determination of Wants and Benefits." *Theory and Decision* 37:333–38.

Broz, J. Lawrence. 1997. "The Domestic Politics of International Monetary Order: The Gold Standard." In *Contested Social Orders and International Politics*, edited by David Skidmore. Nashville, Tenn.: Vanderbilt University Press.

Broz, J. Lawrence. 1998. *International Origins of Federal Reserve Systems*. Ithaca, N.Y.: Cornell University Press.

Bueno de Mesquita, Bruce, and David Lalman. 1992. *War and Reason: Domestic and International Imperatives*. New Haven, Conn.: Yale University Press.

Bueno de Mesquita, Bruce, and Randolph M. Siverson. 1995. "War and the Survival of Political Leaders: A Comparative Study of Regime Types and Political Accountability." *American Political Science Review* 89: 841–55.

Bueno de Mesquita, Bruce, James D. Morrow, and Ethan R. Zorick. 1997. "Capabilities, Perception, and Escalation." *American Political Science Review* 91:15–27.

Burley, Anne-Marie. 1993. "Regulating the World: Multilateralism, International Law, and the Projection of the New Deal Regulatory State." In *Multilateralism Matters*, edited by John G. Ruggie. New York: Columbia University Press.

Burley, Anne-Marie, and Walter Mattli. 1993. "Europe Before the Court: A Political Theory of Legal Integration." *International Organization* 47:41–76.

Burns, Arthur Lee. 1961. "Prospects for a General Theory of International Relations." In *The International System: Theoretical Essays*, edited by Klaus Knorr and Sidney Verba. Princeton, N.J.: Princeton University Press.

Burns, Tom, and Walter Buckley. 1974. "The Prisoners' Dilemma Game as a System of Social Domination." *Journal of Peace Research* 11:221–28.

Cain, P. J. 1980. *Economic Foundations of British Overseas Expansion, 1815–1914*. London: Macmillan.

———. 1985. "J. A. Hobson, Financial Capitalism and Imperialism in Late Victorian and Edwardian England." *Journal of Imperial and Commonwealth History* 13:1–27.

Cain, P. J., and A. G. Hopkins. 1993a. *British Imperialism: Innovation and Expansion, 1688–1914*. London: Longman.

———. 1993b. *British Imperialism: Crisis and Deconstruction, 1914–1990*. London: Longman.

Camerer, Colin F. 1997. "Progress in Behavioral Game Theory." *Journal of Economic Perspectives* 11:167–88.

Caporaso, James A. 1989. "Microeconomics and the International Political Economy: The Neoclassical Approach to Institutions." In *Global Changes and Theoretical Challenges*, edited by Ernst-Otto Czempiel and James N. Rosenau. Lexington, Ky.: Lexington Books.

Carroll, Glenn R. 1984. "Organizational Ecology." *Annual Review of Sociology* 10:71–93.

Chase, Kerry. 1998. "Sectors, Firms, and Regional Trade Blocs in the World Economy." Ph.D. diss., University of California at Los Angeles.

Chatterjee, Kalyan, and Lawrence Samuelson. 1987. "Bargaining with Two-Sided Incomplete Information: An Infinite Horizon Model with Alternating Offers." *Review of Economic Studies* 54:175–92.

Christensen, Thomas J., and Jack Snyder. 1990. "Chain Gangs and Passed Bucks: Predicting Alliance Patterns in Multipolarity." *International Organization* 44:137–68.

Clague, Christopher, Philip Keefer, Stephen Knack, and Mancur Olson. 1995. "Contract-Intensive Money: Contract Enforcement, Property Rights, and Economic Performance," IRIS Working Paper, no. 151, February 10, 1995. Center on Institutional Reform and the Informal Sector (IRIS). University of Maryland, College Park.

Cohen, Benjamin J. 1973. *The Question of Imperialism: The Political Economy of Dominance and Dependence*. New York: Basic Books.

Cohen, P. S. 1976. "Rational Conduct and Social Life." In *Rationality and the Social Sciences: Contributions to the Philosophy and Methodology of the Social Sciences*, edited by S. I. Benn and G. W. Mortimore. London: Routledge and Kegan Paul.

Colman, Andrew M. 1982. *Game Theory and Experimental Games: The Study of Strategic Interaction*. New York: Pergamon.

Conlisk, John. 1996. "Why Bounded Rationality?" *Journal of Economic Literature* 34:669–700.

Conybeare, John A. C. 1984. "Public Goods, Prisoner's Dilemmas, and the International Political Economy." *International Studies Quarterly* 28:5–22.

————. 1987. *Trade Wars: The Theory and Practice of International Commercial Rivalry*. New York: Columbia University Press.

Cooper, Richard N. 1972–73. "Trade Policy Is Foreign Policy." *Foreign Policy*, no. 9: 18–36.

Cooter, Robert, and Daniel Rubinfeld. 1989. "Economic Analysis of Legal Disputes and Their Resolution." *Journal of Economic Literature* 27:1067–97.

Cowhey, Peter F. 1993. "Domestic Institutions and the Credibility of International Commitments: Japan and the United States." *International Organization* 47:299–326.

D'Lugo, David, and Ronald Rogowski. 1993. "The Anglo-German Naval Race as a Study in Grand Strategy." In *The Domestic Bases of Grand Strategy*, edited by Richard Rosecrance and Arthur Stein. Ithaca, N.Y.: Cornell University Press.

Dahl, Robert A. 1956. *A Preface to Democratic Theory*. Chicago: University of Chicago Press.

Damasio, Antonio R. 1994. *Descartes' Error: Emotion, Reason, and the Human Brain*. New York: G. P. Putnam.

Daston, Lorraine. 1980. "Probabilistic Expectation and Rationality in Classical Probability Theory." *Historia Mathematica* 7:234–60.

————. 1988. *Classical Probability in the Enlightenment*. Princeton, N.J.: Princeton University Press.

Davis, Lance, and Robert Huttenback. 1986. *Mammon and the Pursuit of Empire: The Political Economy of British Imperialism, 1860–1912*. Cambridge: Cambridge University Press.

Davis, Philip J., and Reuben Hersh. 1981. *The Mathematical Experience*. Boston: Birkhäuser.

Dennett, Daniel C. 1995. *Darwin's Dangerous Idea: Evolution and the Meanings of Life*. New York: Simon and Schuster.

Depew, David J., and Bruce H. Weber. 1995. *Darwinism Evolving: Systems Dynamics and the Genealogy of Natural Selection*. Cambridge: MIT Press.

Destler, I. M. 1980. *Making Foreign Economic Policy*. Washington, D.C.: The Brookings Institution.

Destler, I. M. 1986. *American Trade Politics: System under Stress.* Washington, D.C.: Institute for International Economics; New York: Twentieth Century Fund.

Dimand, Robert W., and Mary Ann Dimand. 1992. "The Early History of the Theory of Strategic Games from Waldegrave to Borel." In *Toward a History of Game Theory,* edited by E. Roy Weintraub. Durham: Duke University Press.

Downing, Brian M. 1992. *The Military Revolution and Political Change.* Princeton, N.J.: Princeton University Press.

Downs, George W., and David M. Rocke. 1990. *Tacit Bargaining, Arms Races, and Arms Control.* Ann Arbor: University of Michigan Press.

———. 1995. *Optimal Imperfection: Domestic Uncertainty and Institutions in International Relations.* Princeton, N.J.: Princeton University Press.

Downs, George W., David M. Rocke, and Peter N. Barsoom. 1996. "Is the Good News about Compliance Good News about Cooperation?" *International Organization* 50:379–406.

Doyle, Michael W. 1983. "Kant, Liberal Legacies, and Foreign Affairs." *Philosophy and Public Affairs* 12:205–35, 323–53.

———. 1986a. "Liberalism and World Politics." *American Political Science Review* 80:1151–69.

———. 1986b. *Empires.* Ithaca, N.Y.: Cornell University Press.

Dugatkin, Lee Alan, and Hudson Kern Reeve, eds. 1998. *Game Theory & Animal Behavior.* New York: Oxford University Press.

Duverger, Maurice. 1959. *Political Parties: Their Organization and Activity in the Modern State.* 2nd ed. Translated by Barbara and Robert North. New York: Wiley.

Eggertsson, Thráinn. 1990. *Economic Behavior and Institutions.* Cambridge: Cambridge University Press.

Eichenberg, Richard C. 1993. "Dual Track and Double Trouble: The Two-Level Politics of INF." In *Double-Edged Diplomacy: International Bargaining and Domestic Politics,* edited by Peter B. Evans, Harold K. Jacobson, and Robert D. Putnam. Berkeley: University of California Press.

Eichengreen, Barry. 1989a. "The Political Economy of the Smoot-Hawley Tariff." *Research in Economic History* 12:1–43.

———. 1989b. Hegemonic Stability Theories of the International Monetary System. In *Can Nations Agree?,* edited by Richard Cooper et al. Washington, D.C.: Brookings Institution.

———. 1992. *Golden Fetters: The Gold Standard and the Great Depression 1919–1939.* New York: Oxford University Press.

Ellickson, Robert C. 1991. *Order without Law: How Neighbors Settle Disputes.* Cambridge, Mass.: Harvard University Press.

Ellsberg, Daniel. 1960. "The Crude Analysis of Strategic Choices." RAND P-2183. Santa Monica: Rand Corporation.

Elster, Jon. 1979. *Ulysses and the Sirens: Studies in Rationality and Irrationality.* Cambridge: Cambridge University Press.

———. 1985. "The Nature and Scope of Rational-Choice Explanation." In *A Companion to Actions and Events,* edited by B. MacLaughlin and E. LePore. Oxford: Basil Blackwell.

Elster, Jon. 1986. "Introduction." In *Rational Choice*, edited by Jon Elster. New York: New York University Press.

———. 1989. *Nuts and Bolts for the Social Sciences*. Cambridge: Cambridge University Press.

Evans, J. St B. T. 1993. "Bias and Rationality." In *Rationality: Psychological and Philosophical Perspectives*, edited by K. I. Manktelow and D. E. Over. New York: Routledge.

Evans, Peter B., Harold K. Jacobson, and Robert D. Putnam, eds. 1993. *Double-Edged Diplomacy: International Bargaining and Domestic Politics*. Berkeley: University of California Press.

Evans, Peter B., Dietrich Rueschemeyer, and Theda Skocpol, eds. 1985. *Bringing the State Back In*. Cambridge: Cambridge University Press.

Farnham, Barbara. 1994. *Avoiding Losses/Taking Risks: Prospect Theory and International Conflict*. Ann Arbor: University of Michigan Press.

Farrar, L. L. Jr. 1972. "The Limits of Choice: July 1914 Reconsidered." *Journal of Conflict Resolution* 16:1–23.

Fearon, James D. 1990. "Deterrence and the Spiral Model: The Role of Costly Signals in Crisis Bargaining." Presented at the Annual Meeting of the American Political Science Association, San Francisco, August 30–September 2.

———. 1993. "Ethnic War as a Commitment Problem." Manuscript, University of Chicago.

———. 1994a. "Domestic Political Audiences and the Escalation of International Disputes." *American Political Science Review* 88:577–92.

———. 1994b. "Signaling versus the Balance of Power and Interests: An Empirical Test of a Crisis Bargaining Model." *Journal of Conflict Resolution* 38:236–69.

———. 1995. "Rationalist Explanations for War." *International Organization* 49:379–414.

———. 1996. "Causes and Counterfactuals in Social Science: Exploring an Analogy between Cellular Automata and Historical Processes." In *Counterfactual Thought Experiments in World Politics: Logical, Methodological, and Psychological Perspectives*, edited by Philip E. Tetlock and Aaron Belkin. Princeton, N.J.: Princeton University Press.

———. 1997. "Signaling Foreign Policy Interests: Tying Hands versus Sinking Costs." *Journal of Conflict Resolution* 41:68–90.

———. 1998. "Commitment Problems and the Spread of Ethnic Conflict." In *The International Spread of Ethnic Conflict: Fear, Diffusion, and Escalation*, edited by David A. Lake and Donald Rothchild. Princeton, N.J.: Princeton University Press.

Fearon, James D., and David Laitin. 1996. "Explaining Interethnic Cooperation." *American Political Science Review* 90:715–35.

Fenno, Richard F. Jr. 1978. *Home Style: House Members in their Districts*. Boston: Little, Brown.

Ferguson, Niall. 1994. "Public Finance and National Security: The Domestic Origins of the First World War Revisited." *Past and Present*, no. 142: 141–68.

Fieldhouse, D. K. 1961. "Imperialism: An Historiographical Revision." *Economic History Review* 14:187–209.

Finley, M. I. 1973. *The Ancient Economy.* Berkeley: University of California Press.

Frank, Robert H. 1988. *Passions within Reason: The Strategic Role of the Emotions.* New York: W. W. Norton.

——. 1993. "The Strategic Role of the Emotions: Reconciling Over- and Undersocialized Accounts of Behavior." *Rationality and Society* 5:160–84.

Freedman, Lawrence, and Efraim Karsh. 1993. *The Gulf Conflict, 1990–1991: Diplomacy and War in the New World Order.* Princeton, N.J.: Princeton University Press.

Frieden, Jeffry A. 1988. "Sectoral Conflict and U.S. Foreign Economic Policy, 1914–1940." *International Organization* 42:59–90.

——. 1991. 'Invested Interests: The Politics of National Economic Policies in a World of Global Finance." *International Organization* 45:425–52.

——. 1994a. "Exchange Rate Politics: Contemporary Lessons from American History." *Review of International Political Economy* 1:81–103.

——. 1994b. "International Investment and Colonial Control: A New Interpretation." *International Organization* 48:559–93.

——. 1996. "Economic Integration and the Politics of Monetary Policy in the United States." In *Internationalization and Domestic Politics*, edited by Robert O. Keohane and Helen Milner. Cambridge: Cambridge University Press.

Frieden, Jeffry A., and Ronald Rogowski. 1996. "The Impact of the International Economy on National Policies: An Analytical Overview." In *Internationalization and Domestic Politics*, edited by Robert O. Keohane and Helen V. Milner. New York: Cambridge University Press.

Friedman, David. 1977. "A Theory of the Size and Shape of Nations." *Journal of Political Economy* 85:59–77.

Friedman, Milton. 1953. *Essays in Positive Economics.* Chicago: University of Chicago Press.

Froot, Kenneth, and David Yoffie. 1993. "Trading Blocs and the Incentives to Protect." In *Regionalism and Rivalry: The United States and Japan in Pacific Asia*, edited by Jeffrey Frankel and Miles Kahler. Chicago: University of Chicago Press.

Fudenberg, Drew, and Eric Maskin. 1986. "The Folk Theorem in Repeated Games with Discounting or Incomplete Information." *Econometrica* 54:533–56.

Fudenberg, Drew, and Jean Tirole. 1991. *Game Theory.* Cambridge: MIT Press.

Gaddis, John Lewis. 1992–93. "International Relations Theory and the End of the Cold War." *International Security* 17, no. 3: 5–58.

Gallagher, John, and Ronald Robinson. 1953. "The Imperialism of Free Trade." *Economic History Review* 6:1–15.

Gardner, Howard. 1985. *The Mind's New Science: A History of the Cognitive Revolution.* New York: Basic Books.

Garrett, Geoffrey. 1992. "International Cooperation and Institutional Choice." *International Organization* 46:533–60.

——. 1995. "The Politics of Legal Integration in the European Union." *International Organization* 49:171–81.

Garrett, Geoffrey, and Peter Lange. 1994. "Internationalization, Institutions, and Political Change." In *Internationalization and Domestic Politics*, edited by Helen Milner and Robert O. Keohane. Cambridge: Cambridge University Press.

Garrett, Geoffrey, and George Tsebelis. 1996. "An Institutional Critique of Intergovernmentalism." *International Organization* 50:269–99.

Gaubatz, Kurt Taylor. 1993. "Still Hazy after All These Years: Kant's Secret Plan of Nature and the Expansion of Democratic States in the International System." Manuscript, Stanford University.

Gauthier, David. 1986. *Morals by Agreement*. New York: Oxford University Press.

Geanakoplos, John. 1992. "Common Knowledge." *Journal of Economic Perspectives* 6:53–82.

———. 1994. "Common Knowledge." In *Handbook of Game Theory with Economic Applications*, edited by Robert J. Aumann and Sergiu Hart. Vol. 2. New York: Elsevier.

Gerber, Elisabeth R., and John Jackson. 1993. "Endogenous Preferences and the Study of Institutions." *American Political Science Review* 87:639–56.

Gerber, Elisabeth R., and Arthur Lupia. 1997. "Voter Competence in Direct Legislation Elections." In *Democracy and Citizen Competence*, edited by Steven L. Elkin and Karol E. Soltan. College Park: Penn State Press.

Gilbert, Margaret. 1989a. *On Social Facts*. New York: Routledge.

———. 1989b. "Rationality and Salience." *Philosophical Studies* 57:61–77.

Gilpin, Robert. 1975. *U.S. Power and the Multinational Corporation: The Political Economy of Foreign Direct Investment*. New York: Basic Books.

———. 1981. *War and Change in World Politics*. New York: Cambridge University Press.

Ginsberg, Benjamin. 1982. *The Consequences of Consent: Elections, Citizen Control, and Popular Acquiescence*. Reading, Mass.: Addison-Wesley.

Glaser, Charles L. 1994–95. "Realists as Optimists: Cooperation as Self-Help." *International Security* 19, no. 3: 50–90.

Goldstein, Judith. 1988. "Ideas, Institutions, and American Trade Policy." *International Organization* 42:179–217.

———. 1993. *Ideas, Interests, and American Trade Policy*. Ithaca, N.Y.: Cornell University Press.

Goldstein, Judith, and Robert O. Keohane, eds. 1993. *Ideas and Foreign Policy: Beliefs, Institutions, and Political Change*. Ithaca, N.Y.: Cornell University Press.

Goodman, John, and Louis Pauly. 1993. "The Obsolescence of Capital Controls? Economic Management in an Age of Global Markets." *World Politics* 46:50–82.

Gould, Stephen Jay. 1989. *Wonderful Life*. New York: W. W. Norton.

———. 1992. "Punctuated Equilibrium in Fact and Theory." In *The Dynamics of Evolution: The Punctuated Equilibrium Debate in the Natural and Social Sciences*, edited by Albert Somit and Steven A. Peterson. Ithaca, N.Y.: Cornell University Press.

Gould, Stephen Jay, and Richard C. Lewontin. 1979. "The Spandrels of San Marco and the Panglossian Paradigm." *Proceedings of the Royal Society of London* B205:581–98.

Gourevitch, Peter A. 1977. "International Trade, Domestic Coalitions, and Liberty: Comparative Responses to the Crisis of 1873–1896." *Journal of Interdisciplinary History* 8:281–313.

———. 1978a. "The International System and Regime Formation: A Critical Review of Anderson and Wallerstein." *Comparative Politics* 10:419–38.

———. 1978b. "The Second Image Reversed: The International Sources of Domestic Politics." *International Organization* 32:881–912.

———. 1986. *Politics in Hard Times : Comparative Responses to International Economic Crises.* Ithaca, N.Y.: Cornell University Press.

Gowa, Joanne, 1986. "Anarchy, Egoism, and Third Images." *International Organization* 40:167–86.

———. 1989. "Bipolarity, Multipolarity, and Free Trade." *American Political Science Review* 83:1245–56.

———. 1994. *Allies, Adversaries, and International Trade.* Princeton, N.J.: Princeton University Press.

Gowa, Joanne, and Edward D. Mansfield. 1993. "Power Politics and International Trade." *American Political Science Review* 87:408–20.

Grether, David M., and Charles R. Plott. 1979. "Economic Theory of Choice and the Preference Reversal Phenomenon." *American Economic Review* 69:623–38.

Grieco, Joseph. 1988a. "Anarchy and the Limits of Cooperation: A Realist Critique of the Newest Liberal Institutionalism." *International Organization* 42:485–507.

———. 1988b. "Realist Theory and the Problem of International Cooperation." *Journal of Politics* 50:600–624.

———. 1990. *Cooperation among Nations: Europe, America, and Non-Tariff Barriers to Trade.* Ithaca, N.Y.: Cornell University Press.

———. 1993. "Understanding the Problem of International Cooperation: The Limits of Neoliberal Institutionalism and the Future of Realist Theory." In *Neorealism and Neoliberalism: The Contemporary Debate*, edited by David A. Baldwin. New York: Columbia University Press.

Grieco, Joseph, Robert Powell, and Duncan Snidal. 1993. "The Relative Gains Problem for International Cooperation." *American Political Science Review* 87:729–43.

Grief, Abner, Paul Milgrom, and Barry Weingast. 1994. "Coordination, Commitment, and Enforcement: The Case of the Merchant Guild." *Journal of Political Economy* 102:745–76.

Grilli, Vittorio, Donato Masciandaro, and Guido Tabellini. 1991. "Political and Monetary Institutions and Public Financial Policies in the Industrial Countries." *Economic Policy* 6, no. 2: 342–91.

Groenewegen, Peter. 1991. "Political Economy and Economics." In *The New Palgrave: The World of Economics*, edited by John Eatwell, Murray Milgate, and Peter Newman. New York: W. W. Norton.

Grossman, Sanford, and Oliver Hart. 1986. "The Costs and Benefits of Owner-ship: A Theory of Vertical and Lateral Integration." *Journal of Political Economy* 94:691–719.

Güth, Werner. 1991. "Game Theory's Basic Question: Who Is a Player? Examples, Concepts, and Their Behavioral Relevance." *Journal of Theoretical Politics* 3:403–35.

Haas, Peter M. 1992. "Banning Chloroflurocarbons: Epistemic Community Efforts to Protect Stratospheric Ozone." *International Organization* 46:187–224.

Haas, Peter M., ed. 1992. *Knowledge, Power, and International Policy Co-ordination.* Special issue of *International Organization* 46, no. 1 (winter).

Haggard, Stephan. 1988. "The Institutional Foundations of Hegemony: Explaining the Reciprocal Trade Agreements Act of 1934." *International Organization* 42:91–120.

Haggard, Stephan, and Sylvia Maxfield. 1996. "The Political Economy of Financial Internationalization in the Developing World." *International Organization* 50:35–68.

Hall, Peter A. 1986. *Governing the Economy: The Politics of State Intervention in Britain and France.* Cambridge: Polity.

Hall, Peter A., and Rosemary C. R. Taylor. 1996. "Political Science and the Three New Institutionalisms." *Political Studies* 44:936–57.

Hallerberg, Mark. 1996. "Tax Competition in Wilhelmine Germany and Its Implications for the European Union." *World Politics* 48:324–57.

Hamilton, Alexander, James Madison, and John Jay. [1787–88] 1982. *The Federalist Papers,* with an introduction and commentary by Garry Wills. New York: Bantam.

Hammerstein, Peter. 1989. "Biological Games." *European Economic Review* 33:635–44.

Hammerstein, Peter, and Reinhard Selten. 1994. "Game Theory and Evolutionary Biology." In *Handbook of Game Theory with Economic Applications,* edited by Robert J. Aumann and Sergiu Hart. Vol. 2. New York: Elsevier.

Hannan, Michael T., and John Freeman. 1989. *Organizational Ecology.* Cambridge: Harvard University Press.

Hansson, Sven Ove. 1995. "Changing in Preferences." *Theory and Decision* 38:1–28.

Harris, Marvin. 1979. *Cultural Materialism: The Struggle for a Science of Culture.* New York: Random House.

Harsanyi, John C. 1969. "Rational-Choice Models of Political Behavior vs. Functionalist and Conformist Theories." *World Politics* 21:513–38.

———. 1977. "Advances in Understanding Rational Behavior." In *Foundational Problems in the Social Sciences,* edited by R. E. Butts and J. Hintikka. Dordrecht, Holland: D. Reidel.

———. 1988. "Some Recent Developments in Game Theory." In *Theory And Decision: Essays in Honor of Werner Leinfellner,* edited by Gerald L. Eberlein and Hal Berghel. Theory and Decision Library series, vol. 50. Dordrecht, Holland: D. Reidel.

Hausman, Daniel, and Michael McPherson. 1994. "Preference, Belief, and Welfare." *American Economic Review* 84:396–400.

Hayek, Friedrich Von. 1979. *Law, Legislation, and Liberty.* Volume 3: *The Political Order of a Free People.* Chicago: University of Chicago Press.

Heap, Shaun Hargreaves. 1993. "Post-Modernity and New Conceptions of Rationality in Economics." In *The Economics of Rationality,* edited by Bill Gerrard. New York: Routledge.

Heidenheimer, Arnold J. 1957. "German Party Finance: The CDU." *American Political Science Review* 51:369–85.

————. 1964. "Succession and Party Politics in West Germany." *Journal of International Affairs* 18:32–42.

Heidenheimer, Arnold J., and Frank C. Langdon. 1968. *Business Associations and the Financing of Political Parties.* The Hague: Martinus Nijhoff.

Helleiner, G. K. 1977. "Transnational Enterprises and the New Political Economy of U.S. Trade Policy." *Oxford Economic Papers* 29:102–16.

Herz, John H. 1950. "Idealist Internationalism and the Security Dilemma." *World Politics* 2:157–80.

Higonnet, Patrice. 1995. *Truth the Self and the Nation: A Cultural and Political History of Jacobins and Jacobinism During the French Revolution.* Manuscript, Harvard University.

Hillman, Arye. 1989. *The Political Economy of Protection.* London: Harwood Academic Publishers.

Hillman, Arye, and Heinrich Ursprung. 1988. "Domestic Politics, Foreign Interests, and International Trade Policy." *American Economic Review* 78:729–46.

Hintze, Otto. 1906. "Military Organization and the Organization of the State." Lecture to the Gene-Stifung, 17 February. In *The Historical Essays of Otto Hintze,* edited by Felix Gilbert, chap. 5. New York: Oxford University Press, 1975.

Hirschman, Albert O. 1977. *The Passions and the Interests: Political Arguments for Capitalism Before Its Triumph.* Princeton, N.J.: Princeton University Press.

————. 1991a. "Interests." In *The New Palgrave: The World of Economics,* edited by John Eatwell, Murray Milgate, and Peter Newman. New York: W. W. Norton.

————. 1991b. *The Rhetoric of Reaction: Perversity, Futility, Jeopardy.* Cambridge: Belknap.

————. 1993. "Exit, Voice, and the Fate of the German Democratic Republic: An Essay in Conceptual History." *World Politics* 45:173–202.

Hirshleifer, Jack. 1977. "Economics from a Biological Viewpoint." *Journal of Law and Economics* 20:1–52.

————. 1978a. "Competition, Cooperation, and Conflict in Economics and Biology." *American Economic Review* 68:238–43.

————. 1978b. "Natural Economy versus Political Economy." *Journal of Social and Biological Structures* 1:319–37.

————. 1982. "Evolutionary Models in Economics and Law." *Research in Law and Economics* 4:1–60.

————. 1985. "The Expanding Domain of Economics." *American Economic Review* 75:53–68.

Hirshleifer, Jack. 1987a. "On the Emotions as Guarantors of Threats and Promises." In *The Latest on the Best: Essays in Evolution and Optimality*, edited by John Dupre. Cambridge: MIT Press.

———. 1987b. *Economic Behaviour in Adversity*. Brighton: Wheatsheaf.

———. 1993. The Affections and the Passions. *Rationality and Society* 5:185–202.

———. 1995. "Theorizing About Conflict." In *Handbook of Defense Economics*, edited by K. Hartley and T. Sandler. Amsterdam: Elsevier.

Hirshleifer, Jack, and Juan Carlos Martinez Coll. 1988. "What Strategies Can Support the Evolutionary Emergence of Cooperation?" *Journal of Conflict Resolution* 32:367–98.

———.1992. "Selection, Mutation, and the Preservation of Diversity in Evolutionary Games (1)." *Revista Españolade Economia* 9:272.

Hiscox, Michael. 1997. *The Trade War at Home: International Trade, Factor Mobility, and Political Coalitions in Democracies*. Ph.D. diss., Harvard University.

Hodgson, Geoffrey M. 1993a. "Calculation, Habits, and Action." In *The Economics of Rationality*, edited by Bill Gerrard. New York: Routledge.

———. 1993b. *Economics and Evolution*. Ann Arbor: University of Michigan Press.

Holsti, Ole R. 1989. "Crisis Decision Making." In *Behavior, Society, and Nuclear War*, edited by Philip Tetlock, Jo Husbands, Robert Jervis, Paul Stern, and Charles Tilly. Vol. 1. New York: Oxford University Press.

Honkapohja, Seppo. 1993. "Adaptive Learning and Bounded Rationality: An Introduction to Basic Concepts." *European Economic Review* 37:587–94.

Humphreys, S. C. 1969. "History, Economics, and Anthropology: The Work of Karl Polanyi." *History and Theory* 8:165–212.

Huth, Paul K. 1988. *Extended Deterrence and the Prevention of War*. New Haven: Yale University Press.

Huth, Paul K., and Bruce Russett. 1984. "What Makes Deterrence Work? Cases from 1900 to 1980." *World Politics* 36:496–526.

Ikenberry, G. John. 1989. "Manufacturing Consensus: The Institutionalization of American Private Interest in the Tokyo Trade Round." *Comparative Politics* 21:289–309.

Janis, Irving L. 1982. *Groupthink*. Rev. ed. Boston: Houghton Mifflin.

Jervis, Robert. 1970. *The Logic of Images in International Relations*. Princeton, N.J.: Princeton University Press.

———. 1976. *Perception and Misperception in International Politics*. Princeton, N.J.: Princeton University Press.

———. 1978. "Cooperation under the Security Dilemma." *World Politics* 30:167–214.

———. 1979. "Deterrence Theory Revisited." *World Politics* 31:289–324.

———. 1986. "From Balance to Concert: A Study of International Security Cooperation." In *Cooperation under Anarchy*, edited by Kenneth Oye. Princeton, N.J.: Princeton University Press.

———. 1988. "Realism, Game Theory, and Cooperation." *World Politics* 40:317–49.

Jervis, Robert, and Jack Snyder, eds. 1991. *Dominoes and Bandwagons: Strategic Beliefs and Great Power Competition in the Eurasian Rimland*. New York: Oxford University Press.

Jones, E. L. 1987. *The European Miracle*. 2nd ed. Cambridge: Cambridge University Press.

Kahler, Miles. 1992. "Multilateralism with Small and Large Numbers." *International Organization* 46:681–708.

Kahneman, Daniel, and Amos Tversky. 1973. "On the Psychology of Prediction." *Psychological Review* 80:237–51.

Kahneman, Daniel, Paul Slovic, and Amos Tversky, eds. 1982. *Judgment under Uncertainty: Heuristics and Biases*. New York: Cambridge University Press.

Kandori, Michihiro, George J. Mailath, and Rafael Rob. 1993. "Learning, Mutation, and Long Run Equilibria in Games." *Econometrica* 61:29–56.

Kaplan, Abraham. 1967. "Some Limitations on Rationality." In *Nomos VII: Rational Decision*, edited by Carl J. Friedrich. New York: Atherton.

Kaplan, Fred. 1983. *The Wizards of Armageddon*. New York: Simon and Schuster.

Kaplan, Morton A. 1957. *System and Process in International Politics*. New York: Wiley.

———. 1961. "Problems of Theory Building and Theory Confirmation in International Politics." In *The International System: Theoretical Essays*, edited by Klaus Knorr and Sidney Verba. Princeton, N.J.: Princeton University Press.

Kapteyn, Arie, Tom Wansbeek, and Jeannine Buyze. 1980. "The Dynamics of Preference Formation." *Journal of Economic Behavior and Organization* 1:123–57.

Katzenstein, Peter J., ed. 1978. *Between Power and Plenty*. Madison: University of Wisconsin Press.

———. 1985. *Small States in World Markets*. Ithaca, N.Y.: Cornell University Press.

———, ed. 1996a. *The Culture of National Security: Norms and Identity in World Politics*. New York: Columbia University Press.

———. 1996b. *Cultural Norms and National Security: Police and Military in Postwar Japan*. Ithaca, N.Y.: Cornell University Press.

Katzenstein, Peter J., Robert O. Keohane, and Stephen D. Krasner. 1998. "International Organization and the Study of World Politics." *International Organization* 52:645–85.

Kelley, Harold H., and John W. Thibaut. 1978. *Interpersonal Relations: A Theory of Interdependence*. New York: Wiley.

Kennan, John, and Robert Wilson. 1993. "Bargaining with Private Information." *Journal of Economic Literature* 31:45–104.

Keohane, Robert O. 1980. "The Theory of Hegemonic Stability and Changes in International Economic Regimes, 1967–1977." In *Change in the International System*, edited by O. R. Holsti, R. M. Siverson, and A. L. George. Boulder, Colo.: Westview.

———. 1984. *After Hegemony: Cooperation and Discord in the World Political Economy*. Princeton, N.J.: Princeton University Press.

Keohane, Robert O., ed. 1986. *Neorealism and Its Critics*. New York: Columbia University Press.

———. 1993. "Institutional Theory and the Realist Challenge after the Cold War." In *Neorealism and Neoliberalism: The Contemporary Debate*, edited by David A. Baldwin. New York: Columbia University Press.

———. 1996. "Commitment Incapacity, the Commitment Paradox, and American Political Institutions." Paper prepared for a conference on "International Influences on U.S. Politics," Cambridge, Mass., November 2–3.

Keohane, Robert O., and Lisa L. Martin. 1995. "The Promise of Institutional Theory." *International Security* 20, no. 1: 39–51.

Keohane, Robert O., and Helen V. Milner, eds. 1996. *Internationalization and Domestic Politics*. Cambridge: Cambridge University Press.

Keohane, Robert O., and Joseph S. Nye, eds. 1972. *Transnational Relations and World Politics*. Cambridge, Mass.: Harvard University Press.

———. 1989. *Power and Interdependence*. 2nd ed. Glenview, Ill.: Scott, Foresman.

Khong, Yuen Fong. 1992. *Analogies at War*. Princeton, N.J.: Princeton University Press.

Kindleberger, Charles P. 1951. "Group Behavior and International Trade." *Journal of Political Economy* 59:30–46.

———. 1973. *The World in Depression, 1929–1939*. Berkeley: University of California Press.

———. 1974. "*The Great Transformation* by Karl Polanyi" (Book Review). *Daedalus* 103:45–52.

———. 1975. "The Rise of Free Trade in Western Europe, 1820–1875." *Journal of Economic History* 35:20–55.

Kissinger, Henry. 1957. *A World Restored*. Boston: Houghton Mifflin.

Kline, Morris. 1985. *Mathematics and the Search for Knowledge*. New York: Oxford University Press.

Kowert, Paul, and Jeffrey Legro. 1996. "Norms, Identity, and Their Limits: A Theoretical Reprise." In *The Culture of National Security: Norms and Identity in World Politics*, edited by Peter J. Katzenstein. New York: Columbia University Press.

Krasner, Stephen D. 1976. State Power and the Structure of International Trade. *World Politics* 28:317–47.

———. 1978. *Defending the National Interest: Raw Materials Investments and U.S. Foreign Policy*. Princeton, N.J.: Princeton University Press.

———. 1991. "Global Communications and National Power: Life on the Pareto Frontier." *World Politics* 43:336–66.

Krehbiel, Keith. 1987. "Sophisticated Committees and Structure-Induced Equilibria in Congress." In *Congress: Structure and Policy*, edited by Mathew D. McCubbins and Terry Sullivan. New York: Cambridge University Press.

Kreps, David M. 1990a. "Corporate Culture and Economic Theory." In *Perspectives on Positive Political Economy*, edited by James Alt and Kenneth Shepsle. New York: Cambridge University Press.

———. 1990b. *A Course in Microeconomic Theory*. Princeton, N.J.: Princeton University Press.

Kreps, David M. 1990c. *Game Theory and Economic Modelling*. Oxford: Oxford University Press.

Kreps, David M., and Robert Wilson. 1982. "Sequential Equilibria." *Econometrica* 50:863–94.

Kugler, Jacek. 1984. "Terror Without Deterrence." *Journal of Conflict Resolution* 28:470–506.

Kupchan, Charles A. 1994. *The Vulnerability of Empire*. Ithaca, N.Y.: Cornell University Press.

Kusser, Anna, and Wolfgang Spohn. 1992. "The Utility of Pleasure Is a Pain for Decision Theory." *Journal of Philosophy* 89:10–29.

Lagueux, Maurice. 1994. "Friedman's 'Instrumentalism' and Constructive Empiricism in Economics." *Theory and Decision* 37:147–74.

Laitin, David. 1998. *Identity in Formation: The Russian-Speaking Populations in the Near Abroad*. Ithaca, N.Y.: Cornell University Press.

Lake, David A. 1987. "Power and the Third World: Toward a Realist Political Economy of North-South Relations." *International Studies Quarterly* 31:217–34.

———. 1988. *Power, Protection, and Free Trade: The International Sources of U.S. Commercial Strategy, 1887–1939*. Ithaca, N.Y.: Cornell University Press.

———. 1992. "Powerful Pacifists: Democratic States and War." *American Political Science Review* 86:24–37.

———. 1993. "Leadership, Hegemony, and the International Economy: Naked Emperor or Tattered Monarch with Potential?" *International Studies Quarterly* 37:459–89.

———. 1996. "Anarchy, Hierarchy, and the Variety of International Relations." *International Organization* 50:1–33.

———. 1999. *Entangling Relations: American Foreign Policy in Its Century*. Princeton, N.J.: Princeton University Press.

Lake, David A., and Donald Rothchild. 1996. "Containing Fear: The Origins and Management of Ethnic Conflict." *International Security* 21, no. 2: 41–75.

Landes, David. 1961. "Some Thoughts on the Nature of Economic Imperialism." *Journal of Economic History* 21:496–512.

Lane, Jan-Erik. 1974. "Two Kinds of Means-End Contexts: On the Use of Means-End Terminology in Weber, Parsons, and Simon." *Scandinavian Journal of Politics* 9:23–50.

Laplace, Pierre Simon Marquis De. 1951 [1814]. *A Philosophical Essay on Probabilities*. Translated by Frederick Wilson Truscott and Frederick Lincoln Emory. New York: Dover.

Larson, Deborah Welch. 1985. *Origins of Containment: A Psychological Explanation*. Princeton, N.J.: Princeton University Press.

Latsis, Spiro J. 1972. "Situational Determinism in Economics." *British Journal for the Philosophy of Science* 23:207–45.

Legro, Jeffrey W. 1996. "Culture and Preferences in the International Cooperation Two-Step." *American Political Science Review* 90:118–37.

Lenin, V. I. 1939. *Imperialism: The Highest Stage of Capitalism*. New York: International.

Leonard, Robert J. 1992. "Creating the Context for Game Theory." In *Toward a History of Game Theory*, edited by E. Roy Weintraub. Durham: Duke University Press.

Levy, Jack S. 1990–91. "Preferences, Constraints, and Choices in July 1914." *International Security* 15(3):151–86.

———. 1994. "Learning and Foreign Policy: Sweeping a Conceptual Minefield." *International Organization* 48:279–312.

Lewis, David K. 1969. *Convention: A Philosophical Study*. Cambridge, Mass.: Harvard University Press.

Lipman, Barton L. 1991. "How to Decide How to Decide How to . . .: Modeling Limited Rationality." *Econometrica* 59:1105–25.

———. 1995. "Information Processing and Bounded Rationality: A Survey." *Canadian Journal of Economics* 28:42–67.

Lipnowski, Irwin, and Shlomo Maital. 1983. "Voluntary Provision of a Pure Public Good as the Game of 'Chicken.' " *Journal of Public Economics* 20:381–86.

Lipset, Seymour Martin, and Stein Rokkan. 1967. *Party Systems and Voter Alignments*. New York: Free Press.

Lipson, Charles. 1984. "International Cooperation in Economic and Security Affairs." *World Politics* 37:1–23.

———. 1985. *Standing Guard: Protecting Foreign Capital in the Nineteenth and Twentieth Centuries*. Berkeley: University of California Press.

———. 1997. "The Promise of Peace: Why Liberal Democracies Do Not Fight Wars Against Each Other." Draft manuscript, University of Chicago, Department of Political Science.

Lismont, Luc, and Philippe Mongin. 1994. "On the Logic of Common Belief and Common Knowledge." *Theory and Decision* 37:75–106.

Lohmann, Susanne. 1994. "Dynamics of Informational Cascades: The Monday Demonstrations in Leipzig, East Germany, 1989–91." *World Politics* 47:42–101.

Lohmann, Susanne, and Sharon O'Halloran. 1994. "Divided Government and U.S. Trade Policy: Theory and Evidence." *International Organization* 48:595–632.

Lomborg, Bjorn. 1993. "International Cooperation and Relative Gains." Manuscript, University of Copenhagen.

Lowe, E. J. 1993. "Rationality, Deduction, and Mental Models." In *Rationality: Psychological and Philosophical Perspectives*, edited by K. I. Manktelow and D. E. Over. New York: Routledge.

Lowi, Theodore J. 1979. *The End of Liberalism: The Second Republic of the United States*. 2nd ed. New York: W. W. Norton.

Lowry, S. Todd. 1979. "Recent Literature on Ancient Greek Economic Thought." *Journal of Economic Literature* 17:65–86.

Lukes, Steven. 1977. "Power and Structure." In *Essays in Social Theory*. London: Macmillan.

Lupia, Arthur. 1994. "Shortcuts versus Encyclopedias: Information and Voting Behavior in California Insurance Reform Elections." *American Political Science Review* 88:63–76.

Lupia, Arthur, and Mathew D. McCubbins. 1998. *The Democratic Dilemma: Can Citizens Learn What They Need to Know?* New York: Cambridge University Press.

Mack, Andrew. 1975. "Why Big Nations Lose Small Wars: The Politics of Asymmetric Conflict." *World Politics* 27:175–200.

Magee, Stephen. 1980. "Three Simple Tests of the Stolper-Samuelson Theorem." In *Issues in International Economics*, edited by Peter Oppenheimer. London: Oriel.

Magee, Stephen, et. al. 1989. *Black Hole Tariffs and Endogenous Policy Theory.* New York: Cambridge University Press.

Magnus, Philip. 1954. *Gladstone: A Biography.* New York: Dutton.

Mailath, George J. 1992. "Introduction: Symposium on Evolutionary Game Theory." *Journal of Economic Theory* 57:259–77.

Mansfield, Edward, and Marc Busch. 1995. "The Political Economy of Nontariff Barriers: A Cross-National Analysis." *International Organization* 49:723–49.

Mansfield, Edward D., and Jack Snyder. 1995. "Democratization and the Dangers of War." *International Security* 20, no. 1: 5–38.

Maoz, Zeev. 1983. "Resolve, Capabilities, and the Outcomes of Interstate Disputes, 1816–1976." *Journal of Conflict Resolution* 27:195–229.

Maoz, Zeev, and Dan S. Felsenthal. 1987. "Self-Binding Commitments, the Inducement of Trust, Social Choice, and the Theory of International Cooperation." *International Studies Quarterly* 31:177–200.

March, James G. 1978. "Bounded Rationality, Ambiguity, and the Engineering of Choice." *Bell Journal of Economics* 9:587–608.

Mariotti, Marco. 1995. "Is Bayesian Rationality Compatible with Strategic Rationality?" *Economic Journal* 105:1099–1109.

Martin, Lisa L. 1992a. "Interests, Power, and Multilateralism." *International Organization* 46:765–92.

———. 1992b. *Coercive Cooperation: Explaining Multilateral Economic Sanctions.* Princeton, N.J.: Princeton University Press.

———. 1994. "International and Domestic Institutions in the EMU Process." In *The Political Economy of European Integration*, edited by Jeff Frieden and Barry Eichengreen. Boulder, Colo.: Westview.

———. 1995. "The Influence of National Parliaments on European Integration." In *Politics and Institutions in an Integrated Europe*, edited by Barry Eichengreen, Jeffry Frieden, and Jürgen von Hagan. New York: Springer-Verlag.

———. 1997. "Evasive Maneuvers? Reconsidering Presidential Use of Executive Agreements." In *Strategic Politicians, Institutions, and Foreign Policy*, edited by Randolph M. Siverson. Ann Arbor: University of Michigan Press.

Marvel, Howard P., and Edward J. Ray. 1983. "The Kennedy Round: Evidence on the Regulation of International Trade in the United States." *American Economic Review* 73:190–97.

Matthews, R.C.O. 1993. "Darwinism and Economic Change." In *Evolutionary Economics*, edited by Ulrich Witt. Brookfield: Edward Elgar.

Mattli, Walter, and Anne-Marie Slaughter. 1995. "Law and Politics in the European Union: A Reply to Garrett." *International Organization* 49:183–90.

Mayer, Arno J. 1959. *Political Origins of the New Diplomacy, 1917–1918*. New Haven: Yale University Press.

Mayhew, David. 1974. *Congress: The Electoral Connection*. New Haven: Yale University Press.

Maynard Smith, John. 1972. *On Evolution*. Edinburgh: Edinburgh University Press.

———. 1976. "Evolution and the Theory of Games." *American Scientist* 64:41–45.

———. 1982. *Evolution and the Theory of Games*. Cambridge: Cambridge University Press.

———. 1984. "Game Theory and the Evolution of Behaviour." *Behavioral and Brain Sciences* 7:101.

Mayr, Ernst. 1982. *The Growth of Biological Thought*. Cambridge: Belknap.

———. 1988. *Toward a New Philosophy of Biology*. Cambridge, Mass.: Harvard University Press.

McClelland, Peter D. 1975. *Causal Explanation and Model Building in History, Economics, and the New Economic History*. Ithaca, N.Y.: Cornell University Press.

McCubbins, Mathew, Roger Noll, and Barry Weingast. 1987. "Administrative Procedures as Instruments of Political Control." *Journal of Law, Economics, and Organization* 3:243–76.

———. 1989. "Structure and Process, Politics and Policy: Administrative Arrangements and the Political Control of Agencies." *Virginia Law Review* 75:431–82.

McKelvey, Richard. 1976. "Intransitivities in Multi-dimensional Voting Models and Some Implications for Agenda Control." *Journal of Economic Theory* 12:472–82.

McKeown, Timothy. 1983. "Hegemonic Stability Theory and 19th Century Tariff Levels in Europe." *International Organization* 37:73–91.

———. 1986. "The Limitations of 'Structural Theories' of Commercial Policy." *International Organization* 40:43–64.

Mearsheimer, John J. 1983. *Conventional Deterrence*. Ithaca, N.Y.: Cornell University Press.

———. 1990–91. "Back to the Future: Instability in Europe after the Cold War." *International Security* 15, no. 1: 5–56.

———. 1994–95. "The False Promise of International Institutions." *International Security* 19, no. 3: 5–49.

Milgrom, Paul R., Douglas C. North, and Barry R. Weingast. 1990. "The Role of Institutions in the Revival of Trade: The Medieval Law Merchant, Private Judges, and the Champagne Fairs." *Economics and Politics* 2:1–23.

Miller, Gary J. 1997. "The Impact of Economics on Contemporary Political Science." *Journal of Economic Literature* 35:1173–1204.

Milner, Helen V. 1988. *Resisting Protectionism: Global Industries and the Politics of International Trade*. Princeton, N.J.: Princeton University Press.

———. 1997. *Interests, Institutions, and Information: Domestic Politics and International Relations*. Princeton, N.J.: Princeton University Press.

Milner, Helen, and David Yoffie. 1989. "Between Free Trade and Protectionism: Strategic Trade Policy and a Theory of Corporate Trade Demands." *International Organization* 43:239–72.

Mirowski, Philip. 1991. "When Games Grow Deadly Serious: The Military Influence on the Evolution of Game Theory." In *Economics and National Security*, edited by Craufurd D. Goodwin. Durham: Duke University Press.

———. 1992. "What Were von Neumann and Morgenstern Trying to Accomplish?" In *Toward a History of Game Theory*, edited by E. Roy Weintraub. Durham: Duke University Press.

Moravcsik, Andrew. 1997. "Taking Preferences Seriously: A Liberal Theory of International Politics." *International Organization* 51:513–53.

Morgenthau, Hans J. 1948. *Politics among Nations: The Struggle for Power and Peace*. New York: Knopf.

Morrow, James D. 1985. "A Continuous-Outcome Expected Utility Theory of War." *Journal of Conflict Resolution* 29:473–502.

———. 1989. "Capabilities, Uncertainty, and Resolve: A Limited Information Model of Crisis Bargaining." *American Journal of Political Science* 33:941–72.

———. 1991a. "Alliances and Asymmetry: An Alternative to the Capability Aggregation Model of Alliances." *American Journal of Political Science* 35:904–33.

———. 1991b. "Electoral and Congressional Incentives and Arms Control." *Journal of Conflict Resolution* 35:245–65.

———. 1992. "Signaling Difficulties with Linkage in Crisis Bargaining." *International Studies Quarterly* 36:153–72.

———. 1993. "Arms versus Allies: Trade-offs in the Search for Security." *International Organization* 47:207–33.

———. 1994a. *Game Theory for Political Scientists*. Princeton, N.J.: Princeton University Press.

———. 1994b. "Modelling the Forms of International Cooperation: Distribution versus Information." *International Organization* 48:387–423.

———. 1994c. "Alliances, Credibility, and Peacetime Costs." *Journal of Conflict Resolution* 38:270–97.

Mortimore, G. W. 1976. "Rational Action." In *Rationality and the Social Sciences: Contributions to the Philosophy and Methodology of the Social Sciences*, edited by S. I. Benn and G. W. Mortimore. London: Routledge and Kegan Paul.

Mueller, John. 1989. *Retreat from Doomsday*. New York: Basic Books.

Nalebuff, Barry. 1986. "Brinkmanship and Nuclear Deterrence." *Journal of Conflict Management and Peace Science* 9:19–30.

———. 1987. "Credible Pretrial Negotiation." *RAND Journal of Economics* 18:241–75.

———. 1991. "Rational Deterrence in an Imperfect World." *World Politics* 43:313–35.

Nelson, Richard R. 1995. "Recent Evolutionary Theorizing about Economic Change." *Journal of Economic Literature* 33:48–90.

Nelson, Richard R., and Sidney G. Winter. 1982. *An Evolutionary Theory of Economic Change*. Cambridge, Mass.: Harvard University Press.

New Yorker. 1995. "Talk of the Town: Bad Mommies and Other Omens." December 5.

Nicholson, Michael. 1992. *Rationality and the Analysis of International Conflict.* Cambridge: Cambridge University Press.

Niou, Emerson, and Peter Ordeshook. 1994. "Less Filling, Tastes Great: The Realist-Neoliberal Debate." *World Politics* 46:209–34.

Niou, Emerson, Peter Ordeshook, and Gregory Rose. 1989. *The Balance of Power: Stability in International Systems.* Cambridge: Cambridge University Press.

North, Douglass C. 1990. *Institutions, Institutional Change, and Economic Performance.* Cambridge: Cambridge University Press.

———. 1994. "Economic Performance Through Time." *American Economic Review* 84:359–368.

North, Douglass C., and Robert Paul Thomas. 1973. *The Rise of the Western World: A New Economic History.* Cambridge: Cambridge University Press.

North, Douglas, and Barry Weingast. 1989. "Constitutions and Commitment: The Evolution of Institutions Governing Public Choice in Seventeenth-Century England." *Journal of Economic History* 49:803–32.

Nowak, Martin A., and Karl Sigmund. 1993. "A Strategy of Win-Stay, Lose-Shift That Outperforms Tit-for-Tat in the Prisoner's Dilemma Game." *Nature* 364:56–58.

Nowak, Martin A., Robert M. May, and Karl Sigmund. 1995. "The Arithmetics of Mutual Help." *Scientific American* 272:76–81.

Nozick, Robert. 1993. *The Nature of Rationality.* Princeton, N.J.: Princeton University Press.

O'Halloran, Sharyn. 1994. *Politics, Process, and American Trade Policy.* Ann Arbor: University of Michigan Press.

O'Neill, Barry. 1994. "Game Theory Models of Peace and War." In *Handbook of Game Theory with Economic Applications,* edited by Robert J. Aumann and Sergiu Hart. Vol. 2. New York: Elsevier.

Oaksford, M., and N. Chater. 1993. "Reasoning Theories and Bounded Rationality." In *Rationality: Psychological and Philosophical Perspectives,* edited by K. I. Manktelow and D. E. Over. New York: Routledge.

Olson, Mancur C. 1982. *The Rise and Decline of Nations: Economic Growth, Stagflation, and Social Rigidities.* New Haven: Yale University Press.

Ordeshook, Peter C. 1986. *Game Theory and Political Science: An Introduction.* New York: Cambridge University Press.

Osborne, Martin J., and Ariel Rubinstein. 1994. *A Course in Game Theory.* Cambridge: MIT Press.

Oye, Kenneth, ed. 1986a. *Cooperation under Anarchy.* Princeton, N.J.: Princeton University Press.

———. 1986b. "Explaining Cooperation under Anarchy: Hypotheses and Strategies." In *Cooperation under Anarchy,* edited by Kenneth Oye. Princeton, N.J.: Princeton University Press.

Papayoanou, Paul A. 1996. "Interdependence, Institutions, and the Balance of Power: Britain, Germany, and World War I." *International Security* 20, no. 4: 42–76.

Papayoanou, Paul A. 1997. "Economic Interdependence and the Balance of Power." *International Studies Quarterly* 41:113–40.

———. 1999. *Power Ties: Economic Interdependence, Balancing, and War.* Ann Arbor: University of Michigan Press.

Parfit, Derek. 1984. *Reasons and Persons.* Oxford: Oxford University Press.

Paulos, John Allen. 1991. *Beyond Numeracy: Ruminations of a Numbers Man.* New York: Knopf.

Perlmutter, Amos. 1974. "The Presidential Political Center and Foreign Policy: A Critique of the Revisionist and Bureaucratic-Political Orientations." *World Politics* 27:87–106.

Pettit, Philip, and Robert Sugden. 1989. "The Backward Induction Paradox." *Journal of Philosophy* 86:169–82.

Phelps, Edmund S. 1991. "Equilibrium: An Expectational Concept." In *The New Palgrave: The World of Economics,* edited by John Eatwell, Murray Milgate, and Peter Newman. New York: W. W. Norton.

Pinker, Steven. 1997. *How the Mind Works.* New York: W. W. Norton.

Plott, Charles R. 1987. "Rational Choice in Experimental Markets." In *Rational Choice: The Contrasts between Economics and Psychology,* edited by Robin M. Hogarth and Melvin W. Reder. Chicago: University of Chicago Press.

———. 1991. "Will Economics Become an Experimental Science?" *Southern Economic Journal* 57:901–19.

Polanyi, Karl. 1944. *The Great Transformation.* New York: Farrar and Rinehart.

Popkin, Samuel L. 1979. *The Rational Peasant: The Political Economy of Rural Society in Vietnam.* Berkeley: University of California Press.

Posen, Barry. 1984. *The Sources of Military Doctrine.* Ithaca, N.Y.: Cornell University Press.

———. 1991. *Inadvertent Escalation: Conventional War and Nuclear Risks.* Ithaca, N.Y.: Cornell University Press.

Poterba, James. 1994. "State Responses to Fiscal Crises: The Effects of Budgetary Institutions and Processes." *Journal of Political Economy* 102:799–821.

Powell, Robert. 1987. "Crisis Bargaining, Escalation, and MAD." *American Political Science Review* 81:717–35.

———. 1988. "Nuclear Brinkmanship with Two-Sided Incomplete Information." *American Political Science Review* 82:155–78.

———. 1989. "Nuclear Deterrence Theory and the Strategy of Limited Retaliation." *American Political Science Review* 83:504–19.

———. 1991. "Absolute and Relative Gains in International Relations Theory." *American Political Science Review* 85:1303–20.

———. 1993. "Guns, Butter, and Anarchy." *American Political Science Review* 87:115–32.

———. 1994. "Anarchy in International Relations Theory." *International Organization* 48:313–44.

———. 1996a. "Bargaining in the Shadow of Power." *Games and Economic Behavior* 15:255–89.

———. 1996b. "Stability and the Distribution of Power." *World Politics* 48:239–67.

Powell, Robert. 1996c. "Uncertainty, Shifting Power, and Appeasement." *American Political Science Review* 90:749–64.

Putnam, Robert D. 1988. "Diplomacy and Domestic Politics: The Logic of Two-Level Games." *International Organization* 42:427–60.

Quandt, Richard E. 1961. "On the Use of Game Models in Theories of International Relations." *World Politics* 14:69–78.

Radnitzky, Gerard, ed. 1992. *Universal Economics: Assessing the Achievements of the Economic Approach*. New York: Paragon House.

Radnitzky, Gerard, and Peter Bernholz, eds. 1987. *Economic Imperialism*. New York: Paragon House.

Rapoport, Anatol. 1988. "Editorial Comments on the Article by Hirshleifer and Martinez Coll." *Journal of Conflict Resolution* 32:400.

Rapoport, Anatol, and Albert M. Chammah. 1965. *Prisoner's Dilemma: A Study in Conflict and Cooperation*. Ann Arbor: The University of Michigan Press.

Rasmussen, Eric. 1989. *Games and Information: An Introduction to Game Theory*. New York: Basil Blackwell.

Rauch, James. 1995. "Bureaucracy, Infrastructure, and Economic Growth: Evidence from U.S. Cities During the Progressive Era." *American Economic Review* 85:968–79.

Ray, Edward John. 1981. "The Determinants of Tariff and Nontariff Trade Restrictions in the United States." *Journal of Political Economy* 89:105–21.

Reinganum, Jennifer, and Louis Wilde. 1986. "Settlement, Litigation, and the Allocation of Litigation Costs." *RAND Journal of Economics* 17:557–66.

Reiter, Dan, and Allan C. Stam III. 1998. "Democracy, War Initiation, and Victory." *American Political Science Review* 92:377–89.

Rellstab, Urs. 1992. "New Insights into the Collaboration between John von Neumann and Oskar Morgenstern on the Theory of Games and Economic Behavior." In *Toward a History of Game Theory*, edited by E. Roy Weintraub. Durham: Duke University Press.

Reny, Philip J. 1992. "Rationality in Extensive-Form Games." *Journal of Economic Perspectives* 6:103–18.

Rhodes, Edward. 1989. *Power and MADness: The Logic of Nuclear Coercion*. New York: Columbia University Press.

Richards, John. 1997. *The Domestic Politics of International Institutions: The Regulatory Institutions for Trade in Aviation Services*. Ph.D. diss., University of California at San Diego.

———. 1999. "Toward a Positive Theory of International Institutions: Regulating International Aviation Markets." *International Organization* 53:1–37.

Richardson, J. David. 1990. "The Political Economy of Strategic Trade Policy." *International Organization* 44:107–35.

Riker, William H. 1980. "Implications from the Disequilibrium of Majority Rule for the Study of Institutions." *American Political Science Review* 74:432–46.

———. 1992. "The Entry of Game Theory into Political Science." In *Toward a History of Game Theory*, edited by E. Roy Weintraub. Durham: Duke University Press.

Risse-Kappen, Thomas, ed. 1995. *Bringing Transnational Relations Back In: Non-State Actors, Domestic Structures, and International Institutions.* New York: Cambridge University Press.

Robinson, Ronald. 1972. "Non-European Foundations of European Imperialism: Sketch for a Theory of Collaboration." In *Studies in the Theory of Imperialism,* edited by Roger Owen and Bob Sutcliffe. London: Longman.

Robson, Arthur J. 1995. "The Evolution of Strategic Behaviour." *Canadian Journal of Economics* 28:17–41.

Roeder, Philip G. 1993. *Red Sunset: The Failure of Soviet Politics.* Princeton, N.J.: Princeton University Press.

Rogoff, Kenneth. 1985. "The Optimal Degree of Commitment to an Intermediate Monetary Target." *Quarterly Journal of Economics* 100:1169–89.

Rogowski, Ronald. 1978. "Rationalist Theories of Politics: A Midterm Report." *World Politics* 30:296–323.

———. 1987. "Trade and the Variety of Democratic Institutions." *International Organization* 41:203–24.

———. 1989. *Commerce and Coalitions: How Trade Affects Domestic Political Alignments.* Princeton, N.J.: Princeton University Press.

———. 1997. *The Electoral System(s) of the European Union: How Economically Distortionary Are They Likely to Be?* Political Economy of European Integration (PEEI) Working Paper: WP1.58. Berkeley: PEEI.

Romanelli, Elaine. 1991. "The Evolution of New Organizational Forms." *Annual Review of Sociology* 17:93–96.

Root, Hilton L. 1989. "Tying the King's Hands: Credible Commitments and Royal Fiscal Policy During the Old Regime." *Rationality and Society* 1:240–58.

Rosecrance, Richard N. 1961. "Categories, Concepts, and Reasoning in the Study of International Relations." *Behavioral Science* 6:222–31.

Rosecrance, Richard N., and Arthur A. Stein, eds. 1993. *The Domestic Bases of Grand Strategy.* Ithaca, N.Y.: Cornell University Press.

Rosenau, James N. 1968. "National Interest." In *International Encyclopedia of the Social Sciences.* Vol. 11. New York: Macmillan.

———. 1976. "Pre-theories and Theories of Foreign Policy." In *Approaches to Comparative and International Politics,* edited by R. Barry Farrell. Evanston, Ill.: Northwestern University Press.

Rosendorff, B. Peter. 1996. "Voluntary Export Restraints, Antidumping Procedures, and Domestic Politics." *American Economic Review* 86:544–62.

Roubini, Nouriel, and Jeffrey Sachs. 1989. "Political and Economic Determinants of Budget Deficits in the Industrial Democracies." *European Economic Review* 33:903–33.

Rubinstein, Ariel. 1982. "Perfect Equilibrium in a Bargaining Model." *Econometrica* 50:97–109.

———. 1991. "Comments on the Interpretation of Game Theory." *Econometrica* 59:909–24.

Ruggie, John Gerard. 1982. "International Regimes, Transactions, and Change: Embedded Liberalism in the Postwar Economic Order." *International Organization* 36:379–415.

———. 1992. "Multilateralism: The Anatomy of an Institution." *International Organization* 46:561–98.

Russett, Bruce. 1985. "The Mysterious Case of Vanishing Hegemony: Or Is Mark Twain Really Dead?" *International Organization* 39:207–31.

———. 1993. *Grasping the Democratic Peace: Principles for a Post–Cold War World*. Princeton, N.J.: Princeton University Press.

Sagan, Scott. 1986. "1914 Revisited: Allies, Offense, and Instability." *International Security* 11, no. 2: 151–75.

Samuelson, Larry. 1993. "Recent Advances in Evolutionary Economics: Comments." *Economic Letters* 42:313.

Samuelson, Paul A. 1978. "Maximizing and Biology." *Economic Inquiry* 16:174–83.

———. 1985. "Modes of Thought in Economics and Biology." *American Economic Review* 75:166–72.

Schattschneider, E. E. 1935. *Politics, Pressures, and the Tariff; A Study of Free Private Enterprise in Pressure Politics, as Shown in the 1929–1930 Revision of the Tariff*. New York: Prentice-Hall. Reprinted, 1963. Hamdon, Conn.: Archon.

Schelling, Thomas C. 1960. *The Strategy of Conflict*. Cambridge, Mass.: Harvard University Press.

———. 1961. "Experimental Games and Bargaining Theory." In *The International System: Theoretical Essays*, edited by Klaus Knorr and Sidney Verba. Princeton, N.J.: Princeton University Press.

———. 1966. *Arms and Influence*. New Haven: Yale University Press.

———. 1984. "Self-Command in Practice, in Policy, and in a Theory of Rational Choice." *American Economic Review* 74:1–11.

Schoemaker, Paul J. H. 1982. "The Expected Utility Model: Its Variants, Purposes, Evidence, and Limitations." *Journal of Economic Literature* 20:529–63.

Schonhardt-Bailey, Cheryl. 1994. "Linking Constituency Interests to Legislative Voting Behaviour: The Role of District Economic and Electoral Composition in the Repeal of the Corn Laws." In *Computing Parliamentary History: George III to Victoria*, edited by John Phillips. Edinburgh: Edinburgh University Press.

Schotter, Andrew. 1992. "Oskar Morgenstern's Contribution to the Development of the Theory of Games." In *Toward a History of Game Theory*, edited by E. Roy Weintraub. Durham: Duke University Press.

Schroeder, Paul. 1994. "Historical Reality vs. Neorealist Theory." *International Security* 19, no. 1: 108–48.

Schultz, Kenneth A. 1999. "Do Democratic Institutions Constrain or Inform: Contrasting Two Institutional Perspectives on Democracy and War." *International Organization* 53 (2):233–66.

Schumpeter, Joseph A. 1951. "The Sociology of Imperialisms." In *Imperialism and Social Classes*, edited by Joseph A. Schumpeter. New York: Augustus Kelley.

Schweizer, Urs. 1989. "Litigation and Settlement under Two-Sided Incomplete Information." *Review of Economic Studies* 18:163–78.

Scott, James C. 1975. "Exploitation in Rural Class Relations: A Victim's Perspective." *Comparative Politics* 7:489–532.

Scott, James C. 1976. *The Moral Economy of the Peasant: Rebellion and Subsistence in Southeast Asia*. New Haven: Yale University Press.

Seligman, Ben B. 1971. "The Revolt Against Formalism." In *Main Currents in Modern Economics: Economic Thought Since 1870*. Vol. 1. Chicago: Quadrangle Books.

Selten, Reinhard. 1975. "Reexamination of the Perfectness Concept for Equilibrium Points in Extensive Form Games." *International Journal of Game Theory* 4:25–55.

———. 1978. "The Chain Store Paradox." *Theory and Decision* 9:127–59.

Sen, Amartya. 1973. "Behaviour and the Concept of Preference." *Economica* 40:241–59.

———. 1994. "The Formulation of Rational Choice." *American Economic Review* 84:385–90.

———. 1995. "Rationality and Social Choice." *American Economic Review* 85:1–24.

Shafir, E. 1993. "Intuitions about Rationality and Cognition." In *Rationality: Psychological and Philosophical Perspectives*, edited by K. I. Manktelow and D. E. Over. New York: Routledge.

Shepsle, Kenneth. 1979. "Institutional Arrangements and Equilibrium in Multidimensional Voting Models." *American Journal of Political Science* 23:27–60.

Shepsle, Kenneth, and Barry Weingast. 1982. "Structure-Induced Equilibrium and Legislative Choice." *Public Choice* 37:503–19.

Shirk, Susan L. 1993. *The Political Logic of Economic Reform in China*. Berkeley: University of California Press.

Shubik, Martin. 1992. "Game Theory at Princeton, 1949–1955: A Personal Reminiscence." In *Toward a History of Game Theory*, edited by E. Roy Weintraub. Durham: Duke University Press.

———. 1993. "Models of Strategic Behavior and Nuclear Deterrence." In *Behavior, Society, and International Conflict*, edited by Philip E. Tetlock, Jo L. Husbands, Robert Jervis, Paul C. Stern, and Charles Tilly. New York: Oxford University Press.

Sigmund, Karl. 1995. *Games of Life: Explorations in Ecology, Evolution, and Behaviour*. New York: Penguin.

Simmons, Beth. 1994. *Who Adjusts? Domestic Sources of Foreign Economic Policy during the Interwar Years*. Princeton, N.J.: Princeton University Press.

Simon, Herbert A. 1976. "From Substantive to Procedural Rationality." In *Method and Appraisal in Economics*, edited by Spiro J. Latsis. Cambridge: Cambridge University Press.

———. 1978a. "Rationality as Process and as Product of Thought." *American Economic Review* 68:1–16.

———. 1978b. "On How to Decide What to Do." *Bell Journal of Economics* 9:494–507.

———. 1990. "Invariants of Human Behavior." *Annual Review of Psychology* 41:1–19.

Singer, J. David. 1961. "The Level-of-Analysis Problem in International Relations." In *The International System: Theoretical Essays*, edited by Klaus Knorr and Sidney Verba. Princeton, N.J.: Princeton University Press.

Siverson, Randolph M., and Michael P. Sullivan. 1983. "The Distribution of Power and the Onset of War." *Journal of Conflict Resolution* 27:473–94.

Skålnes, Lars. 1998. "Grand Strategy and Foreign Economic Policy: British Grand Strategy in the 1930s." *World Politics* 50:582–616.

———. 1999. *When International Politics Matters: Grand Strategy and Economic Discrimination*. Ann Arbor: University of Michigan Press.

Smith, Alastair. 1995. "Alliance Formation and War." *International Studies Quarterly* 39:405–25.

———. 1996. "Diversionary Foreign Policy in Democratic Systems." *International Studies Quarterly* 40:133–53.

Smith, Tony. 1981. *The Pattern of Imperialism*. Cambridge: Cambridge University Press.

Smith, Vernon L. 1992. "Game Theory and Experimental Economics: Beginnings and Early Influences." In *Toward a History of Game Theory*, edited by E. Roy Weintraub. Durham: Duke University Press.

Snidal, Duncan. 1985. "The Limits of Hegemonic Stability Theory." *International Organization* 39:579–614.

———. 1986. "The Game Theory of International Politics." In *Cooperation under Anarchy*, edited by Kenneth Oye. Princeton, N.J.: Princeton University Press.

———. 1991a. "Relative Gains and the Pattern of International Cooperation." *American Political Science Review* 85:701–26.

———. 1991b. "International Cooperation among Relative Gains Maximizers." *International Studies Quarterly* 35:387–402.

Snyder, Glenn H. 1984. "The Security Dilemma in Alliance Politics." *World Politics* 36:461–95.

Snyder, Glenn H., and Paul Diesing. 1977. *Conflict among Nations: Bargaining, Decision Making, and System Structure in International Crises*. Princeton, N.J.: Princeton University Press.

Snyder, Jack L. 1978. "Rationality at the Brink: The Role of Cognitive Processes in Failures of Deterrence." *World Politics* 30:345–65.

———. 1984a. *The Ideology of the Offensive: Military Decision Making and the Disasters of 1914*. Ithaca, N.Y.: Cornell University Press.

———. 1984b. "Civil-Military Relations and the Cult of the Offensive, 1914 and 1984." *International Security* 9, no. 1: 108–46.

———. 1991. *Myths of Empire: Domestic Politics and International Ambition*. Ithaca, N.Y.: Cornell University Press.

Somit, Albert, and Steven A. Peterson. 1992. *The Dynamics of Evolution: The Punctuated Equilibrium Debate in the Natural and Social Sciences*. Ithaca, N.Y.: Cornell University Press.

Spier, Katherine. 1992. "The Dynamics of Pretrial Negotiation." *Review of Economic Studies* 59:93–108.

Spolaore, Enrico. 1997. "Macroeconomic Policy, Institutions, and Efficiency." Ph.D. diss., Department of Economics, Harvard University.

Spruyt, Hendrik. 1994. *The Sovereign State and Its Competitors*. Princeton, N.J.: Princeton University Press.

Stalnaker, Robert. 1994. "On the Evaluation of Solution Concepts." *Theory and Decision* 37:49–73.

Stam, Allan C. III. 1996. *Win, Lose, or Draw: Domestic Politics and the Crucible of War.* Ann Arbor: University of Michigan Press.

Steele, Cherie J. 1995. "Altered States: Innovation, Power, and the Evolution of the International System." Ph. D. diss., University of California at Los Angeles.

Stein, Arthur A. 1978. *The Nation at War.* Baltimore: The Johns Hopkins University Press.

———. 1980. "The Politics of Linkage." *World Politics* 33:62–81.

———. 1982. "When Misperception Matters." *World Politics* 34:505–26.

———. 1983. "Coordination and Collaboration: Regimes in an Anarchic World." In *International Regimes*, edited by Stephen D. Krasner. Ithaca, N.Y.: Cornell University Press.

———. 1984. "The Hegemon's Dilemma: Great Britain, the United States, and the International Economic Order." *International Organization* 38:355–86.

———. 1990. *Why Nations Cooperate: Circumstance and Choice in International Relations.* Ithaca, N.Y.: Cornell University Press.

———. 1992. "Constraints and Determinants: Realism, Domestic Politics, Levels of Analysis, and International Politics." Paper presented at the Conference on Domestic Politics and Multilateralism, University of California, San Diego, May 1–2.

———. 1993. "Governments, Economic Interdependence, and International Cooperation." In *Behavior, Society, and International Conflict*, edited by Philip E. Tetlock, Jo L. Husbands, Robert Jervis, Paul C. Stern, and Charles Tilly. Vol. 3. New York: Oxford University Press, for the National Research Council of the National Academy of Sciences.

———. 1995. "Ethnicity, Extraterritoriality, and International Politics." Paper presented at the Annual Meeting of the American Political Science Association, Chicago, August 31–September 3.

———. 1996. "Normative Equilibrium and International Politics." Paper presented at the Annual Meeting of the American Political Science Association, San Francisco, August 29–September 1.

Steinbruner, John. 1974. *The Cybernetic Theory of Decision: New Dimensions in Political Analysis.* Princeton, N.J.: Princeton University Press.

Stevenson, R. J. 1993. "Rationality and Reality." In *Rationality: Psychological and Philosophical Perspectives*, edited by K. I. Manktelow and D. E. Over. New York: Routledge.

Stigler, George J., and Gary S. Becker. 1977. "De Gustibus Non Est Disputandum." *American Economic Review* 67:76–90.

Stokes, Eric. 1969. "Late Nineteenth Century Colonial Expansion and the Attack on the Theory of Economic Imperialism: A Case of Mistaken Identity?" *Historical Journal* 12:285–301.

Strange, Susan. 1992. "States, Firms, and Diplomacy." *International Affairs* 68:1–15.

Sutton, John. 1990. "Explaining Everything, Explaining Nothing? Game Theoretic Models in Industrial Economics." *European Economic Review* 34:505–12.

Taagepera, Rein. 1978. "Size and Duration of Empires: Systematics of Size." *Social Science Research* 7:108–27.

Taagepera, Rein, and Matthew Soberg Shugart. 1989. *Seats and Votes: The Effects and Determinants of Electoral Systems*. New Haven: Yale University Press.

Thomas, L. C. 1984. *Games, Theory, and Applications*. Chichester: Ellis Horwood.

Tilly, Charles. 1975. "Reflections on the History of European State-Making." In *The Formation of National States in Western Europe*, edited by Charles Tilly. Princeton, N.J.: Princeton University Press.

———. 1990. *Coercion, Capital, and European States, 990–1990 A.D.* Cambridge: Basil Blackwell.

Tirole, Jean. 1988. *The Theory of Industrial Organization*. Cambridge, Mass.: MIT Press.

Tollison, Robert D., and Thomas D. Willett. 1979. "An Economic Theory of Mutually Advantageous Issue Linkages in International Negotiations." *International Organization* 33:425–49.

Truman, David B. 1951. *The Governmental Process*. New York: Knopf.

Tsebelis, George. 1995. "Decision Making in Political Systems: Veto Players in Presidentialism, Parliamentarism, Multicameralism, and Multipartyism." *British Journal of Political Science* 25:289–325.

Tsebelis, George, and Jeannette Money. 1995. "Bicameral Negotiations: The *Navette* System in France." *British Journal of Political Science* 25:101–29.

Tufte, Edward R. 1973. "The Relationship between Seats and Votes in Two-Party Systems." *American Political Science Review* 67:540–54.

Tversky, Amos. 1972. "Elimination by Aspects: A Theory of Choice." *Psychological Review* 79:281–99.

Tversky, Amos, and Daniel Kahneman. 1974. "Judgment under Uncertainty: Heuristics and Biases in Judgments Reveal Some Heuristics of Thinking under Uncertainty." *Science* 185:1124–31.

———. 1981. "The Framing of Decisions and the Psychology of Choice." *Science* 211:453–58.

———. 1987. "Rational Choice and the Framing of Decisions." In *Rational Choice: The Contrasts between Economics and Psychology*, edited by Robin M. Hogarth and Melvin W. Reder. Chicago: University of Chicago Press.

Van Damme, Eric. 1994. "Evolutionary Game Theory." *European Economic Review* 38:847–58.

Van Evera, Stephen. 1984. "The Cult of the Offensive and the Origins of the First World War." *International Security* 9, no. 1: 58–107.

———. 1986. "Why Cooperation Failed in 1914." In *Cooperation under Anarchy*, edited by Kenneth Oye. Princeton, N.J.: Princeton University Press.

Vaubel, Roland, and Thomas D. Willett. 1991. *The Political Economy of International Organizations*. Boulder, Colo.: Westview.

Verdier, Daniel. 1994. *Democracy and International Trade: Britain, France, and the United States, 1860–1990*. Princeton, N.J.: Princeton University Press.

Wade, Robert. 1990. *Governing the Market: Economic Theory and the Role of Government in East Asian Industrialization*. Princeton, N.J.: Princeton University Press.

Wagner, R. Harrison. 1983. "The Theory of Games and the Problem of International Cooperation." *American Political Science Review* 77:330–46.

Walsh, Vivian. 1994. "Rationality as Self-Interest versus Rationality as Present Aims." *American Economic Review* 84:401–5.

Walt, Stephen M. 1987. *The Origins of Alliances*. Ithaca, N.Y.: Cornell University Press.

———. 1991. "Alliance Formation in Southwest Asia: Balancing and Bandwagoning in Cold War Competition." In *Dominoes and Bandwagons: Strategic Beliefs and Great Power Competition in the Eurasian Rimland*, edited by Robert Jervis and Jack Snyder. New York: Oxford University Press.

Walter, Barbara. 1994. "The Resolution of Civil Wars: Why Negotiations Fail." Ph.D. diss., University of Chicago.

———. 1997. "The Critical Barrier to Civil War Settlement." *International Organization*, 51:335–64.

———. 1998. "Rebuilding States under Anarchy." In *Civil Wars and the Security Dilemma*, edited by Barbara Walter and Jack Snyder. New York: Columbia University Press.

Waltz, Kenneth N. 1959. *Man, the State and War: A Theoretical Analysis*. New York: Columbia University Press.

———. 1979. *Theory of International Politics*. Reading, Mass.: Addison-Wesley.

———. 1990. "Realist Thought and Neorealist Theory." *Journal of International Affairs* 44:21–37.

Watt, Donald Cameron. 1989. *How War Came: The Immediate Origins of the Second World War, 1938–1939*. New York: Pantheon.

Weber, Eugen. 1976. *Peasants into Frenchmen: The Modernization of Rural France, 1870–1914*. Stanford: Stanford University Press.

Weber, Katja. 1997. "Hierarchy Amidst Anarchy: A Transaction Costs Approach to International Security Cooperation." *International Studies Quarterly* 41:321–40.

Weingast, Barry R. 1995. "The Economic Role of Political Institutions: Market-Preserving Federalism and Economic Development." *Journal of Law, Economics, and Organization* 11:1–31.

———. 1997. "The Political Foundations of Democracy and the Rule of Law." *American Political Science Review* 91:245–63.

Weingast, Barry R., and William J. Marshall. 1988. "The Industrial Organization of Congress; Or, Why Legislatures, Like Firms, Are Not Organized as Markets." *Journal of Political Economy* 96:132–63.

Wendt, Alexander. 1992. "Anarchy Is What States Make of It: The Social Construction of Power Politics." *International Organization* 46:391–425.

———. 1994. "Collective Identity Formation and the International State." *American Political Science Review* 88:384–97.

Wendt, Alexander, and Daniel Friedheim. 1995. "Hierarchy under Anarchy: Informal Empire and the East German State." *International Organization* 49:689–721.

White, Lynn Jr. 1962. *Medieval Technology and Social Change*. London: Oxford University Press.

Wight, Martin. 1978. *Power Politics*. New York: Penguin.

Williams, Philip M. 1966. *Crisis and Compromise: Politics in the French Fourth Republic*. Garden City, N.Y.: Anchor.

Williams, Philip M., and Martin Harrison. 1973. *Politics and Society in de Gaulle's Republic*. Garden City, N.Y.: Anchor.

Williamson, Oliver E. 1985. *The Economic Institutions of Capitalism: Firms, Markets, Relational Contracting*. New York: Free Press.

———. 1994. "Transaction Cost Economics and Organization Theory." In *The Handbook of Economic Sociology*, edited by Neil J. Smelser and Richard Swedberg. Princeton, N.J.: Princeton University Press.

Wilson, James Q. 1973. *Political Organizations*. New York: Basic Books.

Witt, Ulrich. 1989. "The Evolution of Economic Institutions as a Propagation Process." *Public Choice* 62:155–72.

Wittman, Donald. 1979. "How a War Ends." *Journal of Conflict Resolution* 23:743–63.

Wong, Carolyn. 1997. *The Politics of Immigration: An Analysis of Policy Reform in Congress, 1965–1996*. Ph.D. diss., University of California at Los Angeles.

Yarbrough, Beth, and Robert Yarbrough. 1992. *Cooperation and Governance in International Trade: The Strategic Organizational Approach*. Princeton, N.J.: Princeton University Press.

Young, David. 1992. *The Discovery of Evolution*. Cambridge: Cambridge University Press.

Young, H. Peyton. 1991. "The Evolution of Conventions." *Econometrica* 61:76–77.

Young, H. Peyton, and Dean Foster. 1991. "Cooperation in the Short and in the Long Run." *Games and Economic Behavior* 3:145–56.

Young, Ruth C. 1988. "Is Population Ecology a Useful Paradigm for the Study of Organizations?" *American Journal of Sociology* 94:1–24.

Zaller, John. 1992. *The Nature and Origins of Mass Opinion*. New York: Cambridge University Press.

Zartman, I. William, and Maureen R. Berman. 1982. *The Practical Negotiator*. New Haven: Yale University Press.

About the Authors

Jeffry Frieden is professor of government at Harvard University. He specializes in the politics of international monetary and financial relations. Frieden is the author of *Banking on the World: The Politics of American International Finance* (1987); and *Debt, Development, and Democracy: Modern Political Economy and Latin America, 1965–1985* (1991); he is co-editor of numerous books on European integration. His articles on the politics of international economic issues have appeared in a wide variety of scholarly and general-interest publications.

Peter A. Gourevitch is professor of political science at the Graduate School of International Relations and Pacific Studies (IR/PS), University of California, San Diego. From 1986 to 1996 he was the founding dean of IR/PS. Gourevitch has published widely in international relations and comparative politics, and is the author of *Politics in Hard Times: Comparative Responses to International Economic Crises* (1986). He is currently co-editor of *International Organization*.

Miles Kahler is Rohr Professor of Pacific International Relations at the Graduate School of International Relations and Pacific Studies (IR/PS), University of California, San Diego. From 1994 to 1996 he was Senior Fellow in International Political Economy at the Council on Foreign Relations. His recent publications include *Capital Flows and Financial Crises* (editor, forthcoming), *Liberalization and Foreign Policy* (editor, 1997), and *International Institutions and the Political Economy of Integration* (1995).

David A. Lake is professor of political science at the University of California, San Diego. During the preparation of this book, he served as research director for international relations at the University of California's Institute on Global Conflict and Cooperation. He is currently co-editor of *International Organization*. Lake has published widely in international relations, international political economy, security studies, and American foreign policy. His most recent book is *Entangling Relations: American Foreign Policy in Its Century* (1999).

James D. Morrow is senior research fellow at the Hoover Institution and professor, by courtesy, of political science at Stanford University. He has published extensively on international relations. He is the author of *Game Theory for Political Scientists* (1994). His current research addresses the role of norms in international politics and how domestic political institutions shape foreign policy.

Robert Powell is professor of political science at the University of California, Berkeley. He has written widely on nuclear deterrence theory and international relations theory. He is the author of *Nuclear Deterrence Theory* (1990) and *In the Shadow of Power* (1999).

Ronald Rogowski is professor and chair of political science at the University of California, Los Angeles. He is the author of *Rational Legitimacy* (1974) and *Commerce and Coalitions* (1989). He was elected in 1994 as a Fellow of the American Academy of Arts and Sciences.

Arthur A. Stein is professor of political science at the University of California, Los Angeles. His publications include *The Nation at War* (1980), *Why Nations Cooperate: Circumstance and Choice in International Relations* (1990), and *Beyond Realism: Domestic Bases of Grand Strategy* (co-editor, 1993).